MW01553777

TABLE OF CONTENTS

Unless otherwise indicated, all Scripture quotations are taken from the King James Version of the Bible.
5,001 Wisdom Quotations of Mike Murdock · ISBN 1-56394-458-8 / B-318
Copyright © 2013 by **MIKE MURDOCK**
Publisher/Editor: Deborah Murdock Johnson
Published by The Wisdom Center · 4051 Denton Hwy. · Ft. Worth, Texas 76117
1-817-759-BOOK · 1-817-759-2665 · 1-817-759-0300
You Will Love Our Website..! MikeMurdockBooks.com

ABSENCE

1 Absentee Authority...Is No Authority.

---

2 Absence~
What You Stop Seeing...You Stop Desiring.

---

3 I Can Accept Your Attitude...
If You Can Accept My Absence.

---

4 My Absence...Explains How Important My Joy
Is To Me.

---

5 You Need Someone...

To Listen To You.
To Speak.
To Comfort.
To Correct.
To Inspire.
To Admire You.
Who Is Missing?

ACCESS

6 5 Door Closers:
   1.   Inappropriate Questions.
   2.   Disinterest.
   3.   Accusatory Tones.
   4.   Ingratitude.
   5.   Controlling Spirit.

7 A Tweet...Is A Door or A Wall.
The Wise...Make It A Bridge.

8 Access~
...Makes Caring Measureable.
...Makes Loyalty Undoubtable.
...Reveals Hidden Needs.

9 Access Answers/Questions...
That Your Imagination Cannot.

10 Access...Creates Opportunity For Conversation.
Conversation...Is Invitation To Credibility.

11 Access Disdained...
Becomes Access Discontinued.

12 Access...Does Not Create Love.
Access...Creates Opportunity To Love.

~

13 Access Does Not...Guarantee Love.
Access...Guarantees Opportunity.
Access Is...A Continual Test.
Only A Fool Forgets It.

~

14 ACCESS...Is A Golden Opportunity To
Reveal Your Worth.
(For Some, This Is Unfortunate.)

~

15 Access Is A Huge Investment...
Someone Makes In You.
Make It Memorable.

~

16 Access...Is A Serious Gift.

~

17 Access...Is An Invitation To Reveal Your
Difference From Others.

~

18 Access...Is An Opportunity For Validation.

~

19 "Access"...Is Bought.
The Currency Is...Honor.

~

20 Access...Is Invitation To Conversation.
Conversation...Is Invitation To Credibility.
Credibility...Decides Trust.

21 Access Is...Invitation To Conversation.
Conversation Is...Invitation To Understanding.
Understanding Is...Invitation To Friendship.

22 Access Is...Not Relationship.
Access Is...
Opportunity To Qualify For Relationship.

23 ACCESS Is...Opportunity.
Continuous Access Is...Continuous Opportunity.
...To Learn.
...To Earn.
Never-Forget-It.

24 Access...Is Opportunity To Build Credibility.
Access Is...The Seed For Credibility...or,
The Loss of It.

25 Access Lost~
When My Instructions...Are Ignored.
When My Opinion...Is Not Honored.
When My Comfort...Does Not Matter.

26 Access Lost...Is Rarely Regained.

27 Your Words...Keep You Linked, Connected.
To Your Past.
To Your Vision.
To Feelings.
To People.
To Disappointment.

28 Access Trivialized...Is Access Lost.

29 Access...Verifies The Hidden Nature of The
Comforting, or...The Contentious.

30 Access...Was Your Door.
Your Reaction...Has Made It A Wall.

31 Familiarity Is The Test...Very Few Pass.

32 Focus...Change...The Criteria For Access.

33 Gatekeeper...Someone Who Will Stand Between
You And An Unpleasant Experience.
Increasing Your Demands...
Will Stop Your Access.

34 Interest...Creates Access.
Inappropriate Requests...Loses It.

35 No Honor...No Access.

36 One Minute of Access...
Determines If You Qualify For More.

37 One Minute of Access...
Determines If You Qualify For One Hour.

38 Palace-Talk~
Guests...Visit.
Servants...Stay.

39 Stop Listening...To A Man Who Has Stopped
Listening.

40 Suppers With Jesus...Did Not Improve Judas.
Access...Does Not Create Loyalty.

41 The "Unwillingness" To Adapt...
Disqualifies You For Access.

42 The "Inability" To Adapt...
Disqualifies You For Access.

ACCUSATION

43 Accusation...Without Verification Is...
Your Explanation.
Think.
What Is The Goal of The Accuser?

44 ACCUSERS~
I Don't Listen To Those I DON'T Know...
Tell Me About Those I DO Know.

45 False Accusation...
Creates Unspeakable Pain.
It Multiplies...
When Someone You Love Believes It.

46 False Accusation...Is Compounded Pain For
Accelerated Entry To The Palace.
Divine.
Joseph Season Is Over.
Prophetic.

47 False Accusation~
Never Embrace The Counsel of An Adversary...
About Someone You Love.

AGING

48 Age...Does Not Make You Seasoned.

49 Aging~
I Am Discovering New Zones of Ignorance...
Much Faster.
:) True.

50 Aging~
I Never Envy...Youth.
They Never Know...What Is Coming Next... :)
(We Do.)

51 AGING...Ahhh.
"Older Men~
...Be Sober
...Reverent
...Temperate
...Sound In Faith
...In Love
...In Patience."
Titus 2:2

52 Aging Is...
Forgetting Faster Than You Are Learning.

ANGER

53 100,000 Necklace "Symbols" Are Wore Around The World.
Yet, Simple "Cross" Creates Profound Conviction, Anger In Rebels.

54 Anger Creates...Instant Energy.
...For Change.
...For Decision-Making.

55 Anger...Is A Very Costly Luxury.
Anger Is...The Seed For Change.

56 Hidden Anger...Is Deadlier.

57 I Can Handle...Your Anger.
Hope You Can Handle Mine.

58 No...You Do Not Make Me Mad.
Only Important People Make Me Mad.
:)

59 No...You Have Not Made Me Angry.
You Are Not...THAT Important.
:)

60 The One Who Can Anger You...Is Powerful.
Increase Your Caution.

61 Those Who Make You Angry...
Belong To Someone Else.
Release Them...With Great Joy.

62 Those Who Unleash Unnatural Anger In You...
May Be The Most Dangerous People In Your
Life.

63 What Excites You...Often Angers Another.

64 Your Anger...Reveals What You Fear.

ANOINTING

65 Amazed...
And Very Thankful For Increase of Anointing.
The Holy Spirit...IS Life.
Singing To Him...Creates Instant Access.

66 I Am Not Anointed...To Control The World.
I Am Anointed...To Control My Mind.

67 In My Early Years, My Cousins Nicknamed Me,
"The Laughing Kid."
That Anointing And Mantle...Is Returning
Tonight. :)

68 No Anointing...Corrects The Fool.
The Anointing...Identifies The Fool.

69 The Anointing You Respect Is The Anointing You
Attract.

70 The Anointing...Does Not Make You Discerning.
Samson.

71 The Anointing...Is Not You.

ANSWER

72 An Answer May Not Really Be...
"Your" Answer.
Does "The Answer" Create Peace...
or Increase Your Stress?

73 Answers...Are Sudden.
A Single...
~Moment of Disrespect
~Look
~Question
~Defiance
~Delay
~Reaction
~Request
~Need

74 Answers Can Escape Anything...
But The Right Question.

75 Answers Can Hide Behind Everything...
Except Questions.

76 Answers To...Why Are You Single?
"...I Start Choking...During Arguments."

77 "...I Have An Obsession...To Be Happy."
:-)

78 Every Answer...Is One Thought Away.
Always.

79 Nothing Satisfies More...Than A Clear Answer.

80 One Word Answers~
"Interesting."
"OK."
"Possibly."
"Really?"
"Amazing."
"Ummm."

81 Sometimes 5 Minutes...Provides Lifetime
Answers.

82 When Answers Come...
Linger No Longer Around The Problem.

83 Your Answer Is...Just One Question Away.
Always.

84 Every "No"...Creates A Yes.

ARGUMENT

85 Arguing...
Increases The Confidence of A Fool.
Don't.

86 Arguing...Does Not "Entertain" Me.

87 Arguing Is Proof...That You Do Not Have An
Explanation.

88 Arguing...Is Not Proof of Intelligence.

89 Arguing ...Shows Hope.
:)

90 DEBATE~
I Don't Enter An Argument Where
Winning Has No Reward.

91 The Difference Between The Fool And The Wise
Is Simple:
...The Passion To Argue.

ASSIGNMENT

92 3:25 a.m...Hotel.
Amazing, Really...45 Years of Traveling And
Hotel Rooms.
An "Assignment"...Explains It.

93 Assignment~
I Don't Belong Anywhere...
I Have Been Undiscerned.

94 Assignment~
Somebody's Future Cannot Begin...
Until YOU Enter.

95 Assignment~
The Damaged...Damage.
The Healed...Heal.
The Deliverer...Delivers.
The Taught...Teach.

96 Assignment~
The Rarer The Jewel...
The More Critical The Setting.
Geographical Location.

97 ASSIGNMENT~
Those Who Unlock Your Compassion...Are
Those To Whom You Are Assigned.

98 Assignment~
Who Do You Long To Protect?
Whose Joy Really Matters?
Whose Pain Do You Feel?
Who Are You Assigned To "Host?"

99 Assignment~
Whose Joy Has Become...Your Obsession?

100 Assignment~
Whose Pain...Do You Long To Remove?
Whose Pleasure...Is Your Obsession?
What Is "The Proof?"

101 Fish Designed...To Swim.
Birds Designed...To Fly.
Deer Designed...To Run.
Humans Designed...To Love.
Rebels Create Chaos.

102 I Do Not Want To Create Discomfort.
May Be Too Big A Price To Pay.
But...This Is A Turning-Point Place For You.
Q. "Where Is Your Assignment?"

103 It Is My Divine Assignment...To Teach Truth.
It Is Your Divine Responsibility...To
Discern It.

104 My Only Assignment Is...To LOVE.
...Not Change.
...Not Correct.
...Not Understand.
...Not Destroy.

105 Turtles...Do Not Talk.
Trees...Do Not Fly.
Divine Design.
Embrace Your Own Design.
Fully.

106 When You Do Not Know Where You Belong...
EXCEL.

107 Your "Eyes" Are Gloriously Important...But
Fail Tragically Every Time You Expect
Them To "Listen."

108 YOUR ASSIGNMENT Is...The Place God
Has Stored Your Eventual Prosperity.
MONEY IS...Anywhere God Wanted You
To Be.

ATHEIST

109 Amazing
...That A Baby In A Manger Intimidates
Atheists.

110 Atheist~
Do You Really Believe That Everything You
Have Not Seen...Does Not Exist..?
Really..?

111 Atheist~
I Am Very SAD...About Your Beliefs.
You Are Very MAD...About Mine.
I Ponder This.

112 Atheist~
I Can Explain...My Joy.
Please Explain...Yours.

113 Atheist~
If I Am Wrong...What Do I Lose..?
If You Are Wrong...What Do YOU Lose..?

114 Atheist Anger Toward The Bible...
Does Not Confuse Me.
Wouldn't You Feel The Same If A Book Called
You..."A Fool?"

115 Atheist Is...It Really True..?
God Has Never...Visited You..?
NEVER..?
Umm...That's Just Not Like Him.

116 Atheist~
Is Your Goal
~Removal...of What Inspires Me?
~Replacement...of What Inspires Me?
Or
~Resentment...of What Inspires Me?

117 ATHEIST~Man With No Memorable
Experience.
AGNOSTIC~Man Who Cannot Remember
His Experience.
CHRISTIAN~Man Changed By His Experience.

118 DO NOT BLOCK...The Atheist; He May Follow
You All The Way To Heaven.

119 The Atheist And The Christian.
"One Is Simply...More Experienced."
One God-Experience Can Create A Chasm.

120 To Atheist~
I Ache For You...Because, I Too, Have Lived In
Doubt...Unspeakable Disappointment In People-
Change...Happens.

121 Atheists...Are Angry.
...About Someone Who Does Not Exist..?
:)

ATTACKED

122 ABUSE~
What You Can Tolerate...
You Cannot Change.

123 I Will Carry No Offenses...Into My New Year.
NONE.
Neither Does God.

124 Silence...Is A Most Effective Weapon.
It Certainly Is...Your Greatest Test.

125 Attack...Is A Signal.
You Are Entering...
"A Season of Radical Change."
Daniel/Joseph/David

126 Attack Is Proof...Satan Just Discovered Your
Future.

127 Every Attack I Have Observed On A Spiritual
Leader...Seems To Come From A Demon
Possessed Person.

ATTITUDE

128 Arrogance...Is Not Simply Thinking
You Are Important.
Arrogance...Is Thinking Others
Are Not Important.

129 Arrogance Is...Pursuing A Withdrawal Where
You Have Never Made A Deposit.

130 Attitude Is...A Fragrance...or An Odor.
A Forever Memory.

131 The Odor of Your Attitude...
Has Blinded Me To Your Beauty.

132 Your Coldness...Has Removed Your Importance
In My Life.

AUTHENTIC

133 Anything Authentic...Is Not Common.

134 Authenticity...Is Always Anointed.
Always.

135 Design The Experience You Want To Become...
To Others.
Authenticity...Is The "Starting Place."

136 Embrace...Your Own Authenticity.
Then...Sculpture The Environment
That Unleashes It.

137 I Will Never Stop Being Me...
So You Can Be You.
Advised.

138 The Anointing On Authenticity~
...Is Strangely Glorious.
...Relentless.
...Divine.

AUTHORITY

139 God Did Not Instruct Me To Understand
The Chain of Authority.
God Instructed Me To OBEY The Chain of
Authority.

140 AUTHORITY...
Over You Becomes Responsible For You.

141 AUTHORITY...Is Only Legitimate If It...
~Protects You From Enemies.
~Provides For You, Your Family.
~Promotes Peace.

142 Give Wisdom...Before Those Under Your
Authority Make Mistakes;
When Those Who Are Not...Ask.

143 Never Give Instructions To Those Under
The Authority of Another.
(Job...Home...Relationships)

144 Pharisee Style~
The Willingness To Challenge Someone...
Superior To You.

145 Rebellion To Authority...Explains Most Chaos.

146 Rebellion...Is A Decision,
Not Merely A Mistake.

147 Rebellion...Is Deadlier Than Ignorance.

148 Submission Is...A Business Exchange...
For Sponsorship With Rewards.

149 Submission To Authority...Is Permission To
Promote.
Rebellion To Authority...Is Instruction To
Remove.

BATTLE-TALK

150 Battle Should Be An Event...
Not A Lifestyle.

151 Battles...
Have Not Been My Greatest Problem.
Using Wrong Weapons...
Has Been My Greatest Problem.
Right Weapons...Matter.

152 BATTLES...Are Either Bridges or
Distractions.
Discern Difference.

153 Choose...WHEN You Will Fight.
Choose...WHERE You Will Fight.
Choose...WEAPONS You Will Use.
(Not Carnal~Mighty)

154 Those Who Attack You...Have Found You More
Interesting Than Their Own Future.

155 Never Enter A Battle...
That Has No Obvious Reward.

156 Your Movement...Creates A Tired Enemy. :)

157 Stay...Where You Find Joy.
Battle...Softly.
Verify...Accuracy.
Don't Overload...A Day.

158 What Battle Have You...Decided To Win?
What Are The Rewards For Winning It?
How QUICKLY Could You Win It?

BEAUTY

159 Beauty...
God Gave Women Different Personalities...
To Make Decision-Making Easy For Men.

160 Beauty...Decides If He Looks.
Mystery...Decides If He Reaches.
Reactions...Decides If He Stays.
Few-Get-It.

161 Beauty...Is A Divine Gift To You.
Humility...Is Your Gift Back To God.

162 Beauty Is...Always Pursued.
So, Beauty...Rarely Learns To Reach.

163 Beauty...Is An Opinion.
...Created By A Mood.

164 Beauty...Placed Esther On The Throne.
Mentorship...Kept Her There.
Mordecai

165 Beauty Sabotages...Your Ability To Discern.
And, You Will Pay Dearly For It.
(Samson/Delilah)

166 Beauty Unleashes...Energy.
Ugly Unleashes...Creativity.
Both...Inspire.

167 Beauty...Without Energy~
Is Like An Ocean...Without Water.

168 Men Are Swift To Embrace Beauty.
Because It Is Plentiful?
No.
They Simply Fear...
"Kindness" May Never Arrive.

169 The Tragedy of Beauty...Is That It Delays
Further Discerning.
(Men Stop...At Beauty And Rarely Pursue More
of What Is Hidden.)

BIBLE

170 Biblical Standards...
Are More Important Than Your Like-ability.

171 Every Part of The Bible I Believe...Is Working
For Me.
Thankful.

172 Have Read Bible Through Over 100 Times.
It Corrects...Strengthens...Heals...Increases
Patience...Energizes...Calms.
W-I-S-D-O-M.

173 I Doubt Any Man...Who Doubts The Bible.

174 I Will Say It Again...
Some Have...A Political Persuasion.
I Have A...Biblical Persuasion.

175 From The Mouth of God...
The Day of The Eagles...
Soaring.
Landing.
Surprises.
Harvests Hurtling Toward Every "Yes."

176 NEWS...
Tells Me What Is Important To Others.
BIBLE...
Tells Me What Is Important To God.

177 Read 40 Chapters Daily In The Bible.
Completes~30 Days.
~My Favorite Schedule.
~Profound.
~Did It First Day of Obedience.

178 She Sighed, "Do You Have A Word From The
Lord...For Me?"
I Smiled, "Yes, 800,000.
The Bible." (Smile.)

179 The Bible Is...
~Healing My Mind.
~Increasing My Confidence.
~Purifying My Character.
~Making Me Wiser Than Enemies.
~Calming My Chaos.

180 The Bible Is...A Book About Receiving.
...Forgiveness.
...Divine Favor.
...Opportunities.
...Wisdom.
...Money.

181 The Disobedient...Are Unqualified
For Any Biblical Promises.
So, Do Not Give False Hope. That Is Cruel.

~

182 The Most Important Verse In The Bible
Is...Numbers 23:19...

~

183 WHAT PART OF THE BIBLE...
Have You Decided Not To Believe?
(It May Be Linked To What Is Missing
In Your Life.)

~

184 What Part of The Bible...
Have You Refused To Embrace..?
You Know Just Enough...
To Get Where You Are.

~

185 What Part of The Bible Do You Think Is
Unnecessary..?
...To Read?
...To Believe?
...To Practice?
...To Teach?

~

186 CONFIDENCE:
When I Quote God...I Am Never Wrong.
Bible.

~

BITTERNESS

187 BITTERNESS...Has An Unhideable Odor.
Thankfulness...Is The Only Known Cure.

188 BITTERNESS...Is Deadlier Than Injustice.

189 BITTERNESS...Is The Seed For Loss.
(Access/Job/Friendship)

190 Bitterness Is Deadlier Than Betrayal.
(Internal/External)

191 Bitterness...Is The Seed For Sadness.

192 The Odor of Bitterness Is Unmistakable Nor
Delayed When The Unhappy Enter Our
Environment.

BOSS-TALK

193 4 Agitations:
...Avoiding My Questions.
...Manipulative Affection.
...Correction From Non-Achievers.
...Ignored Instructions.

194 A Good Employee...Works Well.
A Great Employee...Works Well With Others.

195 Are You...
Dismissive...Toward My Needs?
Unneedy...of My Difference?
Self-Absorbed?
Determined To Train To Qualify
For My World?

196 Are Your Repeated Requests...Completely
Ignored By Those Who Work With You?
It Will Greatly Damage You...Over Time.

197 Boss Hires When He Hears:
1) I Am Easy To Correct.
2) You Will Never Have To Repeat An Instruction.
3) I Am A Completer.

198 Don't Try...To Make Me Happy.
Follow My Instructions...And I Will Be Happy.

199 Learn How Your Boss Makes Decisions.
...Information Needed.
...Deal Breakers.
...Negotiation.
...Vendor Trust.

200 Only Fools Ignore Who The King Enjoys.

201 What Problem Has Your Boss...Requested You
To Solve?
Why Have You...Not Solved It?

202 Those Who Reach...Are Wiser
Than Those Who Wait.

203 Those Who Play With My Instructions...
Are Adversaries To My Assignment.

204 Make Truth...An Obsession.
Guard...Your $.
Please...Your Boss.
Treasure...Favor.

205 Do Not Abuse The Diligent On Your Team.
Leave Nobody Unrewarded.
Nobody.
Nobody.
Nobody.

206 I Have No Hope...For People
Who Cannot Follow A Checklist.
None.

207 I Hear Every Demand...
And Compare It With Your Productivity.
If Someone Else Can Do It...Do Not Do It.
Focus...On What Others CANNOT Do.

208 Manager-Talk~
Dead Branches...Are To Be Removed,
Not "Encouraged."

209 Manager-Talk~
Hire...Slowly.
Fire...Quickly.
Replace...Disloyalty.
Swiftly. Silently.

210 Office Managers~
1) Nurture Your Managers~
   Not Their Tasks.
2) Teach Managers The Art of
   Problem-Solving~Questions!

211 When Your Happiness Is Unimportant To
Them...They Have Made The Decision For You.

212 You Cannot Change The Nature of Judas...But
You Can Change His Salary.

213 Can God...Do Business Through You On The
Earth?
Does He..?

CARING

220 CARING...Decides What You Discern.
...What You See.
...What You Change.
...What You Protect.
...What You Say.

221 Caring Is...
...An Anointing, Not A Feeling.
...Instantly Discernable.
...Magnifies The Uncaring.
...Irreplaceable.

222 Caring Is...
Not An Instruction To Marry Someone.
Caring Is...
Often An Instruction To Intercede.

223 Caring Is...Instant Credibility.
Understand This...And Failure Is Impossible.

224 I Have Never Succeeded In Training An
Uncaring Person...To Become A Caring Person.

225 If You Ever Find Someone Who Really, Really
Cares...Stay Close.

226 Caring...Cannot Hide.
Uncaring...Can.

227 The Uncaring...Do Not Belong In My World.

228 The Uncaring...Do Not Discern You.
The Undiscerning...Require Constant
Explanations From You.
Exhausting.

229 Uncaring...Always Documents Itself.

230 When You Care Enough...
You Will Write A Book About It.

CHANGE

231 Change Begins...
One Decision From Right Now.
...An Offense You Ignore.
...Somebody You Honor.
...Protégé You Train.

232 Change Begins...One Question From Now.

233 Change Begins...When You Start Doing What You Admire In Others.

234 Change Is A Divine Reward...
For Confronting A Deception.
Think. Again.

235 Change Is Always...One Question Away.

236 CHANGE...Is One Decision Away.
YOUR Decision.
Marriage.
Finances.
Stress.

237 Change…Is Simpler Than You Know.
The Pain of Life…Can Stop INSTANTLY.
Changes…Are Always Proportionate To Your
Pain.

238 Changes In My Words…
Have Created Changes In My Life.
The Secret of The Mouth.

239 Changing One Daily Habit…
Will Change Your Whole Life.
Dramatically.

240 The Difference In People…Is "Routine."

241 Do You Really Want To Change Yourself..?
Simple.
Just Change…Your FOCUS.

242 EVERY PLEASURABLE CHANGE YOU
DESIRE IN YOUR LIFE…Is Only 3 Decisions
Away.
Think.

243 Hope Without A Change…Is A Mere Fantasy.

244 I Do Not Try...To Change "Me."
I Simply Change...Something I Am Doing.
Daily.

245 I Never...Never...Never...Wait For Change.
Never.
I Birth Change.

246 The FASTEST Way To Change Your Life Is...
Asking Questions.
...Relentlessly.
...About Yourself.
...Your Dreams.

247 The ONLY Thing That Will Change This Year...
Is A New Habit.
Something You Do Differently...Daily.
That Is All.

248 What 3 Daily Routines...
...Would Create A "Change" In 30 Days?
Health?
Productivity?
Family?
Focus?

249 You Met God...And Did Not Change?
You Met...An Imposter.

250 Your Tattoo Is A Clue...That You Expect No
Changes In Your Future.
:)

251 Changing The "World"...Is A Fantasy.
Changing Yourself...Is Not.

CHARACTER

252 DearDaughter~

A Ring...Does Not Create A Covenant.

Character...Creates Covenant.

253 CHARACTER Is...Revealed By Your Reaction To Human Weakness.
(Comedy Focused On Human Pain Is Sickness.)

254 Charisma...Is Not Character.

255 "Eating...Made Judging You Unnecessary."
"A Good Tree Cannot Bring Forth Evil Fruit..."

256 Etiquette...Is Not Character.

257 Flawed Character In People...Will Create More Pain Than A Lifetime of Tragedies.

258 Your Confidence In Them...Makes Them Bold.
It Does Not Change Their Character.
Give Respect, Earned or Not.
It Is Your Gift, Not An Honorarium.
Respect Reveals YOUR Character,
Not Another's.

259 How To Discern Character In Others?
1) Find The Voice They Trust...
2) The Hero They Most Admire...
3) Whose Counsel They Honor.

260 How You Treat Me...
Conscience...Controls Character,
Not Contracts.
A Contract...Does Not Create Character.

261 Nothing Reveals Character As Quickly...As A
Reaction To An Instruction.

262 The Character of God Satisfies Me...
More Than His Power.

CHOICE

263 Choose Goals Easy Enough...
To Enjoy Quickly.
Hard Goals...Do Not Increase Your Joy.

264 Choose ONE Focus...Daily.
Build Your Day Around It.
It Diminishes Disappointment, Depression
And Loneliness.
Magnify.

265 Choose...Those You Want To Inspire.
FOCUS.
(Leave Everybody Else Alone.)

266 CHOOSE...What You Want To Experience.
Make A List.
Set A Date.
Tell Others.
Seek Advice.
Keep Pictures On Wall.

267 Destiny?
World Is...Restaurant.
God Did Not Pre-Order.
You Choose Every Ingredient You Want For Your
Own Omelette.

CHRISTIAN

268 Boldness Is...Possibly The Most
Misunderstood Words In Christianity.
(Disrespect/Inappropriate)

269 CHRISTIAN Couples Do Not Live Together
Before Marriage.
Religious Couples May. (Smile)

270 Christian Fantasies~
Those Who Hate God...Will Enjoy You.
:)

271 Christianity...Is Being Challenged.
No Muslim...Would Accept Such.

272 Christianity Is Very Different...From Islam.
Choice.
Conquering.

273 This Generation of Unbelievers Has Not Yet
Experienced...A Militant Church.
Not Yet.

274 Christians...Are "YES! YES! People"...
In A No No World.
Yes...To Peace.
Yes...To Love.
Yes...To Honor.
Yes...To GOD.

275 Christmas Tips~
Do Not Hurry Through Presents.
Comment On Each One.
Hug Constantly.
Make Love Calls.
Musicalize..!

276 Mystery of Christianity~
We Applaud The Greatness of God.
Then, Scorn And Belittle Ourselves...
The CROWN of His Creativity.

277 Mystery of The Gospel~
Something Used...Can Be Exchanged For
Something New.
Something Dirty...Can Be Exchanged For
Something Pure.

278 No True Christian...Hates A Muslim.

279 THE CLOSEST THING TO SATAN...Is Often A Misguided Christian.

280 The Difference Between A Christian And An Atheist Is Simply...An Experience. Amazing.

281 Tim Tebow ...Amazing How One Christian Can Inspire Blasphemy On TV...

282 Two Sinners Who Agree...Are More Powerful Than 1,000 Christians Who Do Not (Agree). Stunning, Really.

283 Unlearned Christians...Permit Bullying. God...Fears No Bully.

284 When Sinners Sin...We Love Them And Pray. When Christians Sin...We Kick Them Out of Church.

CIRCLE

285 Circle of Comfort.
Circle of Counsel.
Circle of Conversation.
Circle of Companionship.
Circle of Contentious.
Which Circle Are You In?

286 Circles~
Who Do You...LOVE To Talk To? Why?
Who Is Difficult...To Talk To? Why?
Who Do You...ENJOY Listening To? Why?

287 CIRCLES of PEOPLE...Who
1) You Need.
2) Need You.
3) Motivate You.
4) Comfort You.
5) Mentor You.
6) Trust You.
7) Critique You.
8) Enjoy You.
9) Explore You.
10) Admire You.

COMPLAIN

288 Complainers~
If The Gospel Is Not Working For You...Why
Are You Still Hanging Around It?
Duh. :)

289 Complainers~
You Are Never Responsible For The Pain of
Those...Who Ignored Your Counsel.

290 Complaining~
Never Advertise...The Success of Your Enemy.

291 Men Lament The Mountains They Face...
But Ignore The Pebble That Makes
Them Stumble.

292 NEVER COMPLAIN...About What You Permit.
Change It...or Shut Up.

CONDUCT

293 Conduct Permitted...Is Conduct Taught.

294 Conduct You Permit...Is Conduct You Approve.

295 Poise...Can Take You Where Passion
Is Not Welcomed.
Do Not Riot With Peasants.
Stay In Your Chariot.
Kingly Poise.

296 Poise Is Speaking Right Words...
When You Have Wrong Feelings. :)

297 Poise Is Staying Calm...During Dinner With
Judas.

298 POISE Is The Ability To Recognize Disrespect...
Without Revealing It.

299 Poise Is...The Ability To Stay Silent In The
Presence of Fools.

CONFRONTATION

300 6 REASONS FOR CONFRONTATION~
~Attempt To Preserve A Relationship.
~Remove Confusion.
~Prevent A Tragedy.
~Establish Order.
~Confirm Leadership.
~Begin Healing.

301 CONFRONTATION~
I Will Not Stand Silent...And Permit You To
Dismantle My Dream.
Believe Me.

302 CONFRONTATION...Is An Attempt To Preserve
A Relationship.

303 CONFRONTATION...Is Rarely The Tool For
Change; It Is Merely A Release Valve That
Births A Silent War.

304 "Confrontation Is...The Seed For Healing."
Apostle Renê Terra Nova

CONFUSION

305 CONFUSION...
Requires Another To Survive.
Cannot Succeed Alone.

306 Confusion Is Always...A Conspiracy.
Astounding.

307 Confusion Is A Strategy...
For Conquering.
~In Politics.
~In Marriage.
~In Mind.

308 Confusion...Is Proof A Deceiver Is Present.

309 Confusion Is The Inevitable Odor...
of Every Deceiver Present.
Fools Are Clueless.

310 Confusion...Is The Odor of A Deceiver.
Do No Business In That Environment.

CONSEQUENCES

311 Flirtation Is...The Most Pleasurable Part of A Tragedy.

312 What Area of Your Life...Are You Openly Defiant?
When Do You Anticipate...The Consequences?

313 What Area of Your Life...Are You Willingly Ignorant?
When Do You Anticipate...The Consequences?

CONTROL

314 A Controlling Spirit...Is Speaking
Authoritatively Over Someone~
Who Is Not Under Your Authority.
Demonic.
Divisive.

315 FIRE...Cooked Food That Fed 6 Billion People
Yesterday.
Fire...Killed 5 Last Night In Apartment Fire.
Control Matters.
YOU.

316 Water Controlled...Creates Life.
Water Uncontrolled...Destroys Life.
(Tsunami) People. Energy.

CONVERSATIONS

317 An Effective Listener...Is Someone Who Unlocks Your Passion To Talk.

318 An Hour Conversation...Is 32 Page Book. Do Not Exit The Earth...Until Your Experiences And Persuasions Are In A Book.

319 Communication~ Always Speaking To The 9 Year Old "Mind"... Will Greatly Diminish Your Disappointments. Advised.

320 Intelligence Is... Understanding The Information. Clever Is...Manipulating The Information.

321 A Woman Talks...To Get Close. A Man Talks...To Get Admiration.

322 Do Not Expect "Honda" Conversations... To Produce A "Mercedes" Relationship.

323 I Listen~
~For Tone.
~For Falsehood.
~For Diversionary Tactics.
~For Honor.

324 I Extract Knowledge From Every Moment.
If You Do Not Speak...I Will Not Know.

325 Speak Fast...
When Your Words Are Unimportant.
The Faster You Speak...
The Less I Will Remember.
:)

326 Keys To Changing Your Mood...
1. Music
2. Candles
3. One Good Conversationalist
4. Sleep :)

327 The Bridge To Hope Is...Very Short.
Advised.

328 The Need For Explanation Reveals...
The Absence of Discernment.
Wisdom.

329 Whatever You Talk About MOST Today...Is The Most Serious Problem In
Your MIND.

330 Whatever You Talk About Most...
Is The Most Important Thing In Your Life.

331 When I Ask One Question...
I Want One Answer.

332 Your Words...Are Creating Your Experiences.
Profound.

333 Your Words...Keep Your Past Alive.
Your Words Decide...How Long An Offense
Lives.

334 Conversation Can Reveal...What Your
Discerning Has Not.

335 Conversation...Decides The Enjoyment of
A Relationship.
INTEGRITY...Decides The Longevity of
A Relationship.

336 Conversation Decides...Your Energy or Emptiness.

337 Conversation...Describes The Eventuality of Every Relationship.

338 Conversation...Describes The Quality of Every Relationship.
Listen Longer.

339 Conversation...Doth Not Cure A Fool.

340 Conversation Is...
The Oxygen For Relationship.
Without It, Love Is An Illusion.

341 Conversation...Is An Investigation
...To Determine Who Cares.

342 Conversation...Is An IQ Test.

343 Conversation...Is An Irreplaceable Information Source.
...Clarity.
...Mutual Interest.
...Competence.
...Compatibility.

344 Conversation...Is Like A Ping-Pong Game.
Your Returning The Ball...Matters.
It Decides...If I Stay At The Table.

345 Conversation Is...Research For A Future
Investment.

346 Conversation...Is The #1 Obsession of
The Holy Spirit.
Oh, When You Discover This,
Your World Changes.

347 Conversation...Is The Most Powerful Thing On
Earth.
QUESTIONS...Are The Most Important Part of
Any Conversation.

348 Conversation Is...The Birthplace For Every
Change In Your Life.

349 Conversation Is...Your Personal Profile.
...of Your Passion.
...of Your Discerning.
...of Your Servanthood.

350 Conversation Should Be A Reward...
Not A Burden.

351 Avoid Speaking...The Unnecessary.
Make Your Words...Purposeful.

352 Conversation...Should Have A Reward.
My Search For It Is...Relentless.
Every Moment of My Life.

353 Conversation...Summons.
Your Past.
Your Future.
Success.
Failure.
Prosperity.

354 Conversations Are...Maps.
Revealing Where You Have Been, or...
Where You Are Going.

355 Any Conversation That Provides Useable
Information...Has Value.
(Listen/Ask/Persist...or Too Costly.)

356 Conversations...Are Encyclopedias of
Knowledge...If You Listen.
...And, I Do.

357 Conversations...Reveal Limitations.
Quickly.

358 Conversations~
...Birth Seasons (Peter/Lame).
...Stop Pain (Jesus/Well).
...Create Miracles (Naaman/Maid).
...Unleash Love (Ruth/Boaz).

359 There Is A Reason...I Don't Enjoy Talking
To You.
Figure It Out.

360 Your Words Are Doors...or Walls.

361 Dramatic Change...Will Occur One
Conversation From Now.

362 A Missing Conversation...Explains Most
Conflicts.

363 Every Conversation Contains A Giver...And A
Receiver.

364 Every Conversation Is A Deposit or A
Withdrawal...From The Bank of Credibility.

365 Every Conversation Is...
A Presentation of What Matters Most To You.

366 Every Conversation Is...
A Major Investment.
I Scrutinize The Profit.
...And The Loss.
Always.

367 Every Conversation Is...
An Opportunity To Build Credibility.
...or Destroy It.

368 Every Conversation...
Is Another Page of Your Resumé.

369 Every Conversation...Is A Door.
YOU...Decide The Room.

370 How Do You Make A 2-Minute
Conversation...Unforgettable?

371 Every Conversation...Is An Interview.
...For Confidentiality.
...For Trustworthiness.
...For Interest.
...For Love.

372 I Analyze Conflicts:
One Is Always...The Killer.
One Is Always...The Healer.
I Side...With The Healer.

373 If You Were My Daughter~
Invest Conversation...Before You Invest Your
Presence.
Verify...His History.

374 I Could Easily Become Addicted To Meaningful
Conversation...If It Happened Often Enough.

375 I Have Never Seen A Problem...
Conversation Could Not Solve.
Counsel Delivered.

376 I Heard...What You Said.
Be Thankful.
I Heard...What You Did Not Say.
Be Concerned.

377 If "Conversation" Could Cure Stupid...
Satan Would Still Be A Choir Director.

378 If I Permit You To Talk To Me...
Make It A Good Experience For Me.
Advised.

379 If You Cannot Understand Me...
My Conversations Will Stop.
If I Cannot Understand You...
My Conversations Will Stop.

380 If You Listen Well...One Conversation Will Often Reveal Enough.

381 Keep Talking...I Had No Idea What You Have Been Hiding Inside You.

382 Listen For 7 Sounds...In Every Conversation.
~Focus
~Ideas
~Pain
~Honor
~Need
~Humility
~Opportunity

383 Never Discuss...The Unnecessary With Me. Never Say Anything About Yourself That You Do Not Want Anyone Else To Believe.

384 Not Everything Is Worthy of...Conversation.

385 Nothing Is Rarer Than...
Meaningful Conversation.
When You Find It...Embrace It.

386 One Conversation...Can Turn Every Wall Into A Door.

387 Every "Wall"...Is A Potential Door.

388 One Effective Conversation...Can Move Almost Any Mountain You Are Facing.

389 One Good 10-Minute Conversation... Often Reveals 90% of Everything You May Need To Know. (Invest.)

390 One Meaningful Conversation... Can Solve Your Biggest Problems.

391 SOUNDS IN CONVERSATIONS~
Envy?
Hints For Aid?
Kindness?
Hunger For Attention?
Control?
Joy?
Concern?
Servanthood?
Self-Love?
Speak Only...What Your Ears Love To Hear.

392 The Difference In Inner Chaos And Peace Is...One Effective Conversation.

393 The Frequency of Conversation...Describes The Healthiness of The Relationship.

~

394 The Fruit of Conversation Is...The Revelation of Character.

~

395 Politics~
Long Conversations...Do Not Solve Problems.
Truthful Conversations...Solve Problems.

~

396 What Missing Conversation...Would Have Made A Huge Difference In Your Life?
...With Your Father?
...With Your Pastor?

~

397 Why Would I Desire A Conversation With Someone...Who Would Not Read My Books..?
I Would Not.

~

398 You Can Close My Conversation With You...In 10 Happy Seconds.
(Just Start Reading Your Phone Texts.)
Time Is Up.

~

399 You Have The Freedom To Speak Your Mind...
And...I Have The Freedom To Evaluate It.

400 You Made Our One Conversation Very
Thorough...Satisfying All My Questions.

401 Your Conversation...
Decides The Size of Your "Mountain."
Huge.
Small.
So, Downsize It.
Words...Create Mastery.

402 Your Conversation With Me...
Explains Your Discerning of Me.

403 Your Conversations Reveal Where You Hope...or
Where You Hurt.

404 Your Conversation...Reveals Your Opinion
Matters To You.
Your Book...Reveals Others Matter
To You.

405 To Change Your Feelings...Simply Change Your
Conversation.

CORRECTION

406 3 PEOPLE YOU MUST NEVER CORRECT
1) Someone You Don't Love.
2) Someone Who Won't Listen.
3) Someone Not Under Your Authority.

407 Correct Me...
...When You Pay My Salary.
...When You Are My Scriptural Authority.
...When I Ask You For Counsel, Ideas.

408 Correct...What You Can Change.
Prepare...For What You Cannot.

409 Correcting A Man...
Can Keep You Single For A Lifetime.

410 95%...of Those In My Life ENDURE My
Correction.
4%...Accept It.
1%...Apply It.
Difference Is Obvious.

411 Correction...Is An Investment.
I Always Critique The Returns.

412 Correction~
It Is Entirely Proper To Not Address Wrong...
Until The Appropriate Time.
Karate Kid.
Judas/Jesus.

413 CORRECTION...Is An Investment;
Study The Profits or Loss.

414 CORRECTION...Is The Seed For Excellence.

415 "Enduring" My Correction...
Is Very Different Than "Embracing"
My Correction.
Very Few Embrace.

416 The Difference In Men...Is In What Offends
Them.

417 I Do Not Correct...Where I See Error.
I Correct...Where I See Humility.
(Jesus/Pharisees-Zacchaeus)

418 If Your Goal Is Acceptance...
All Correction Is Painful.

COUNSEL

419 Counsel~
Thinking With Only One Mind...Is The Slowest
Way To Get Into Your Future.

420 Every Counseling Session, There Is An Attempt
To Hide Information From You.
Stay Relentless.

421 If Your Counsel Is Ignored...
So Will Your Needs.

422 It Is Difficult For Me To Stay Interested In The
Success of Anyone...
Who Ignores My Counsel.

423 My Deadliest Losses...Occurred When I
Distrusted Worthy Counsel.

424 Never Pour Water...Until There Is
A Glass To Receive.
Wasted Counsel.

425 Sleep Often Provides...What Counsel Does Not.
:)

CREDIBILITY

426 Apologies...Increase Credibility.

427 Every Time You "Slither" To Avoid Answering A Question...You Destroy Your Own Credibility. Advised.

428 Credibility...
Has Never Known A Closed Door.
~Is Greater Than Genius.
~Never Denied Access.
~More Influential Than $.

429 Credibility Is The Highest Currency Possible...
Exchangeable In Every Environment.

430 Credibility...Is Currency In Every Nation.
Relentless...In Usability.

431 Credibility...Is More Powerful Than Your Desires.
(Joseph-Rebekah-Jesus)

432 Credibility...Is The Seed For Endorsement.

433 Credibility...Is World Currency.

434 Credibility...Is Worth Any Price.
ANY Price.
The Wise Will Pay For It.

435 Credibility Tips~
Every Time You Forget An Instruction...
Inform And Apologize And Compensate.

436 Credibility-Tips~
Every Time You Make A Mistake...Inform
Those Who Were Affected By The Mistake.

437 Every Completed Instruction...
Builds Credibility.
Credibility...Is Currency In Your Future.
Few-Get-It.

438 I Stop Trusting Anyone...Who Trivializes An Opportunity To Build Credibility With Me.

439 Let Us Make A Deal~
When You Provide Credibility...
I Will Provide You My Trust.

440 My Approval...Without Your Credibility...Will Not Happen.

441 Never Mistake My Love...
For Your Credibility.
Two Very Different Things.
I Love Some...That I Cannot Trust.

442 Reputation Rape~
His History Has More Credibility Than His Accusers.

CRISIS

443 3 Questions...Can Resolve Your Crisis.
Ask Them.

444 Crisis~
1.   Find 7 Advisors.
2.   Find 3 Intercessors.
3.   Involve Your Pastor/Mentor.
4.   Get ALONE-In The Secret Place.
It Is A "Wisdom" Problem...Not $ Problem.

445 CRISIS?
1. Create Your Top 10 Questions.
2. Review With 5 Intelligent People.
3. Follow Their Do-able Instructions.

446 Crisis...Accelerates Your Wisdom.

447 Crisis...Contains Divine Secrets.

448 Crisis Introduces Your Greatness...
To Others.
David/Goliath

449 Crisis Is...A Birth Place.
Crisis...Purges Disloyal People From Your Life.
Crisis Happens...As Birth Pains.

450 Crisis Is...An Opportunity For Creativity.

451 Crisis...Is Condensed Knowledge.
Lifetime of Knowledge...In A Single Problem.

452 CRISIS...Is One of The Few Opportunities
Greatness Has.

453 CRISIS Is The First Evidence...
of Favorable Change.
False Accusation...Joseph.
Adversity...David/Goliath.

454 Crisis Times~
1) Identify Your Desired Future.
2) Examine Your Decisions.
3) Admit Any Ignored Instruction.

455 Crisis...Summons Your Greatness.

456 Crisis-Talk~
1. Find 3 Decisions...That Reduce Your Pain...10%.
2. Identify Any Divine Law Broken.
3. Involve God.
4. SING.

457 Every Crisis Can Be Resolved...In 3 Decisions. Never Forget It.

458 Every Crisis...Can Be Traced To A Missing Conversation.

459 Every Crisis...Contains A Divine Secret.

460 PROBLEM?
What Instruction Was Dishonored?
What Is Biblical Solution?
Who Was Wronged?
What Will Stop It From Reoccurring?

461 Storms...Expose The Jonah On Your Boat.

462 Where Did Your Crisis Begin?
What Decision Birthed Crisis?
Whose Counsel Did You Ignore?
Who Is The "Problem Person?"

CRITICS

463 A Critic...Is Someone Who Finds You More
Interesting Than Themselves.

464 A Critic...Wants To Be Included In Your Life.
...Even At The Lowest Level.
:)

465 A Truthful Critic...Is An Unrewarded Genius.
Priceless.
They Do Not Require The Burden of Friendship.
Think. :-)

466 Analyzing The Achievements of Your Critics...
Will Create A Very Humorous Moment In
Your Life.

467 Critic: "Pastor, Why Did You Talk About Money
Today...For 30 Minutes?"
Pastor: "Same Reason You Worked For It...
40 Hours This Week."

468 Critics~
You Are The Most Interesting Event In
Their Life.
Critics...Just Feel "Left Out."
:)

469 CRITICISM From New Christians Toward
Leaders Is Humorous~Kinda Like Privates In
Boot Camp...Advising General Patton.

470 Criticism Hurts.
But, When You Study The Credibility of
Your Critics...All The Pain Goes Away.

471 Criticism Is Often Free Counsel...
Without The Stress of Relationship. :)

472 Criticism Is Usually The Death Gargle...of
A Non-Achiever.

473 Criticism Is...Simply The Reaction
From A Disappointed Life.

474 Criticism Weakens Your Influence With Him.
Men Stop Listening To Sounds of Disapproval.
Survival Technique.

475 Criticism...The Only Time A Fool Thought About You.

476 Critics~
A Lion...Ignores A Barking Dog.

477 Critics~
Don't Stop By A Sewer...On Your Way To The Ocean. (Dream)
Reactions.
Distractions.

478 Critics~
I Would Respond To You...
If Your Opinion Mattered.

479 Critics~
No Elephant...Fears A Mousetrap.

480 Dear Critic~
Am Investing My Attention And Energy...
In My Friends.
Have Had None Left Over...To Invest In Fools.

481 Him: "Have You Read What Your Critics Say?"
Me: "I Do Not Research Opinions of...
The Unlearned." :)

482 I Am Too Strong To Be Destroyed...
By A Stupid Sentence From Your Lips.
:)

483 I Only Read...What I Want To Remember.
Criticism

484 Never Give More Time To A Critic Than You
Would Give To A Friend.

485 Never Give Up A Rose...To Satisfy A Cactus.

486 Never Live A Single Day...To Satisfy A Critic.
Never.
Never.
Never.
Never.

487 No Lion...Notices A Barking Dog.
I Know.
I Raised Them Together. :)

488 Response To Your Critics...
"Your Words Would Have Hurt Me...
If You Mattered."

489 The Closer You Come To Your Canaan...
The More Shrill The Voice of Your Critics.
:)

490 You Are The Most Interesting Event In Your
Critics Life.
:)

491 Your Critic...Is Just Trying To Be Remembered.
:)

492 Your Criticism Only Hurts...If Your Mind Is
Superior To Mine.
:)

493 Your Critics...Always Verify Your True Friends.
Irreplaceable Joy.

494 Your Critics...Crave Your Attention.

495 Your Best NEVER Satisfies...Critics.
Your Best ALWAYS Satisfies...God.

DATE-TALK

496 7 Tones That Stop Weddings~
~Argumentative.
~Dismissive.
~Scornful.
~Corrective.
~Accusatory.
~Disinterest.
~Condescension.

497 A Date Is An Experiment...Not
A Decision.

498 A Single Conversation...Disqualifies Most.

499 Are You Dating For A Mere Experience...
or Training For A Lifestyle?
(Esther/Joseph)

500 Beware The Man Who Deftly Avoids:
...Easy Questions.
...Questions About His Past.
...Discussion of His Goals.

501 Dating~
"Attention" Alone...Satisfies Some People.
Their Heart...Remains Uninvolved.

502 Checklist:
History of Honor.
Her Mentors.
Her Fear of God.
Agreeable Temperament or Contentious.

503 Commitment~
No Man Will Commit...
If Investment Is Not Equal.
I Will Not Trade My Rolls-Royce...
For Your Wal-Mart Bike.

504 Dating~
Criticism...Is The Assassin of Intimacy.

505 Damaged...Is When You Match An Old Scar To A
New Face.

506 Date-Talk~
It Is Simple, Really.
You Need A Worshipper...Not A Friend.

507 Dating~
3 World-Class Needs.
Intelligence.
Integrity.
Inspiration.

508 Dating~
A 747 Jet And A Bicycle...Don't Belong On
The Same Runway.
:)

509 Dating~
A God-Connection...Will Not Disqualify
Themselves For Relationship.
That's How You Recognize It Is God.

510 Dating~
A Man Does Not Marry The Woman Who
Turns Him On.
A Man Marries The Woman Who...
Does Not Turn Him OFF.

511 Dating~
A Woman...Decides How A Man Feels.
That Feeling...Determines
Their Entire Future Together.

512 Dating~
Are You Looking For Someone To Endure
The "Devil-Part" of You...or Inspire
The "God-Part" of You..?

513 Dating~
Caring...Increases Compatibility.

514 Dating~
Desire...Is Not Always Love.
(Lion Chasing Antelope)

515 Dating~
Disinterest...Is A Divine Conclusion.

516 Dating~
Disinterest...Is Divine Permission To
Disconnect.

517 Dating~
Do Not Buy A House...Because You Love
The Front Door.

518 Dating~
Do Not Risk Losing A Garden...Just Because
You Discovered Weeds.

519 Dating~
Even The Untrustworthy...Desire
The Trustworthy.

520 Dating~
First Impressions...Are Curable.
:)

521 Dating~
~How Do They Improve Me?
~What Secret Fears Are Emerging?
~Do They Show Honor? Dishonor?
~Do I Feel Need For Caution?

522 Dating~
How Do You Build Credibility...With Someone
Who Cannot Speak Your Language..?

523 Dating~
How Many Times Does A Snake Have To
Bite You...Before You Kill It?

524 Dating~
I Provided...The Bridge.
You...Did Not Cross It.

525 Dating~

ICE...Can Make A Sensuous Relationship
Quite Stressful.
(Integrity, Compassion, Excellence.)
:)

526 Dating~

I Have Found Some Pleasures...Worthy of
The Chase.
I Never Found A "Puzzle"...Worth The Chase.

527 Dating~

I Have Never Met A Man Who Was Turned Off...
By Humility.

528 Dating~

If Trust Is Not Important...
Your Opportunities Are Endless.
:)

529 Dating~

Invest "Time"...Before You Invest Your "Life."

530 Dating~

If You Need An Ocean...
Don't Camp By A Creek.

531 Dating~
In The Multitude of Conversations...
There Is Understanding.

532 Dating~
Invest Time...Before You Commit.
Nobody Is Ever As They First Appear.

533 Dating~
Kissing Reveals Skill...Not Love.

534 My Opinion of You...Concerns Me Far More
Than Your Opinion of Me.
:):)

535 Dating~
Never Stop Comparing...
Investments In The Relationship.
Never.
Think.

536 Dating~
Not Every Mountain...Is Worth The Climb.

537 Dating~
One Gives...
One Receives...
Not An Equal Investment.

538 Dating~
Please Keep Talking.
You Are Confirming...My Unspoken Concerns.

539 Dating~
Reaching Is...The Seed For Reaction.
Reactions...Reveal Hidden Truth.

540 Dating~
Sarcasm...Kills Desire.

541 Dating~
Skill At Love-Talk Is...Not Love.
Few Know This.

542 Dating~
Some...Find Immaturity of Youth
Exhausting.
Some...Find "Older" Age Boring.
Find What Excites Your "Heart."

543 Dating~
Sometimes An Inner Voice Insists..."You
Still Do Not Really Know The True Hidden Part
of Him."

544 Dating~
The Invitation To Enter...Is To Qualify You For
The Invitation To Stay.
The Joseph Journal.

545 Dating~
The More You Listen...The More You Know.
The More You Know...
The Easier The Decision.
Simple, Really.

546 Dating~
The Right One...Isn't Dangerous
...Removes Fear.
...Is Easy To Trust.
...Inspires Conversation.
...Feels Your Pain.

547 Dating~
The Right Person...Is Worth Any Price.
ANY Price.

548 Dating~
...The Stage Where Honor Is Displayed.
...Where Reactions Expose.
...Where Difference Is Revealed.

549 Dating~
The Undiscerning...Are The Unqualified.

550 Dating~
The Wise Test...And Test...And Test.
Until Peace Comes.

551 DATING?
What Interest Do They Show In MY
Problems?
Do I Have A Desire To Discuss My QUEST
With Them?
Do They Lie, Slither or Avoid?

552 Dating~
When I Know What You Enjoy...I Can Predict
Our Future.
When I Know Who You Honor...I Can Predict
My Joy.

553 Dating~
When I Saw What Created Her Excitement...
I Lost Mine.
:)

554 Dating~
When I Saw Who You Enjoyed...I Realized You
Would Not Enjoy Me.

555 Dating~
When You Make Our Relationship...Hard.
You Make My Decision...Easy.

556 Dating~
When You See Who They Loved Before You...You
May Not Feel So Special.
:)

557 Dating~
When Your Request Is Unimportant To Them...
You Are Unimportant To Them.

558 Dating~
You Shop At The Store...
That Has What You Need.

559 Dating~
You Will Never Stay Close To Someone...
You Are Not Around Daily.

560 Dating~
Your Investment In Me...Was Too Small To Do
Business.

561 Dating~
Your Obsession To Criticize...Is A
Costly Pleasure.

562 Dating~
Your Reactions Have Well Answered...
My Unasked Questions.

563 Dating A Successful Person Requires:
Accuracy...In Communication.
Attentiveness.
Adaptation...To Changing Focus.

564 Dating...Is Exploring For Possible Investment.

565 Dating Is...Interrogation For Investment.
Dating Is...Interviewing For A Lifetime
Confidante.

566 Dating Is Research...For Your Greatest Lifetime
Investment.
~Expensive.
~Deceptive.

567 Dating Is...Training.
But, Nobody Believes It.

568 Dating...Is Interviewing For Your Next Owner.
:)

569 Dating...Is To Qualify Someone For All of You.

570 Do You Really Want A Mate...
Who Cannot Find You..??

571 Dating Questions~
What Percentage of Them Do You...Enjoy?
Endure?
How Soon Do You Experience...Enough of
Them..?

572 Do You Really Want A Mate Too Dumb To
Discern You..?

573 Fool or King
When The Fool In Me Arises...
I Know She Is Not My Queen.

574 Her Ability To Discern...Will Remove Your Need
To Persuade.

575 Her Ability To Make You Feel Kingly...
Is Not Always Proof She Is A Queen.
Proverbs 7

576 Dating...Becomes A Lifetime Search For The
Sound of Gratitude.
Good Luck :)

577 Unspoken Love...Is Hardly Love At All.

578 Her Preparation For Her Moments With You...
Explains Her Value of You.
(Queen of Sheba/Solomon)

579 Your Unwillingness To Talk...Explains
My Unwillingness To Reach.

580 Her Skill At Creating Desire Within You...Is Not
Proof of "Destiny."
(Delilah)

581 Her~"A Stalker Follows Me!"
Me~"He Wants A Memorable Experience.
Create One For Him...The Taser Experience."

582 Her: "He Was...Uninteresting."
Him: "I Was...Uninterested."
A Difference.

583 How Did They Exit Their Last Relationship?
~Is Conversation Burdensome?
~Is Their "Hunger" For Attention?
~Is Their "Hunger" For God?
~Is Their "Hunger" For Aid?

584 I Wanted...Romance.
She Wanted...Debates.
:-)
I Wonder If Romance...And Reality Ever Agree?

585 If He Wants To Talk To You, He Will Call.
If He Wants To Talk To You, He Will Call.
If He Wants To Talk To You, He Will Call.

586 If I Do Not Enjoy Lunch...
I Will Not Be Returning For Dinner.

587 If You Are Considering "Two"...
...The Right "One" Has Not Yet Arrived.

588 If You Do Not Have A Strong Desire
To Talk To Them...There Is A Reason.
Explainable or Not.

589 If You Do Not Know How To Talk To Me...You Would Not Know How To Live With Me.

590 If You Need More Than I Am Offering...
You Need What I Do Not Have.

591 In What Scenario Would They Embarrass Me?
~In A Crisis, Could They Pray Effectively For Me?
~Are They Successful or Needy?

592 Is There A Camel You Have Refused To Water..?
Costly Reaction.

593 Is Meaningful Talk A Struggle?
~Do They Energize You, or Are You
   Just Lonely?
~Do Their Questions Show True Interest
   In Your Passion?

594 Never Marry Someone...Who Does Not Treat You Better Than You Would Treat Yourself.

595 Some...Belong Together.
Some...Belong To Another.
The Bait...Reveals The Kind of Fish Desired.

596 The Standards of Your Marriage...Are
Established In Your Courtship.

597 The World-Class Man...
Will Require The World-Class Woman.

598 The-Samson-Journal~
You Can Fall In Love With Someone
Who Will Destroy Your Life.
Evangelistic Dating...Is Deadly.

599 The-Samson-Journal~
3-Minute Pleasure...Can Become Lifetime Pain.

600 The-Samson-Journal~
Her Unpredictability Is~
...Stimulating.
...Sensuous.
...Provocative.
And Deadly.

601 Think Twice Before Marriage...
...If He Has Not Established A History of Honor.
(Authority-Parents-You-God)

602 Think Twice Before Marriage~
...If Their History Is Hidden.
...If They Are Scornful of Authority.

603 Think-Twice-Before-Marriage:
~If They Are Uncomfortable
In The Presence of God.
~If They Never Ask Quality Questions
About Your Assignment.

604 Think Twice Before Marriage~
...If They Show No Desire To Give To You.
...If You Have No Longing To Discuss Your
Dreams.

605 When I Am Not Attracted To Someone...
It Costs Me Big.
:) :)

606 When You Explained What You Needed...
I Realized I Was Not.

607 Withhold Affection...
Until You Prove Character.

608 Yes...A Younger Mate...Is Often More Adaptable.
~Older...Usually Unteachable.

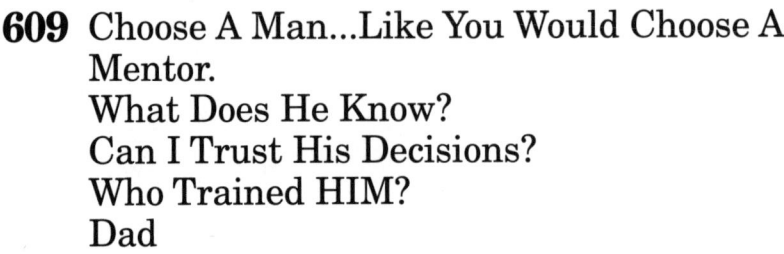

DEARDAUGHTER

609 Choose A Man...Like You Would Choose A
Mentor.
What Does He Know?
Can I Trust His Decisions?
Who Trained HIM?
Dad

610 Never Submit...To An Unqualified Man.
Dad

611 A Man Who Dishonors...Will Become Your
Lifetime Pain.
Dad

612 All Men...Look.
Few Men...Listen.
Advised.
Dad

613 An "Interested" Woman...Will Outlast
An "Interesting" Woman.
Dad

614 An Exceptional Man...
Will Have Exceptional Needs.
Dad

615 A Smart Man...Is Not Fascinated With A Coy
Woman.
Sincere? Yes.
Clever? No.
Dad

616 A Strong Woman...
Has No Need To Discuss It.
Dad

617 Asking Appropriate Questions...
Will Distinguish You To A Man.
(Queen of Sheba)

618 Beauty...Does Not Make A Woman
Interesting.
But, An Interesting Woman...
Is Always Beautiful.

619 Beware The Man...Who Wants To Look At You,
But Does Not Want To Listen To You.

620 Crazy...Multiplies.
Crazy Men...Are Never Extinct.
Do Not Run.
Consider Them...A Divine Zoo.
:)
Dad

621 Criticism...Instantly Destroys Any Affection He
Had Toward You.
Few-Get-It.
Dad

622 Dishonoring You...Reveals He Views You As A
Toy, Not An Investment.
His Odor...Will Increase.
Dad

623 Do Not Despair If You Miss "The Right One."
There Is More Than One Possibility.
:)
Dad

624 If He Does Not Understand Honor...He
Understands Nothing.
Dad

625 Do Not Stop For A Crumb...On Your Way To
Your Banquet.
Dad

626 Do You Want His Attention...or
His Heart?
Dad

627 Do You Make Him...
...Want To Talk?
...Listen?
Or...
...Watch TV?
:)

628 Do You Really Want A Man...
Incapable of Understanding You?

629 Does His History...Confirm Good Decisions?
How Does He React...To Authority?
Who...Trained Him?
Dad

630 Don't Let Your Loneliness Tempt You...To Reach
For Yesterday Pain.
Dad

631 Don't Look For...Young.
Don't Look For...Old.
Don't Look For...Handsome.
Look For...A Man Who Honors.

632 Don't Marry A Man...You Don't Want To Learn
From.
Dad

633 Every Man...Has A Different Interest.
And, It Can Change Instantly.
Dad

634 Every Man Secretly Dreams of Marrying...
An Uncritical Wife.
Few-Get-It.
Dad

635 Find A Man...Other Men Admire.
Dad

636 He Is Quite Gifted...In "Talking" To You.
Is He As Gifted...When He "Listens" To You?
Dad

637 His Ability To Discern You...Will Remove
Your Burden To Persuade Him.

638 His Ability To Talk...
Does Not Guarantee His Ability To Love.
The Young...Trust.
The Wise...Test.
Dad

639 His Admiration Costs Far More...Than
His Attention.
A "Quarter" On The Pavement...Gets
His Attention.
Dad

640 His Faithfulness...Is Not Your Responsibility.
His Faithfulness...Is HIS Responsibility.
Dad

641 His Friends...Explain His Needs.
Dad

642 His Fascination With You...Is Not Proof He Will
Honor You.
Dad

643 His "Potential"...Means ZERO.
NOTHING.
Even Lucifer...Had Potential.
Dad

644 His Reaction To You...Reveals
Your Desirability.
His Reaction To Your Pain...Reveals
His Love.
Dad

645 His Reactions...Reveal His Wisdom.
His Words...Reveals His Persuasions.
His Tone...Reveals His Honor.
Dad

646 His Shoes...Reveal His Style.
His Watch...Reveals His $$$.
His Mentors...Reveal His Future.
Discern.
Dad

647 If FUN Is Your Focus...He Is Perfect.
If "Future" Is Your Focus...Throw The Fish Back
Into The Water.

648 If He Cannot Discern Your Difference...
He Does Not Desire Your Difference.
Advised.
Dad

649 If He Enters Your Body Before Your Covenant...
He Will Exit Your Life Before The Marriage.
Dad

650 If He Resents Those You Enjoy...It Will Not
Work.
Dad

651 If You Cannot Trust Him...Drop Him.
Case Closed.
Dad

652 If You Do Not Have Passion For His Mission...
He Will Lose His Passion For You.
Advised.
Dad

653 If You Do Not Know His Daily Responsibilities...
...You Still Do Not Know Him.
Dad

654 If You Know How To Talk To A Man...He
Will Desire Your Presence For A Lifetime.
Dad

655 If You Want A King...Master His Domain.
Dad

656 Immerse Yourself In His World...
And He Will Never Want You To Leave It.
Ruth's Diary

657 Is He Willing...To Train You?
Are You...Willing To Be Trained?
Is He Worthy...of Your Investment?
Dad

658 Know His Yesterday...Before You Imagine His Tomorrow.
Dad

659 Love Is...When He Wants To "Service" Your Heart.
Wisdom Is...When He Knows How.
Dad

660 Many Girls Have Access To...A Good Man.
Few..."Discern" Him.
Dad

661 Many May Love Your Mouth...
But The Right Man Will Love Your Words.

662 Marry A
~Golfer...He Is So Easily Satisfied.
~Motorcyclist...He Trusts The Entire World.
~Boxer...Others Hit Him For You.
Dad

663 "Master His Domain" Means...
...To Study His World, His Interests.
...Know How To Discuss His Concerns.
Dad

664 Moments...Matter.
Esther Had 2 Meals...To Persuade A King.
A Moment...Can Decide A Lifetime.

665 Most Men Are...Demanding.
WHAT They Demand...
Reveals Their Difference.
Dad

666 Never Doubt The Future of A Man Who
Understands Protocol And Knows How To Honor
Appropriately.
Dad

667 Never Invest Rolls-Royce Time...In A
Honda Relationship.
Dad

668 Never Marry...Who You Cannot Discern.
Dad

669 No Man...Dishonors A Lady.
His Dishonor...Reveals He Does Not View You As
A Lady.
Dad

670 No Man Stays Silent...If You Are Talking
About Something He Loves.
Dad

671 None of His Gifts...Can Replace His Heart.
Dad

672 Nothing Is More Torturous Than Living With A
Man...Who Is Not Trained By God.
Dad

673 One Wrong Conversation...Can Lose
Your "Garden."
Adam/Eve.
Dad

674 If You Attempt To Train A Fool...Who Is The
Bigger Fool?
Dad

675 Replace...Any Machine That Does Not Work.
Replace...Any Man That Does Not Work.
Dad

676 Ruth Created Credibility With Employees
Boaz Trusted...Before He Trusted Her.
Dad

677 Ruth Trained In The Fields of Boaz...
Before She Qualified For The House of Boaz.
Dad

678 Some Men...Are Not Men.
Dad

679 Some...Want An Experience.
Some...Want A Servant.
Some...Want A Queen.
His Investment...Reveals.
Dad

680 Sometimes Their Departure...Is Just A Divine
Colonic.
Dad

681 STUDY...
~His Reactions...To Discern His Character.
~His Watch, Shoes To Assess $.
~His Mentor To Predict His Future.
Dad

682 Why Trust...The Unproven?
Dad

683 Submission...Is Simply Permission To Protect.
(He Better Understand This.)
Dad

684 Getting His Attention...Is Easy.
Getting His Heart...Is Divine.
Dad

685 The Difference In Men...Is Not The Past They
Survived...But The Future They Design.
Dad

686 The Greater The Prize...
The Greater Your Preparation.
Dad

687 The Greatest Investment You Can Make In Your
Man Is...A Question.
Dad

688 The Longer You Look...The More You Will See.
Research Reduces Risk.
Dad

689 The Man Who Loves Looking At You...
May Hate Listening To You.
Dad

690 The "Perfect Man"...Would Not Choose You, Would He?
:)
Kinda Obvious, Huh?
Dad

691 The Right One...Increases Order In Your Life.
The Wrong One...Increases DISorder In Your Life.
Dad

692 The Right One...Will Not Look For Another.
You Are Enough.
Dad

693 The Right One...Will Unleash Unexplainable Energy For Meaningful Conversation.
Consistently.
Dad

694 A Man That Cannot Discern Your Difference...
Certainly Will Never Reward You For It.
Dad

695 Your Feeling...Is Not A Fact. Verify Your Opinion...Before You Make A Commitment.
Dad

696 Those Who Enjoy You...May Not Want To Know
You.
Dad

697 Those Who Provoke...Will Not Yoke.
Dad

698 Train...With The "Trained."
"The Boaz Secret"...By Mrs. Ruth Boaz.
Dad

699 Until You Speak Right Words...
His Imagination Will Rule.
Dad

700 Until You Understand His Responsibilities...
Most of Your Reactions Will Be Inappropriate.
Dad

701 What He Does...Is Who He Is.
Duh. :)
Dad

702 When A Man Discerns A True Listener...
He Never Leaves.
Dad

703 When You Know Who He Admires...
You Will Know What He May Become.
Dad

704 Why Are You "Explaining" Your Difference To Him?
Even The Peasant...Recognizes The Queen.
Dad

705 You...Decide Your "Field."
Your Field...Decides Your Favor.
Ruth
Dad

706 You Have Invested...Your Very Best.
His "Best"...Has Not Satisfied You.
Leave.
Dad

707 You Must Qualify For Access...
Before You Can Qualify For Love.
Dad

708 You Say, "But, He Loves Talking To Me!"
But...Do YOU Love Talking To Him..?
The Test.
Dad

709 Your Admiration Will Increase...
With The Right One.
Your Admiration Will Decrease...
With The Wrong One.
Dad

710 Attack...Will Not Increase His Trust.
Dad

711 You Are Not...His Only Problem.
So Do Not Become His Biggest Problem.
Dad

712 Wrong Timing...Will Kill The Perfect
Relationship.
Nobody Believes It.

713 Your Reactions...Schedule His Solitude.
Dad

DearSis

714 Who Unlocks The Worst In You...And Why Do You Stay Around Them..?

715 The Difference In A Good Man And An Evil Man...Is The Way He Treats A Woman.

716 The Worthy...Will Discern Your Worth. The Unworthy...Cannot. Think.

717 The Immature...Do Not Listen.
The Ignorant...Do Not Know.
The Fool...Does Not Care.
The Proud...Do Not Ask.

718 100 Conversations Will Not Erase...His Request You Ignored.

719 A Boy...Cannot Delay Gratification.
A Man...Can.

720 A Busy Man...
Has Very Different Expectations.
(Make Moments Memorable For Him.
An Achiever Values It.)

721 A King Never Forgets The Queen's
Excitement...Towards The Court Jester.

722 A King...Knows He Is.

723 A Real Man...Does Not Require Permission To
Lead.

724 Age Difference=Perception Difference.
You Are 20,000 Experiences...Behind.
Seeds For Indescribable Stress.

725 An Experience With A Man...Does Not
Guarantee Your Influence On Him.
Admiration Has Greater Reward Than
Attention.

726 An Unromantic Man...
Is Like A Car Without Wheels.
No Reason To Own One.
:)

727 Two Success Secrets.
Who...Do You Trust?
Who...Can Trust You?

728 Arguments Will Get His Attention...
But Not His Admiration.

729 Attack...Is When You Force Him To Defend
Himself.
It Attracts...His Attention.
It Destroys...His Admiration.

730 Beauty Is...Never Unimportant.
Never.
(If He Denies It, He Is Simply Using A
Different Strategy.)

731 Become The Rare Woman Who Resists The
Overwhelming Urge...To Instruct Him Like A
Little Boy.

732 Boaz Watched Ruth In His Fields~
Long Before She Was Welcomed To His Home.
Credibility Is...Seed For Availability.

733 Do You Really Feel Protected...By The Man
You...Trapped?

734 Do You Really Want A Life Journey...With
Someone Who Cannot Even Find...YOU?

735 Do Not Build...A Web.
Build A NEST.
One Energizes Him To Leave.
One Energizes Him To Stay.

736 Entertain Him.
Comfort Suffocates Creativity.
A Man Thrives On The Sensation of...New.
Counsel Delivered.

737 Establish His Reward System...
Before Investing Your Submission.

738 Eve Was Not The Only Woman Who Talked
Herself...Out of A Paradise.

739 God Loving You...Brings No Joy.
You Loving God...Will.

740 Stay Close...To Those You Admire.
If They Are Trustworthy.

741 Every Man Is...Very Different.
So, Deal With Them...Accordingly.
...For A Rewarding Relationship.

742 Every Man Wants Something Different...
From A Woman.
~Nurse?
~Cook?
~Conversationalist?
~Momma?
~Confidante?
~Playmate?

743 Every Warrior Needs A~
~Cave of Comfort.
~Nest Without Thorns.
~Voice Without Scorn.
~Pleasure Without Caution.
Every Word He Speaks...
Helps Reveal The Hidden Part of Him.

744 Explaining Your Greatness...
To An Undiscerning Man Is Kinda Amusing,
Don't You Think..?

745 God Often Uses One Hour of Their Anger...
To Save You A Lifetime of Heartache.

746 He Is Unromantic?
Nah.
Just Unaroused.

747 Ask MORE Questions. Insist.
What Is The Quality of People Who Enjoy
Him?
You Are Investing Your LIFE Into Him.

748 He Who Trivializes Your Words...Will Greatly
Sadden Your Life.
Believe Me, Sis.

749 He Is Hostile Toward The Presence of God?
Who Will Develop His Conscience?
Trust No Man Without Keen Conscience.

750 His Interest...Decides If He Reaches.
Your Words...Decide If He Keeps Reaching.

751 His Music...Reveals His Philosophy.
His Talk...Reveals Who He Honors.
His Friends...Reveals His Trust.
His Right Words...Do Not Guarantee
A Right Heart.

752 His Treatment of You...Reveals HIS Character.
NOT...Your Value.

753 How Can You Be In Love...With A Man You Do
Not Know?
You Are Not.
You Are In Love With...Your "Perception" of Him.

754 I Notice...
...Her Reaction To My Preference List.
...Her Playfulness Toward Males.
...Her Evasion of My Questions.

755 I Will Not Exit Earth...
...Until I Find Every Way Possible...
...For You To FEEL My Love.

756 If Conversation Could Cure A Violent Man...
Lucifer Would Still Be Leading The Choir In
Heaven.
Do Not Stay Stupid.

757 If He Did Not Ask...He Does Not Want To Know.

758 If He Is Really Your King...You Will Invest All To
Qualify For Him.
If He Will Not Give You Flowers...

759 He Will Never Give You His Heart.
If You Are Not In His Fields...Do Not Expect To
Be In His Future.
Secrets-of-Ruth

760 If You Could Train A Fool...Don't You Think God
Would Have Held A Seminar...
For Lucifer?
Do Not Stay Stupid.

761 Improving Someone...Requires
Their Permission.

762 If You Know How To Talk To A Man...You Will
Have Access To Him...The Rest of Your Life.
Believe It.

763 If You Stay With An Abusive Man...
The Damage Has Already Been Done.

764 If You Want A King...Know His Domain.
(Ruth/Boaz...Abigail/David...Pro. 31)

765 If Your Presence Has Not Improved Him...
Remove It.

766 Invest Time...In Him.

767 Access...Exposes Weaknesses And Reveals His Heart.
Phone Creates "Perception."

768 Is Your Goal To Be An Experience...or His Friend..?

769 Loneliness...Makes An Average Guy Seem Spectacular.

770 Lonely Women...Make Bad Decisions.
Men Too.

771 Marry The Man Capable of Training You...
For His World.
My Counsel.

772 Men Interpret Kindness...As Honor.
...Control As Dishonor.
If It Matters To You.
Advised.

773 Never Become So Bitter...That You Quit Admiring A Successful Man.

774 Beautiful Women...Exude The Elusive Elixir of Hope. Without One Ounce of Guilt.

775 No Man of Honor...Will Live With Dishonor.
...In Conversation.
...In Tone.
...In Countenance.
Ever.

776 No Man...Marries The Woman Who Embarrasses Him.
No Man.
(And, He May Never Tell You When You Did.)

777 OK, Sweet Sis...
Talkers.
Stalkers.
Gawkers.
Balkers.
Walkers.
Which Is He..?
Brother

778 Only A Fool Marries A Man...Who Has No Mission.

779 Ruth Earned Credibility...In His Fields~
Before She Qualified...For His Name.
(Boaz/Marriage)

780 Ruth Was In The Fields of Boaz...BEFORE
She Was In His Heart.
Credibility...Before Commitment.

781 Ruth...Positioned.
Boaz...Decided.

782 Submission Is...Not Ownership.
Submission Is...Merely Authorizing Him
To Protect You.

783 Test Him: Your Future Is In His Hands.
Listen For Slither, Skillful Maneuvering In
Elusive Conversation.

784 The Difference In Men...Is Not Their
Background.
The Difference In Men...Is Their Future.
Advised.

785 The First Evidence of His Wisdom...Is If He Has
Identified Who He Should Honor.
Enough Said.

786 The Lovable Man Is...Not Always Loving.
Please...Please...Believe Me.

787 The Man That Never Talks To You...
Will Never Marry You.
Believe Me.

788 The Right One...
Dreads Being Away From You.
For Real.

789 The Right One...Will Not Be At The Wrong
Places.
Geography Matters...In Your Quest.
Your Big Brother.

790 The Woman...Who Gets In His Face...
Will Never Get Into His Heart.

791 The Wrong One CANNOT Discern You.
He Is Incapable.
That Will Be THE Difference In...
The Right One.

792 To Know His Future, Look At His Goals.
To Know His $, Look At Watch/Shoes.
To Know His Heart, Look At His Worship.

793 Treating Him Like A King...Does Not Make Him
One.

794 The Easiest Relationship In My Life...Is
The Holy Spirit.

795 Verbal Abuse...Does Not Make Him A Better
"Slave."
Advised.

796 What Do You Need Most?
The Appearance of Caring...or Caring?
How Do You Distinguish...The Difference?

797 When He Does Not Respond...
Stop Talking.
~Do Not Yell.
~Do Not Whine.
~Do Not Cry.
~Do Not Pout.
~Just STOP.

798 When He Is In Love With You...Your Joy
Becomes His Obsession.
His Constant Obsession.

799 When You Learn Him...You Will Earn Him.

800 Love Does Not Thrive...In Solitude.

801 The More The Planning...The Quicker
Love Dies.

802 You Have...High Expectations..?
Imagine His.

An Uncommon Man...Will Have
Uncommon Expectations.

Ready..?

803 Love...Is Deadly Afraid of Scrutiny.

804 Your Countenance of Pain...Influences A Man 10
Times More Than Your Look of Anger.
Influence.

805 Your Credibility...Is Built Through The Naomi
You Serve.
Your Boaz...Will Research The Quality of Your
Servanthood.

806 Your DIFFERENCE...From Other Women Is
The Magnetism.
Identify It...To Treasure It.

807 Your Imagination...Has Turned A Peasant
Into A King.

Walk Slower, Sweet Sis...

808 Your Territory of Divine Responsibility...Is Very
Different Than Expectations of Others.
Simplify.

809 The Difference In Men...Is What They Are
Willing To Live Without.

810 Excitement...Can Be Scheduled.

811 Doing Right Things...Satisfies More Than Doing
Many Things.

812 Genius Is...The Ability To Find Great Pleasures
At Low Prices.
:)

DearSon

813 A Love Letter...Is Not Love.
It Is The Ability To "Describe" Love.
Daddy-Knows.

814 A Queen...Will Manage Your Palace.
This One...Cannot Even Clean Her Car.
Dad

815 Attention...Is The Goal
of The Common Woman.
Integrity...Is The Goal
of The Uncommon Woman.
Dad

816 Beauty Is Not Always...Your Harvest.
Beauty Is Sometimes...Your Trap.

817 The Son...Chooses.
He Is "The Follower."
i.e. Prodigal Son.

818 Delilah "Talks."
Never Forget It.
Dad

819 Do Not Ask Her...For "Permission" To Lead.
Give Her An Opportunity...To Follow.
Dad

820 Do Not Judge Her...For Not Listening To You.
Listening Requires...A Certain IQ.
A Divine Gift. :)
Dad

821 Do Not Let Your Loneliness Tempt You...
To Reach For Yesterday Pain.
Dad

822 Do Not Linger At The Door...If She Does Not
Invite You In.
Dad

823 Do Not Search For Someone..."To Love."
Search For Someone..."To Enjoy."
Dad

824 Does She Love What You Do...or Who You Are?
Dad

825 Every Woman Is A Rose/Thorn Combo.
Thorns Increase Caution...When Handling
The Rose.
Dad

826 Every Woman...Is An Event.
~Inspiration.
~Interrogation.
~Conversation.
~Confrontation.
~Celebration.
Dad

827 Cynicism...Has Kept Many Unhappy People
Alive.
Much Longer Than Necessary.
:)
Dad

828 Fortunately, She Is A Master
Conversationalist...
(Since She Does Not Listen At All.)
:)
Dad

829 Get Close Enough To Her...To Verify Her
Trustworthiness.
...or Lack of It.
Dad

830 Her Adaptation Will Always Be...
Proportionate To Her Desire To Please.
Dad

831 Her Affection Is Not Proof of Her Love... But,
Proof of Her Need.
Dad

832 Her Appearance...Explains What She Wants You
To Remember.
Dad

833 Her Behavior...Is Her Training You.
Your Reactions...Will Train Her.
Dad

834 Her Disinterest Deserves...An Appropriate
Response.
Dad

835 Her Interest Today...Does Not Guarantee Her
Interest Tomorrow.
Advised.
Dad

836 Her Quiet Rebellion...Will Soon Diminish Her
Beauty~Greatly.
Advised.
Dad

837 Her Reactions Will Decide Your Joy...or
Your Pain.
Dad

838 Her Words Reveal Her Skills...Not
Her Heart.
Proverbs 7
Dad

839 Him: "Nothing In Life...Happens By Accident."
Me: "You Are Wise To Avoid The Freeways."
:-)
Think Twice.
Dad

840 I Know...She Is An "Ocean" To You.
But, You Seem To Be...Just A "Drop"
To Her.
Dad

841 I Saw Her Past Boyfriends...And How Little
She Requires.
You May Be A Bit...Overqualified.
Dad

842 If Beauty Is Your Standard...
Decision Will Be Hard.
If Trust Is Your Standard...
Decision Will Be Easy.
Dad

843 If Her Beauty Has Made Her A Skilled
Receiver...
She Will Probably Never Develop
The Nature of A Giver.
Dad

844 If She Bores You For An Hour...She Will Bore
You For A Lifetime.
Dad

845 If She Cannot Even Make A Video Letter For
You~She Certainly Could Not Make A Future
For You.
Duh. :)
Dad

846 If She Cannot Feel Your Pain...
She Cannot Create Your Joy.
Dad

847 If She Cannot Manage Her Mouth...
She Cannot Manage Your Wealth.
Dad

848 If She Cannot Stay Out of Your Personal
Business...You Received A Divine Answer.
Dad

849 If She Does Not Even Have Energy To Text
You...She Would Not Have Energy To "Twirl" For
You. :)
Dad

850 If She Does Not Love What You Do...
She Will Never Know Who You Really Are.
Dad

851 If She Does Not Love Who You Are...
She Cannot Love What You Do.
Dad

852 If She Does Not Make You Feel Kingly...
She Is Not Your Queen.
Dad.

853 If She Does Not Resurrect "The Giver" Within You...She Is Too Weak For Your Future.
Dad

854 Feelings...Lie.
Reactions...Don't.

855 If She Is Unhappy...Working With You~
She Would Be Unhappy...Living With You.
Dad

856 If She Kills The "Giver" In You...
She Has Killed You.
Dad

857 If She Loves What You Do Not...
She Will Hate What You Do...
Think.
Think.
Think.
Dad

858 If You Do Not Enjoy Her For A Day...You Would Not Enjoy Her For A Lifetime.
Dad

859 If You Have Not Learned Honor...You Have
Learned Nothing.
Dad

860 If You Saw Her "Heroes"...You Might Change
Your Mind.
Dad

861 If Your Pain Does Not Matter To Her...Neither
Will Your Pleasure.
Dad

862 If Your Small Bicycle Request Created A 747
Reaction...I Would Give Her A Pass.
(To Small Claims Department.)
Dad

863 Invest One Minute...
Before Investing One Hour.
Invest One Hour...Before Investing A Day.
Invest One Day...
Before Investing Anything.
Dad

864 Is She Humble Enough...To Be Trained For
"Your" World?
(Eleazar/Rebekah)
Dad

865 Is YOUR Comfort...Important To Her?
Does She ANTICIPATE...Your Needs?
Does She PURSUE Your Personal Training?
Dad

866 Just One More Conversation...Can Reveal The
Hidden Chapter of Her Character.
Dad

867 Keep Two Fears...Forever:
Fear...of Being Wrong.
Fear of Being Wrong...About A Woman.
Dad

868 Keep Your World Small Enough...To Keep Order.
Dad

869 Kitchen.
Bedroom.
Prayer Room.
Game Room.
Library.
Which Is Her Field of Expertise, Son?
Dad

870 Kitten Eyes...Can Hide A Tiger Heart.
Dad

871 Know Your Dominant Difference From Others.
Excel...In Your Authenticity.
It Attracts "Real"/Purges Others.
Dad

872 Let Her Talk Long Enough...To Reveal Her
Heart.
You May Be Stunned.
Dad

873 Let The World...Aim High.
You...Aim RIGHT.
That Is Joy.
And, Joy Is Success.
Dad

874 Life Is...Not Your Struggle.
The Unwilling...Are Your Struggle.
Move Around Them.
Not Through Them.
Dad

875 Love Is...When You Want Her To Keep
Talking.
Dad

876 Make No Decision...Until You Watch
The Comedian She Enjoys Most.
Disappointment.
Dad

877 Many Will Fight You.
A Few Will Fight...Beside You.
ONE...Will Fight For You.
Your Comfort. Peace. Honor.
Dad

878 Most Can Pass Every Test...Except One.
The Test of Time.
Dad

879 Never Confuse Her Love...With God's Love.
A Normal Mistake.
Dad

880 Never...Never...Hurt Her.
Protect Her.
At ANY Cost.
Her Heart.
Her Reputation.
Her Confidences.
Dad

881 Never Interrupt...Her Anger.
It Contains Too Many Secrets.
Dad

882 Prodigal Son...Lost The Father's Blessing
Through Dishonor.
Absalom Lost...The Father's Blessing
Through Dishonor.
Be Careful.
Dad

883 She Desires Somebody...That You Are Not.
And Has A Divine Right To Do So.
Dad

884 She Is Showing You...The Best Parts of Her.
...Words.
...Looks.
...Honor.
...Tone.
It Will Not Improve.
Dad

885 She Will Unleash Your Authenticity...or
Suffocate It.
Dad

886 Silence Is The Appropriate Response...
To The Disinterested.
Dad

887 Some Belong…In Your Day.
Some Belong…In Your Past.
One Belongs…Inside Your Heart.
Dad.

888 Some…Make You Look.
Some…Make You Listen.
Some…Make You Long.
One…Makes You "Love."
Dad

889 Some People…Are A 3 Minute Pleasure.
Dad

890 Some Women…Want To Sleep With You.
Some Women…Want To Dream With You.
The Difference Is Profound.
Dad

891 Some You Enjoy For "A Minute"…You Would
Despise For "A Day."
:)
Dad

892 Tell Me 4 Ways Her Presence Has Improved…
…Your Joy.
…Your Finances.
…Your Productivity.
…Your Health.
Dad

893 Test.
Test.
Make "Small" Requests.
Her Reaction...Is Your Answer.
Accept It. Save Your Life.
...And Hers.
Dad

894 The Danger of Beauty...Is That It Paralyzes
Male Logic.
Advised.
Dad

895 The Difference Between Decision And
Indecision Is...
One Effective Conversation.
Dad

896 The Fool...Will Study Her Walk.
The Wise...Will Study Her Work.
Dad

897 The Fragrance of Her Perfume...
...Cannot Remove
...The Odor of Her Lies.
Dad

898 The Indiscreet Woman...Is Your Delilah.
Dad

899 The Ocean Is Very Full of A Variety of
Beautiful Fish.
Don't Quit Swimming...Because One Bit You.
Dad

900 The Right One...
...Comforts Your Heart.
...Stimulates Your Mind.
...Excites Your Body.
...Empowers Your Spirit.
Dad

901 The Right One...
...Will Be Your Greatest Temptation.
...And Worthy of Your Greatest Discipline.
Dad

902 The Right One...Has No Fear of Comparison.
Secrets-of-Esther
Dad

903 The Right One...Is Whoever You Enjoy
Talking To The Most.
Dad

904 The Right One...Is Willing To "Become"
The Right One.
Training.
Dad

905 The Right One...Treasures Credibility
With You.
At Any Cost.
Dad

906 The Right One...Will Accept YOUR Timing.
Secrets-of-Ruth
Dad

907 Dating~
Discerning Your Potential...Is Easy.
Discerning Your Heart...Is Impossible.

908 The Right One...Will Not Agitate You.
Enough Said.
Dad

909 Some Enjoy...What You Say.
Some Enjoy...What They See. :)
Somebody...Will "Need" Who You Really Are.

910 The Right One...Will Not Leave.
Dad

911 The Sound of Honor...Will Make Every Other
Sound Unbearable.
That Will Be...Her Difference.
Dad

912 The Trustworthy...
Are Rare, Rare, Rare.
Dad

913 The Unteachable Woman...Will Become Your
Hell.
Dad

914 The Wisest On Earth...Can Be Deceived.
Never...Never...Forget It.
Dad

915 The Woman Passionate To Please You...
...Is Very Different Than...
The Woman "Willing" To Please You.
Dad

916 The Woman You Trust...Will Decide If Your Life
Is A Heaven or A Hell.
Dad

917 Those Who Can "Obtain" Through Their
Beauty...Will Refuse To Obtain Through Honor.
Dad

918 Those Who Enjoy Your Money...May Hate Your
Assignment.
Dad

919 To You...She Is A "Possibility."
To Her...You Are Simply An "Experience."
Learn.
Dad

920 To You...Your Reaching Revealed Your Desire.
To Her...Your Reaching Exposed Your
Weakness.
Dad

921 Two Reasons To Marry A Woman~
1) How You Feel In Her Presence. :)
2) How You Feel In Her Absence. :(
Dad

922 Watch Her Work.
Her Productivity Will Explain Her.
(Rebekah/Ruth/Proverbs 31)
Dad

923 Beauty Is A Door~Not The House.
Dad

924 Watching A "Man Crawling Event"...May Be Her
Favorite Recreation.
Dad

925 What Does She Enjoy MOST..?
Your Assignment...or Your Weakness..?
Dad

926 What Is...Her "Selling Point?"
The Part...You "Bought."
:) Dad

927 What She Is...Matters Least.
What She Is Willing To Become...Matters Most.
The Esther Diary
Dad

928 When You Discover The Other Men Who Excite
Her...Your Interest Will Change.
Radically.
Suddenly.
Dad

929 Relationship~
Plant A Part of Yourself...BEFORE...You Plant
All of Yourself.

930 When You See Others Who Excite Her...
You Will Not Feel So Special Anymore.
:) Dad

931 When Your Words...Do Not Matter To Her,
Neither Will Your Pain.
Dad

932 Wise Dating Is...Simply Keeping The
Investments Equal.
Dad

933 You Are Not Her Only Interest.
Never Forget It.
Dad

934 You Can Calm...An Angry Woman.
You Cannot Cure...An Embittered Woman.
Dad

935 You Need A Woman...Who Can Live With You.
You Need A Woman...Who Cannot Live Without
You.
Dad

936 Your Disrespect Will Close More Doors...Than
1,000 Enemies Can Close.
Dad

937 Your Inability To Inspire Her...Is Your Answer.
Dad

938 Your Queen...
Is Whoever Inspires You Most.
Dad

939 Your Queen Will Not Have...
The Tone of An Interrogator.
Dad

940 Your Requests...Are Her Opportunities.
Her Reactions...Are Your Answers.
Dad

941 You Respond...To Her Beauty.
But, You Do Not Respond...To Her Opinions.
A Wife Is...Divine Balancer.
Dad

942 Her Enjoyment of Your Company...Does Not
Guarantee She Will Enjoy Your Assignment.
Dad

943 You Will Crave Her Admiration...
If She Is The Right One.
If She Is The Wrong One...
She Won't Give It.
Dad

944 Your Joy Revealed...You Saw Her
Possibilities.
Your Sorrow Revealed...You Discerned Her
Probabilities.
Dad

945 Dating~
Money
Investigate...Before You Invest.

946 Do Not Use Your Palace To Attract A Queen;
You Will Always Wonder If She Really Loves
You...or The Palace.
Dad

947 If Passion, Real AND Kind Arrive...
In Same Package...Linger.
It Is Almost Irreplaceable, Son.
Dad

948 If She Does Not DISCERN You...
She Has Not EARNED You.
Dad

949 If She Does Not Trust Your Decisions~
She Will Feel Unsafe.
If She Feels Unsafe~
She Will Confide In Another.
Dad

950 If She Giggled...You Are Her Audience.
If She Confided...You Are Her Confidante.
If She Questioned...You Are Her Project.
Dad

951 The Difference In Men...Is How Often They
Consult God.

DECEPTION

952 A Deceiver Is Someone Who Will Not Tell You...
Enough.

953 A Single Question...Can Expose A Lifetime
Deceiver.

954 DearDaughter~
Every Snake...Is Interesting.
Deceivers...Never Bore.
Garden of Eden.

955 A Deceiver...Is Very Different Than The
Deceived.
(Serpent/Adam, Eve)

956 Bold...Is Not "Real."
Deceivers Are Often Bold.

957 Deceivers Dread Hearing, "I Will Wait A Little
Longer To Gather More Facts."
"Waiting...Suffocates The Deceiver."

958 Deception Is...Purposeful/Strategy.
Truth Is...Effortless/Spontaneous.

959 Deception...
At 24...I Confronted Liars.
At 64...I Simply Identify Them.
(Never Tell Thieves Where Security Cameras
Are.)

960 Deception Is...
The Birthplace For All Pain.

961 Deception...Gives Gifts To Control Decisions.
Integrity...Gives Gifts To Reward Excellence.

962 Deception...Is Disloyalty.

963 Deception...Thrives On Misplaced Mercy.

964 Delilah's Diary~
"He Is Just A Man.
My Persistence Will Pay Off...If I Can Just
Remember The Money...The Money."

965 Discerning A Deceiver...Is Not Empowerment
To Change Them.
Everybody...Takes A Side.
Deceivers...Simply Hide It.

966 In The World of Deceivers...Knowledge Is
An Enemy.

967 You Are...Deceivable.
Never Forget It.
We All Are.
Unfortunately.
So...Invest What It Takes.

968 You Stabbed Me.
And, You Want Me To Buy The Knife..?

DECISIONS

969 3 Decisions Create Success~
~Who You Decide To Honor.
~Weakness You Decide To Overcome.
~Voice You Decide To Trust.

970 3 Good Decisions...
Train Team Via Personal DVD's.
Replace Disloyalty Swiftly/Quietly.
Identify Your "Elisha."

971 4 Decisions Create Success...
...Who You Honor.
...Who You Train.
...What You Stop Doing.
...Voice You Believe.

972 4 Decisions That Remove Stress~
...Change Deadlines.
...Change Access.
...Change Goals.
...Change Expectations.

973 A Decision To Care Is...A Decision To Hurt.
But, No Alternative Exists.

974 A Delayed Decision...Is Delaying Your Future. (How Much Longer Do You Want Your Present Season To Last..?)

975 A Man Who Forces His Wife To Make A "Man-Decision"...May Fear The Consequences of A Wrong Decision.

976 A Single Decision...Will Launch Your Next Season.

977 A Wrong Decision...Creates Your Pain.
A Right Decision...Removes It.
Think.

978 Astrology...Can Be Comforting To Those Who Dread The Consequences of Their Decisions.

979 Culture Is Established For Those Who Cannot Make Decisions.

980 Most Problems Need Decisions...
Not Prayers.

981 "Decisions...Decide Wealth."
Holy Spirit Changed My Life With These Words.

982 Decision-Making...Is A System of Questions.
What Is My True Goal?
What Matters Least?
What Are My Options?

983 Decisions Delayed...Are Pleasures Postponed.

984 Decision-Making~
Identify 3 Options~
Creates...A Consequence.
Creates...A Continuance.
Creates...A Calm.

985 Decision #1...Created Your Problem.
Decision #2...Corrects The Problem.
Think.
Again.

986 Every Decision You Make...Reveals Your Doubts
or Your Faith.

987 Decisions...Are Seeds For Hope.

988 Decisions...Schedule Divine Activity In Your Life.
Think.
Again.

989 When You Have Asked Enough Questions...
Decision-Making Is Easy.
(Questions Are Doors To Knowledge.)

990 Rejection Is...A Wise Decision Another Made For Me.

991 Decisions~
Some Things Are...Right or Wrong.
Some Things Are...Wise or Unwise.
Some Things Are...Now or Later.

992 Decisions~
The Obvious Thing To Do Is...Often Not The Wisest Thing To Do.
Revisit ALL Options.

993 Decisions~
Your Present Season...Happened With Your Permission.

994 Depression...Is Not Always A Disease.
Depression...Is Often A Decision.

995 Destiny Is A...Divine Desire~
...Not A Divine Decision.

996 Destiny Is...Decided By Your Decisions,
Not God.

997 Your Potential Is...Not Your Destiny.
Your Decisions Are...Your Destiny.
(Satan/God...David/Absalom)

998 DIVORCE Is...The Decision of ONE.
God And Israel.

999 Divorce Is A Decision, Not An Attitude.

1000 Doing The Right Thing...
Is Never A Wrong Decision.

1001 DUMB...Is A Decision.
...To Ignore Mentors.
...To Silence Your Conscience.
...To Defy Scripture.
...To Refuse Correction.

1002 Equation For Destiny Is Simple:
Divine Desires + Your Decisions=Destiny.
Bible Is An "If" Book of Possibilities.

1003 Every Decision...
Creates A Reward or A Consequence.
Now...or Eventually.
How Far AHEAD...Will You Think?

1004 Every Decision...Complicates Your Life.
Or...
...Simplifies It.

1005 Every Decision Increases Order...or Disorder
In Your Life.
Or In...
Your Day.
Your Marriage.
Your Finance$.

1006 Every Decision Is...Easy...
...If
...If
...IF...You Ask Enough Questions.

1007 Every Decision...Reveals Your Faith or Your
Fears.

1008 Every Right Decision...Creates Instant Peace.

1009 Is Your Life A Drip...or A Wave..?
Your Own Decision.

1010 It Is Always A Right Decision...
To Remove Wrong People.

1011 Keeping The Uncaring In Your Life...
Is A Dangerous Decision.

1012 Listening Well...Makes Decision-Making Very
Easy.

1013 Mastery Is A Decision, Not An Anointing.

1014 Most Problems Do Not Require Prayer...Just "A
Scriptural Decision."

1015 My Decisions...Are Instant.
My Changes...Are Eventual.

1016 No Decision Is Hard...
When You Ask Enough Questions.
None.

1017 Simple Decisions...Create Instant Change.

1018 Sometimes Your Decision...Is More Important Than Your Prayers.

1019 Something Deep Within Me...Believes The Next 90 Days Will Be Stunningly Glorious. EVERY Decision...Will Be Perfect.

1020 Sooooooooo......Where Have You Decided To Fail..?

1021 Struggle Is Usually...The Proof of A Bad Decision.

1022 The Consistency of Your Inaccuracy...Has Helped Me Finalize An Important Decision.

1023 The Entire World...Is Your Personal Kitchen. Your Own Decisions...Are Creating Your Meals.

1024 The World Is...A Menu of Ingredients. Your Decisions Are Creating...The Life Omelette You Are Cooking For Yourself.

1025 The World Is...My Kitchen.
My Decisions...Create The Buffet.
Chef Michael.
Kinda Nice.

1026 The World You Are Experiencing...
Is The World YOU Created For Yourself.
(Through Decisions-Focus-Faith-Doubt-Attitude)

1027 Time...Changes Little.
Decisions...Change Everything.

1028 Until You Have Had My Experiences...You May
Never Understand My Decisions.

1029 When A Decision Creates Unrest Within
You...Make Another Decision.
God Does.
"I Will Do A NEW Thing."

1030 When You Care...You Find A Way.

1031 When You Decide What Matters MOST...
You Will Discern What Matters Less.
Power Is...The Ability To Release
"The Less."

1032 Writing Me...Was Your Decision.
Answering You...Is My Decision.

1033 You Decide...Who Matters.
This Explains Your Joy.
And...Sorrow.

1034 Your Decision To Believe The Wrong
Person...Was "Your" Own Decision.
Adam/Eve

1035 Your Decision To LOVE...Makes You The
Authority In Every Environment.

1036 Your Decision To Simply "Love"...Could Solve
The Top 5 Problems In Your Life.
Home.
Job.

1037 YOUR Decisions
...Are Creating Your Own Destiny.
Who You Honor.
Who You Ignore.
Who You Train.
Who You Trust.

1038 Your Decisions...Are Not My Responsibility.
Remember That.

1039 Your Decisions...Reveal Your Persuasions.

1040 Your Decisions...Schedule Your Desired
Experience.
Think Again.

1041 Your Destiny Begins...With Your Next Decision.
Think.

1042 Your Destiny...Is Not A Divine Decision.
Deuteronomy 28:1-14/Isaiah 1:17-19

1043 Your Problem Is The Size You Decide To Make
It.

1044 Destiny...Is A Decision.
Yours.

1045 Those Who Disagree With Your Goals...Will
Resent Your Decisions.

1046 Questions...Make Decision-Making Easy.

DESIRE

1047 Never Put In Front of You...What Does Not
Belong In You.

~

1048 DESIRES...Are Deadly Tyrants.
(Stay Parental Toward Them...
Harnessing/Supervising.)

~

1049 Desire...Hopes.
Passion...Pursues.

~

1050 Desire Is Birthed Through The PERCEPTION of
Someone.
Do Not Commit Until You Know~
History.
Conversations.
Experiences.

~

1051 Desire...Is Not Always Divine.

~

1052 Desire Is...Neither An Instruction Nor A
Prophecy.

~

1053 Desire Is...The Unbroken Stallion...
Champions Decide To Master
And Harness.

1054 DESIRE Is...Too Unpredictable To Be My Boss.
So, I Have Made It...My Servant.
Am Parental And Authoritative Toward It.
Greed...Is Not The Desire For "More."
Greed...Is Keeping What Belongs To Another.
Duh.

1055 My Desire Is...Not A Prophecy.

1056 My Desires Have Flawed My Discerning.
Often.

1057 My Desires...Are Not Me.
Nor, My Master.
Merely Unpredictable Children...
Needing Continuous Supervision.

1058 QUEST~
What Is...Your STRONGEST Desire?
What Is Proof...of Its Importance?
What Is...Its Cost?
Will You Pay The Price?

1059 Sustained Intimacy Is...Impossible With
Someone Who Ignores Your Desires.

1060 What You Desire...Chooses What You Believe.

1061 YOU Are The Only Person In Your Life...Who
Will Be Militant Toward Your Desires.

1062 Real Desire...Is The Seed For Discovery...
Desire...Discerns "The Path"...
Desire...For Peace...Makes You Reach For God.

DIFFERENCE

1063 Different Experiences=Different Persuasions.
Different Information=Different Opinions.
A Zoo For God; A Buffet For Us.

1064 Jesus Instructed Us...To Love Enemies.

1065 Do Not Explain Your Difference...
To Someone Incapable of Discerning It.

1066 If You Cannot State Your
Dominant Difference In A Sentence...
You Have Not Yet Discovered It.

1067 Know-Your-Difference~
I Am...Always Gracious.
I Am...Rarely Stupid.
:)

1068 Know-Your-Difference~
I Am Not...A Very Smart Man.
But...
I Am...An Attentive Man.

1069 Know-Your-Difference~
If You Cannot Follow My Instructions...
You Would Never Follow Me.
:)

1070 Know-Your-Difference~
Productivity...Excites Me.
Laziness...Nauseates Me.

1071 Know-Your-Difference~
When You Underestimate My Discerning...You
Become Very Unattractive.

1072 Recognition of Your Difference...
Creates Confidence.
Recognition of Your Weakness...
Creates Humility.

1073 Some Are Addicted...To Your Divine Difference.
Some Are Angered...By Your Divine Difference.
Simplifies Your Life.

1074 The Difference In Men Is...In The Kind of
Woman They Strive To Impress.

1075 The Difference In Men Is...In What They Want
To Destroy.
Think.
Again.
I Interpret Men Through This.

1076 The Difference In People Is...
The Voice They Trust.

1077 The Difference In People Is...Whose Comfort
Matters Most To Them.

1078 The Difference In Success And Failure...
Is Who Likes You.
Joseph/Esther/Daniel/Ruth.

1079 The Difference In Those Who Succeed And
Those Who Fail Is Quite Simple:
...The Voices They Trust.

1080 The Dominant Difference I Have Observed In
Women Is...How They Talk To A Man.

1081 The Dominant Difference In People Is Not Their
Opinions...But, Their GOALS.
Life-Changing.

1082 The Dominant Difference In People Is...Who They Have Decided To Honor.

1083 Your Difference...
Will Be The Secret To Your Success.
~What Do You Love To
...Think About?
...Learn About?
...Talk About?

1084 Your "Difference"...Decides Your Value.

1085 Your Difference From Others...Is Who God Has Assigned You To Protect.

1086 Your Difference...Is More Important Than Your Weakness.

1087 Your Difference...Is Whose Happiness Matters To You MOST.

1088 The Difference In People Is...What They Are Unwilling To Live Without.

1089 Never Study Your Weakness...Study Your Difference.

DISAGREEMENT

1090 Disagreement Is Normal...Whenever There Is
An Intelligence Gap.
:)

1091 Disagreement...Does Not Bother Me.
Disagreement Without Thought...Bothers Me.

1092 Disagreement...Is Proof of Difference.
...In IQ.
...In Experiences.
...In Goals.

1093 Disagreement...Is The Seed For Loss.

1094 If I Thought We Had The Same Opinion...
You Would Not Have Needed Mine.

1095 Him: "I Disagree With You..!"
Me: "I Understand Totally. I Remember My
Own Season of Ignorance Very Well."
:)

1096 Him: "I Do Not Agree With You..!"
Me: "How Could You With Such Limited
Experience?"
:)

1097 Him: "I Do Not Agree With You..!"
Me: "Oh, Son...I Would Never Expect A Man of
Your Inexperience To Grasp This."
:)

1098 Him: "I Do Not Think...I Agree With You."
Me: "Your First 3 Words...Explain Why."

1099 I Never Expect Those With Limited
Knowledge...To Agree With Me.
:)

1100 Those Who Disagree With What You Do...
Will Probably Despise Who You Are.

DISAPPOINTMENT

1101 1,000 Disappointments...
In Your Life Have Not Stopped You.
The New One Today...
Will Not Stop You Either.

1102 Disappointment Confirms...
My Flawed Discerning. :)

1103 Disappointment Is Merely...
Unexpected Discovery.
Profound.

1104 Disappointment Is Proof...
Our Discerning Is Flawed.

1105 DISAPPOINTMENT...Is Always
Financial Wisdom.
(Stunning Understanding. Meditate On This.)

1106 Disappointment...Is Proof of Progress.
Unexpected Progress.
:)

1107 Every Disappointment Contains 3 Success
Secrets:
~Flawed Discerning.
~Misplaced Mercy.
~Opportunity To Replace.

1108 Every Disappointment...Is Concentrated
Wisdom; Extract Its Secrets And Bitterness Is
Impossible.

1109 Loving God...Does Not Make You Intelligent.

Some Christians...Are Absolutely Stupid.

Ashamed. :)

1110 The Greatest Disappointments...
Contain The Greatest Wisdom.
A Divine Reimbursement To You.

DISCERN

1111 My Investment In You...Reveals My Hopes
For Us.
Your Reactions...Reflect The Quality of My
Discerning.

1112 Discern The God-Deposit In Everyone.
But, Do Not Ignore The Devil...
Hiding In The Corner.
:)

1113 Your Needs...Determine What You Discern.

1114 Discerning His Character...
The Goals...He Sets.
The Hero...He Admires.
The Mentor...He Pursues.

1115 Discerning Is...For Your Private
Decision-Making, Not Discussion.

1116 Discerning Motives Is...A Very Painful Anointing
To Experience.
Torture.
...But Necessary For Decision-Making.

1117 Discernment Is...Divine Direction.
Act On It.

1118 How Long Does It Take You...
To Discern Error In Your Belief-System?
Would You Really...Want To Discover It?

1119 I Am Not Assigned...
To Change The Hypocrite.
Merely To Discern Him.

1120 I Am Not...Awesome.
But...
I Am...Attentive.

1121 I Speak Very Little...About What I Discern.
I Use My Discerning...For Making Decisions.

1122 The Greater Your Love...
The More Accurate Your Discerning.

1123 The Greater Your Sensitivity...
The Greater Your Pain.
The Greater Your Pain...
The Greater Your Opportunity.
...To Heal.
...To Learn.

1124 The More Undiscerning Someone Is...The More You Will Have To Explain Yourself.

1125 The Spider Is Discerned...Last.

1126 The Unimpressed...Are The Undiscerning.

1127 Those Who Cannot Discern Your Heart...
Will Never Discern You.
Never. Never. Never.

1128 UNREST...Occurs When Your Spirit Has Discerned Information That Your Mind Has Not Yet Reported.

1129 When You Really Care...You Will Discern.
When You Do Not Discern...You Do Not Belong.

1130 You Cannot Help Anyone...
Who Does Not Discern You.
(Jesus/Pharisees...David/Absalom)

1131 Your Reluctance To Make Her Your Confidante Is...Significant.
Your Spirit Has Discerned...What Your Mind Cannot Explain.

DISCOVER

1132 Discovery Is...IMMEDIATE Success.
Anywhere.
Anytime.
Proverbs 4:7/Isaiah 1:17

1133 Enjoy Mystery; It Delays The Pain of Discovery.

1134 Every Significant Discovery...Creates Regret.
Every Regret...Increases Humility.
Humility...Makes You Attentive.

1135 In Discovering Those Who Dislike Me;
I Discover That I Have The SAME
Feelings...Toward Them!
Agreement!
Ahhh...Such Peace.

1136 The Most Successful Day of Your Life...
Is The Day You Discover What You Despise.

1137 When You Discover Something Wonderful...
You Reach Again.
When You Discover Something Irreplaceable...
You Stay.

1138 You Don't "Decide"...What Excites You.
You "Discover"...What Excites You.

1139 You Don't Choose Who Motivates You...You
Discover Them.

1140 Your Most Profound Discoveries...Are Very
Close.
"I Told You So."
:)

1141 Sometimes, You Do Not Need An Ocean...A
Single Swallow Often Satisfies...

DISCRETION

1142 Discretion Is...Silence.
Deception Is...Secrecy.
Never Confuse The Two.

1143 Discretion Is...The Ability To
Discern The Ignorant...
Without Revealing It.

1144 Discretion...Is The Ability To
Discern The Ignorant...
Without Reacting To Them.

1145 DISCRETION~
"The Smaller The Small-Print...
The Bigger The Headline."
Never Confuse The Two.

1146 Dating~

Caution...Is A Divine Message.

DISHONOR

1147 It Is Not The Ungodly...Who Show Dishonor.
It Is The Untrained...Who Show Dishonor.

1148 DISHONOR~
The First Evidence of Dishonor Is...
When Someone Requests
What They Did Not Earn.
(Prodigal Son)

1149 Dishonor Is...The Expiration Date For
Relationship.
(Absalom/Korah/Ananias/Demas)

1150 Dishonor...Creates Loss.
Of...
...Access
...Opportunity
...Credibility.

1151 Dishonor...Destroys Future Favor.

1152 Dishonor...Has Created Every Loss In Your Life.

1153 DISHONOR...Is An Explanation...of Character, Prejudice And Perception.

1154 Dishonor...Is Seed For Loss.
Disobedience...Is Seed For Pain.
Disinterest...Is Seed For Replacement.

1155 Dishonor...Makes You Memorable.
(Judas/Absalom)

1156 Dishonor...Will Explain Every Loss In Your Life.

1157 Dishonor...Will Kill Every Good Thing Favor Birthed.

1158 Disrespect Closes More Doors...Than 1,000 Demons Have Closed.

1159 Disrespect Is...A Divine Instruction Only The Fool Ignores.

1160 Disrespect Is...Irreplaceable Wisdom~ Reusable For Your Lifetime.

1161 Disrespect Is...The Seed For Your Replacement.

1162 Disrespect...Has An Obsession For Attention.

1163 Disrespect...Is Not A Mistake. Disrespect...Is A Very Costly Decision.

1164 DISRESPECT...Is The Favorite Weapon of Character Assassins.

1165 Disrespect...Makes You Memorable.

1166 Disrespect...Provides A Fortunate Discovery.

1167 Disrespect...Reveals Displaced Trust.

1168 Ignoring My Instructions...Is Silent Dishonor. Dishonor...Has A Consequence.

1169 If He Will Steal Your Tweet Publicly...
What Would He Do If You Invited Him Into Your Home?
:)

1170 Only One Reason Divorce Occurs:
DISHONOR.
Every Sin Is A Sin of...DISHONOR.

1171 Sadness~
I Do Not Know Who Dishonored You...But
The Holy Spirit Has A Recovery System.
He Really, Really Does.

1172 Signs-of-DISHONOR~
...Trivialized Desire.
...Substitution For Preference.
...Contempt For Difference.
...Disdain For Protocol.

1173 The Odor of Dishonor...Never Lingers Long In
The Palace.
Any Palace.
(Esther/Absalom)

1174 There Is No Greater Dishonor Than...
Disobedience. (Parental/Authority)

1175 What Is Your Single Greatest...Skill?
Dishonor...Creates Instant Loss of Favor.

1176 You Have Been Dishonored...
When They Text Someone During
Your Conversation To Them.

1177 You Have Been Dishonored...
...When Someone Makes No Apology For Being
Late To The Appointment.

1178 Your Lifestyle Does Not Reveal What You Were
Taught...But What You BELIEVED.

DISINTEREST

1179 5 Mistakes Employees Make :)
1)Not Listening
2)Not Listening
3)Not Listening
4)Not Listening
5)Not Listening

1180 Disinterest Is...Divine Protection.

1181 Disinterest...Is Divine Closure.

1182 Disinterest...Creates Disinterest.
(Fathers...Toward Children)
(Conversations/Dating)

1183 Disinterest...Has Deadly Consequences.
Relationships.
God.
Job.
Government.

1184 Disinterest...Is A Divine Instruction.

1185 Disinterest...Is An Instruction.
(Jesus Told Disciples To Withdraw
From Homes Where They Weren't Valued.)
Sow Your Presence Carefully.

1186 Disinterest...Mesmerizes Me.
...For About 5 Seconds.

1187 Disinterest...REMOVES My Interest.

1188 The Most Common Force That Makes
You...Stoppable.
Almost Every Time...Disinterest.

1189 The Uninterested...Are The Unworthy.
No Mystery.
(Jesus/Disciples/Shake Dust Off)

1190 Their Disinterest...Does Not Make You
Unneeded.
Their Disinterest...Makes You Powerless.

1191 Your Disinterest In My Assignment...
Explains Your Role In It.

1192 Your Disinterest In My Assignment...
Will Explain My Absence.

DISLOYALTY

1193 Absalom Spirit~
The Willingness To Oppose/Rally Opposition To
Decisions of The Spiritual Leader.
First Step Downward.

1194 DISLOYALTY Is...Incapable of Discretion.

1195 Disloyalty Is...Not A Decision.
Disloyalty Is...A Reaction To Greatness.
(Judas/Jesus...Absalom/David)

1196 Disloyalty Is...Not Treatable.
(Lucifer/God...Judas/Jesus)

1197 DISLOYALTY Needs An Exit...
Not A Conversation.

1198 The Goal of The 3rd Voice Is...
To Be The Only Voice.
(Serpent/Garden of Eden...Absalom/David)

1199 Those Who Disagree With Your Decisions...Do
Not Qualify For The Rewards of Them.

1200 The Palace Environment...
Quickly Exposes The Odor of Disloyalty.
(David/Absalom...King/Vashti)

DISTRUST

1201 Distrust...Creates Emotional Bankruptcy.
Distrust...Occurs When Your Heart Discerns.
Information Your Mind Has Not Yet Reported.

1202 Distrusting People...
Increases Your Discussions With God.

1203 Distrusting The Right Person...Is Far Deadlier
Than Trusting The Wrong Person.

1204 Distrust...Is Often Divine Protection.

1205 An Untrusted Mentor...Is Not Your Mentor.

1206 I Distrust Those...Who Distrust Me.

1207 Whenever You Have Created Distrust...You
Have Destroyed Favor.
Loss of Trust=Loss of Favor.

1208 Divine Answers...Are Never Complex.
Never.
The Simplicity...Blinds Us.

1209 Divine Authorization For Promotion...
Has Been Given To Your Boss Alone.
Joseph/Daniel

1210 Divine Creativity...Included Your Weakness.
Never Forget It.

1211 Divine Replacements...
Are Always An Improvement.
Singles...Relationships.
Career...Your Job.

1212 Divine Treasures...Can Be Lost
Quite Easily.
It Happens Every Single Day.

1213 Divine-Dictionary
Rejection Is..."A Divine Rescue."

1214 Do Not Expect Divine Rewards...For Doing The Job of Another.

1215 Human Words...Control Divine Behavior.
"Draw Nigh To Me...I Will Draw Nigh To You."
James 4:8

1216 I Have Fully Accepted And Agreed To The Terms of...Divine "Sponsorship" While I Am On Earth.
Deuteronomy 28:1-14

1217 I Have Greatly Overestimated...
My Influence On Others. :)
Fortunately, I Greatly Underestimated...
Divine Love.

1218 Healing...Is Divine Responsibility.
Health...Is Human Responsibility.

1219 Something Divine And Incredible...
Lies Hidden In Your Immediate World.
One Lingering Moment Remains For You
To Discern It.

1220 Something Gloriously Unexpected...
Is Very, Very Close.
:)
Feel It, Too, Don't You..?!

1221 Something God Invested In You Is Keeping Him Excited...
Really Hope You Discover It...Soon.

⁓

1222 Something INSIDE You...Is Keeping God Excited About You.
Identify It.
Protect It.
Promote It.

⁓

1223 The Divine Explanation For Pain Is...
Disobedience.
Deuteronomy 28

⁓

1224 The Divine Purpose For Money Is To...CREATE.
...Experiences.
...Environments.
...Memories.
...Changes.
...Improvements.

⁓

1225 The Divine Role of Memory...Is To Re-Visit Pleasures.

⁓

1226 The Rocky Terrain Exhausting You...
Has A Divine River Within.
"He Cutteth Out Rivers...
Among The Rocks."
Job 28:10

1227 Your Conscience...Is A Divine "Tool."
It Is NOT...A Divine Voice.

1228 Your Sleep...Does Not Stop Divine Activity.
Joseph/Solomon/Dreams

DOORS

1229 A Knock...Does Not Open A Wall.
One Key...Often Opens 1,000 Different Doors.

1230 Close Wrong Doors.
Close Every Door...
With Expectation of Promotion.
Close Every Door...
In The Timing of The Holy Spirit.

1231 Do Not Stare...At The Wall In Front of You.
Circle...Until You Find The Door.

1232 Do Not Walk Through A Door...
Until You Are Invited.

1233 Open Doors...Can Close Suddenly.
Arrogance.

1234 There Are No Walls...On Earth.
Merely..."Uncommanded Doors."

DREAMS

1235 When You Decide What Will Live...
You Have Decided What Will Die.
(Your Dream vs Rejection)

1236 How Do You Kill A Man...With A Dream?
Give Him A Second Dream.
(Broken Focus)

1237 What Does It Take...To STOP You..?
(In Your Pursuit of A Goal...Job...
Relationship..?)

1238 Romance...The Dream Within You.
Caress It.
Stroke It.
Pamper It.
Talk Softly To It...Unceasingly.
Bathe It.

1239 The Greater Your Dream...
The More Excited God Becomes.

EAGLE-TALK

1240 A True Eagle Is Not Arrogant;
Aloneness...Cures Arrogance.

1241 Agony To An Eagle...
Is The Sound of A Clucking Chicken.

1242 Eagles And Chickens~
Living In The Barnyard...Excites The Chicken.
Leaving The Barnyard...Excites The Eagle.

1243 Eagles And Chickens~
Mastering The Barnyard...
Excites The Chicken.
Soaring...Excites The Eagle.
:)

1244 Eagles Discern Chickens Easily;
They Are The Ones...Who Despise Eagles.
(Envy Is Odor of...The Intimidated.)
Eagles...Soar.

1245 A Chicken...Has No Aspirations To Fly.
An Eagle...Has No Tolerance For The
Barnyard.

1246 A Chicken...Is An Experience.
An Eagle...Is A Turning-Point.

1247 Adapt...Until It Diminishes Your Authenticity.
Barking Seminars Are Very Stressful...
For Cats To Attend.

1248 Chickens...Cluck.
Eagles...Soar.
Simple, Really.
:)

1249 Chickens Do Not Admire You.
That Is How You RECOGNIZE...A Chicken.

1250 Chickens...Do Not Know How Long It Took You
To Build Your Nest.
:)
Nor Do They Care. :)

1251 Eagle..."We Are Flying High Today..!"
Chicken..."Why..?"
:)

1252 Eagles And Chickens...Simply Despise
What The Other Loves.

1253 Eaglet: "Mommy, Why Are You Looking...At That Chicken?"
Mother Eagle: "Just Needed To Giggle, Baby."
:)

1254 Eaglets...Discern Eagles.
They Will Find You.

1255 Enlarging The Barnyard...Does Not Excite An Eagle.
Even Eaglets Want To Advise...Eagles.
:)

1256 Mastering Your "Nest"...Is Not Mastering The Skies.

1257 If Clucking Chickens Are Distracting You...
You Are Flying Too Close To The Barnyard.
Mount UP...

1258 Leaders: Yelling At A Chicken Does Not Turn It Into An Eagle.
:)

1259 Longest Recorded Flight of A Chicken Is 13 Seconds.
But...They Can Give Advice To Eagles...For Hours. :)

1260 Never Give A Chicken...An Eagle Instruction.
Leadership-Talk.

1261 Never Tell A Chicken It Cannot Fly...
It May Be An Eagle In Disguise.
:)

1262 No Chicken...Enjoys An Eagle's Diary.
i.e. "Spent The Day...Soaring.
Could Barely See The Barnyard."

1263 No Investment In A Barnyard
Environment...Can Persuade The Eagle To
Leave The Sky.

1264 Recognizing A Chicken...Is Fairly Easy.
THE CHICKEN...Asks No Questions About
Flying.
:)

1265 Recognizing A Chicken...Is Fairly Easy.
THE CHICKEN...Feels Out of Place...
In "High Places."
It Is.

1266 Recognizing A Chicken...Is Fairly Easy.
THE CHICKEN...Is Absent
At Flight Parties.
Kinda Sick. :)

1267 Recognizing A Chicken...Is Fairly Easy.
The Chicken...Is Excited Over The Egg It Laid
"Last Year."
:)

1268 Recognizing A Chicken...Is Fairly Easy.
The Chicken...Is The First One At
The Time Clock At 4:59pm.
:)

1269 Recognizing A Chicken...Is Easy.
The Chicken...Is The First One Journalizing
Barnyard Quarrels.
:)

1270 Recognizing A Chicken...Is Fairly Easy.
THE CHICKEN...Is The One Who Reports
Possible Hurricanes.
:)

1271 Recognizing A Chicken...Is Fairly Easy.
The Chicken...Is The Unhappy One When The
Eagle Enters The Room.

1272 Recognizing A Chicken...Is Fairly Easy.
The Chicken...Opposes BIG Nests.
Prosperity :)

1273 Recognizing A Chicken...Is Easy.
THE CHICKEN...Wants 17 More Meetings
About Flight Plans.
Does Not Want To Fly.

1274 Recognizing A Chicken...Is Fairly Easy.
The Chicken...Wants A "Raise" For Flying.
:). :). :).

1275 Recognizing A Chicken...Is Fairly Easy.
The Chicken...Wants To Advise Eagles.

1276 Recognizing A Chicken...Is Easy.
The Eagle Wants...To "Fly."
The CHICKEN...Wants To Be "Understood."
:)

1277 Recognizing A Chicken...Is Fairly Easy.
THE CHICKEN...Wants To Postpone
Flying Lessons For A Year.
:)

1278 Recognizing A Chicken...Is Fairly Easy.
THE CHICKEN...Wants To Visit Another
"Barn." :)

1279 Rooftop Roosters Have The Illusion...
They Are Now Eagles.
:)

1280 Study Your "Difference"~
Not Your Weakness.
Everyone Knows Their Weakness.
Few Know Their Difference.

1281 The Most Beautiful Chicken On Earth...
Cannot Excite An Eagle.

1282 The Mysterious Trait of Chickens Is...Their
Unending Boldness In Correcting Eagles.
Kinda Cute.

1283 The Presence of An Eagle...
Has Never Excited A Chicken.
Do Not Expect It.
Just-FYI.

1284 What Is Motivating You...To Argue With
Chickens..?
:)

1285 Wounded Eagles With Bloodied Feathers...Are STILL Eagles.

1286 You Are Not Equipped To Enjoy The Barnyard...Because God Has Not Authorized You To Live There.
Chickens :)

1287 Your Patience...Does Not Improve The Chicken.
Just-FYI

1288 Your Role Is To Fly...Not Explain How To Chickens.

1289 Never Invite A Chicken To An Eagle Conference.
~Chicken Gets Credibility.
~Eagles Are Too Paralyzed To Fly.

1290 No Eagle...Can Adapt To A Barnyard.

1291 ONE HOUR With An Eagle Is...Worth More Than A Lifetime With A Chicken.
(Never Forget It.)

1292 Sarah Palin~
I Have Never Seen One Eagle...Upset
So Many Chickens At One Time.
:)

1293 Sooo...You Really Think You Can Understand
The Decisions of "Chickens?"
The Barnyard That Thrills A Chicken...
Will Kill An Eagle.
Even Eagles...Cannot Improve A Barnyard.

1294 The Chickens Diary.
Have Not Read It.
Eagle View Lane.

1295 Wake Up The Eagle In You...
Do Not Fly Close To The Barnyard And Get In
Chicken Conversations.

1296 Your Soaring Higher...Never Excites A Chicken.
Eagles...Never Become Heroes...
To Chickens.

ENDURANCE

1297 Endurance Is A Bridge...Not A Destination.

1298 Endurance Rules...Until You Create Change.

1299 Endurance...Is The Seed For Credibility.

1300 ENDURANCE...Should Be A Season, Not Your Lifestyle.
(Re-Visit Your Decision Skills.)

1301 ENDURANCE...Should Be A Seed Only...Not Your Harvest.
(A Transition...Not A Destination.)
(Jesus~ "MY Yoke Is Easy.")

1302 Your Endurance...
Embarrasses Your Adversaries.
Battle Simply...Documents Your Strength.

1303 Your Endurance...Is Very Painful
To Your Enemies.
:)

ENEMIES

1304 Addiction Is...When You Become Bonded To An Enemy.

1305 Adversary~
You Scheduled...Your Entry.
I Will Schedule...Your Exit.
Comfortable On Battlefield.

1306 An Enemy Is...Anyone Jealous of Your Credibility.

1307 An Enemy...Is Anyone Unexcited By Your Successes.

1308 An Enemy...Is Anyone Who Felt Uninvited To Your Party.
:)

1309 An Enemy Is Proof...Your Banquet Is Beginning.
"Thou Preparest A Table Before Me In The Presence of Mine Enemies." (Psalm 23:5)

1310 An Enemy...Is Simply A Test of Your
Friendships.
True Friends Stay.

⁓

1311 An Enemy Is Someone Desperate...For
Your Attention.
An Enemy Is Someone Who Finds You...
Gloriously Intimidating.

⁓

1312 An Enemy Is Someone Who Has Never
Discerned...The Rewards of Your Favor. :)

⁓

1313 An Enemy Is Someone Who...
Is Jealous of Your Favor.
Resents Your Difference. Researches...Your
Mistakes.

⁓

1314 An Enemy...Purges The Undecided From Your
Friendship List.

⁓

1315 An Ignored Enemy...
Becomes More Dangerous.

⁓

1316 Anything You Trivialize...
Will Become Your Enemy.

⁓

1317 Attention...Excites Your Adversary.
Sooo...Starve Him.
:) :)
Attention...Is Food To An Unwanted Dog.

1318 David's-Diary~
The Jealous...Become Your Enemy.

1319 Diplomacy~
Attack...Does Not Improve An Enemy.

1320 Do Not Worry...About Your Enemies.
Someday...They Will Be Your Friends.

1321 Enemies...
~Are Seeds For Recognition
(David-Goliath).
~Magnets For Favor (Esther-Haman).
~Introductions To Greatness (Joseph).

1322 Enemies...
Permit God...The Retaliation Schedule.
He Is Far More Creative.
:)
(Earth Opening Up...Etc.)

1323 Enemies~
Their Interest In You...Does Not Make Them
More Interesting.

1324 Enemies Are Doors...To Next Seasons.

1325 Enemies Are Often People...
Who Simply Do Not Know You Yet.
Get Closer.
:)

1326 ENEMIES...Create Heroes.
Heroes Are Overcomers...
(David/Goliath...)

1327 An Enemy...Can Give You In A Day...
...What A Friend Cannot Give You In A Lifetime.
...Wisdom.
...Credibility.
...Access.

1328 Enemies Often Provide Remarkable
Mentorship...If You Are Attentive.
Not Mentors.
Mentorship.

1329 Enemies Qualify For Your Reaction...
Not Your Investment.

1330 Enemies...Unleash Your Passion For Research.

1331 Every Enemy...Is An Opportunity.

1332 First Sign of An Adversary Is...
Their Willingness To Withhold Important
Information.

1333 He Who Believes The Slander of Your
Enemy...Was Never Your Friend.

1334 He Who Does Not Warn You About An
Enemy...Is A Deadlier Enemy.

1335 Your Deadliest Enemy...Is The Unknown Enemy.

1336 He Who "Justifies" Your "Enemies"...Is Also Your
Enemy.

1337 I Do Not Fear...My Enemies.
I Fear...For Their Future.

1338 I Have Always Had Enemies.
But, I Never Discerned Who They Were.
Ever.

1339 Lesson: Prepare For Surprises.
I Have...Enemies.
But, I Am Not One.

1340 I Have Never Found An Enemy...As Fascinating
As They Find Me.
:)

1341 The Success of Your Enemy...Is Decided By You.

1342 In Old Testament...David Killed His Goliath.
In New Testament...We Pray For Them.
Ever Wish For The "Good Ole Days?"
:)

1343 Just Took A Picture...
...of The Home of My Enemies.
Under My Feet.
:)

1344 Killers...Come In Many Forms.
...of Your Joy.
...of Your Dreams.
...of Your Hopes.
...of Your Trust.
...of Your Confidence.

1345 Laughter...Instantly Demoralizes The Morale of Your Enemy.

1346 Laughter...Is The Surprise Weapon Your Enemy Never Expected.

1347 Most Enemies...Are Hidden.
My ENEMIES Are Those...
Who Agree With My Enemies.

1348 My Enemies Have Been So Neglected.
Trying To Catch Up On Backlog of...
Reward Celebrations For All My Friends.

1349 Neglecting Your Adversaries...
Can Become A Habit. :)

1350 Never Allow An Enemy...To Choose Your Friends.
Never.

1351 Never Believe The Enemy...of A Friend.

1352 Never Confide...In An Enemy.
Nor Their Friends.
Never Fear...Enemies.
Fear...Not Discerning Them.

1353 No Enemy...
...Can Choose My Weapons.
...Will Decide The Timing of My Response.
...Will Select The Place of My Conquest.

1354 No Enemy Can Not Be Satisfied...Merely
Delayed.
Israel
Iran

1355 Predators...Have More Than One Prey.
Remember.

1356 Some Enemies...Are Necessary Bridges To Your
Destiny.
David/Goliath.
Joseph/Wife of Potiphar.

1357 The Ability To Excite Your Enemies...
Is A Profound Gift.

1358 The Command: Pray...For An Enemy.
Not Understand Them. :)
Studying Insanity...Is Not Your Assignment.

1359 The Happier You Make God...
The Angrier Your Enemies Become.
:)

1360 The Low Quality of My Enemies...
Is Becoming Embarrassing.
:)

1361 The Most Dangerous Enemy...Is Disguised As
A Friend.

1362 Those Who Believe Your Enemies...Have Never
Been Your Friend.

1363 Those Who Enjoy Your Enemies...Are Not Your
Friends.

1364 Those Comfortable Around My Enemies...Are
Not My Friends.

1365 Those Who Are Comfortable With My
Enemies...Are Also My Enemies.

1366 To Your Enemies...You Are The Most Exciting
Thing In Their Life.
:)

1367 You Cannot Satisfy...An Enemy.
Goliath

1368 You Will Never Find Your Enemy...
As Intriguing As He Finds You.
:)

1369 Your Ability To Excite Your Enemy...
Is Unexplainable, But Incredibly Exhilarating.
:)

1370 Your Attack Does Not Bother Me...
If My Winning Does Not Bother You.

1371 Your Attack...Did Not Turn You Into An
Adversary.
Your Attack...Revealed That You Are An
Adversary.

1372 Your Deadliest Enemy...Stays Well-Hidden.

1373 Your Enemy Does Not Desire...
Your Explanation.
Your Enemy Desires...Your Annihilation.

1374 Your Enemy Is Angry...Because Your Weakness
Did Not Stop Your Success.

1375 Your Enemy...Studies You.
Fascinated And Dazzled By You.
They Find You More Important Than Their Own
Future. :)

1376 Your Enemy Views Your Weakness...As More
Exciting Than His Own Future.
:)

1377 Your Enthusiasm...Is The Greatest
Discouragement Your Enemies Experience. :)

1378 Your Progress Can Often Be Measured By...The
Emergence of Adversaries.

1379 Your "Reaction" To Your Enemies...Decides Their
Success.

1380 Your Waiting Reveals The Weaknesses...
of An Impatient Enemy.

ENVIRONMENT

1381 Always Assess An Environment...
Before You Attempt To Change It.
(Or Conversation)

1382 Assess An Environment Well...
Before You Attempt To Influence It.

1383 DOMINATE...Your Turf.
Identify Your Divine Boundaries.
Discern Potential Adversaries.
Stay Attentive.

1384 Environment Can Hide Flaws...or Magnify
Them.
(Romantic Lights Restaurant...
Prayer Room)

1385 Environment
...Does Not Change A Fool.
Lucifer/Heaven

1386 ENVIRONMENT...Does Not Change The Nature
of A Fool.
Judas/Jesus

1387 Every Environment...Has A Code of Conduct For
Entering or Remaining In It.
(Beauty Made Esther Queen;
Obedience KEPT Her Queen.)

1388 Every Environment...Has A Saboteur.

1389 Every Environment...Has Expectations.
Know Them...Before You Attempt To
Change It.
One Mistake.

1390 Every Environment...Welcomes A Servant.

1391 Great Men Become Weak...In Wrong Places.

1392 Home...Is A Person.

1393 I Am...Territorial.
...Unapologetically.
I Created...MY World.
Why Should I Fear It..?

1394 I DO NOT STAY~
~In The Presence of The Disinterested.
~Near Odor of The Disrespectful.
~Accessible To The Unthankful.

1395 I Have Decided To Be...The Environment.
Think :)
Decide To HAPPEN...Everywhere You Are.

1396 I Have Decided To Be...The Environment.
Enter...And Enjoy.

1397 If Everything You Ever Wanted Was In Your
Present Environment...
Would You Find It?

1398 If You Do Not Control Your Own Environment
...Someone Else Will.
~Sounds.
~Music.
~Colors.
~Views.

1399 If You Do Not Create Your Own
Atmosphere...Someone Else Will.

1400 In Every Environment...
The Unthankful...Are Always The
Unhappy.

1401 In Some Environments...
Sensuality Is The Currency.
In Other Environments...
Trust Is The Currency.

1402 MY 6 DISCOMFORT ZONES~
Time-Wasters.
Meaningless Conversation.
The Deceptive.
The Self-Obsessed.
Non-Learners.
The Unthankful.

1403 Never Enter...Uninvited.
Even God Doesn't.

1404 Never Enter...Uninvited.
(Room/Relationship/Pursue/Conversation/
Intimacy)

1405 Never Linger...Where You Are Ignored.

1406 Never Stay In An Environment...
That Magnifies Your Weakness.
:)

1407 Never Stay...Where You Are Not Heard.

1408 No Environment Changes The Nature of A Fool.
(Heaven/Lucifer...Jesus/Judas)

1409 Observe...The Obvious.
Search...For The Hidden.

1410 Peasants Act Different...
Away From The Palace.

1411 Peasants Protest...Palace Protocol.
That's How You Discern They Are Peasants.
:)

1412 Prep Your Environment~
I Love 3 Things In Every Room I Enter~
...Light.
...Movement.
...Sound.

1413 Prolonged Elegance Is...Depressing.
...Furniture
...People
It Is Why God Created Skunks, Not Just
Elk.
:-)

1414 Something You Are Ignoring...
Should Be Faced.
Strange Surroundings...Often Create
Strange Dreams.

1415 Territorial Attitude Is Needed...For Your Own
Divine Domain.
It Is Satanic...When Invading
Unauthorized Terrain.

1416 Territorial...Is Not The Proof of Love.

1417 When You Cannot Control Your
Environment...Control Your Mind.
Pictures On iPad...In Front of Me Corrects
My Focus.

1418 When You Remove A Rebel From Your
Environment...Your Entire Life Will
Change.
In A Single Day.

EVIL

1419 Abortion~
Silence Toward Evil...Is The Greatest Evil.

1420 Abortion...Is The Assassination of The Human Future.

1421 Abortion...Is Simply Legal Murder.
Assassins of The Future.

1422 Abortion...Is Simply The Legal Right To Kill.
Anything Good...Intimidates Evil.

1423 Wrong Always Feels Inferior...To Right.
Always.
(Cain/Abel...Absalom/David)

1424 As Hunters Plan And Relish Their Killing of One Innocent Deer...So,
Evil Men Plan The Death of Christian Influence.

1425 Do Not...Fear Evil.
Fear...The Inability To Discern It.

1426 Gun Control~
Disarming Good Men...Is The Goal of Evil Men.

1427 Evil Men...Have Never Loved The Godly.
That Is How You Discern An Evil Man.
Cain/Abel

1428 Evil People Are Pleasured...
By Your Exposure.
Godly People Are Pleasured...
By Your Recovery.

1429 Evil Survives...By Alliance.

1430 EVIL...Birthed Your Past.
YOU...Are Keeping It Alive. Memory.

1431 Evil...Is Not Ugly.
Evil...Is Adaptive.
Evil...Shows Interest.
Rare...Is The Man Who Detects It Early.
Samson

1432 Evil...Never Removes Itself.

1433 Evil Men Can Be Discerned;
They Resent The Righteous.

1434 Goal of Evil Men...
Is To "Destroy" Good Men.
Goal of Good Men...
Is To "Change" Evil Men.
Wisdom Is: Awareness of Difference.

1435 I Distrust Silence...About Evil.
"He Who Conceals His Hatred Has Lying
Lips..." (Proverbs 10:18).

1436 I Have Never Met The Devil...
But Met His Representatives In Every Country
On Earth.

1437 Never Expect Truth...From An Evil Man.

1438 Never Permit An Evil Person...To Create
Your Philosophy.

1439 Only Men Who Are Fools...Ignore Evil Men.
Or, Maybe...They Are The Same Men.
:)

1440 Insanity~
The Most Effective Way To Empower Evil Men...
Is Disarming Good Men.

1441 Satan...Is Not Unattractive.
The Cruel...Are Gratified Through It.
Demonic.

1442 Terrorists~
If Evil Men Can Achieve Their Goals...
Have NO Doubts You Will Achieve Yours.

1443 The First Sign of An Evil Woman...Is Her
Contempt For A Good Man.

1444 The Sweeter The Sugar...The Deadlier The
Poison.

1445 Those Who Are Not Good...Are Very Proud of
Being Bad.

1446 Those Who Murder "Children of The Womb"...
Do It For Money, Not Pleasure.

1447 There Is War...Anywhere There Is An Evil
Person.

EXCELLENCE

1448 ...Pour "Best" Into EVERY Moment.
...No Hurry...Do It Right...The First Time.
...No Regrets.
...Lifestyle.

1449 Excellence Increases...At The Speed of Your
Correction.

1450 Excellence Is Not An Opinion.
It Is A Philosophy.

1451 Excellence Can Become An Addiction.
A Satisfying One.

1452 Excellence...Does Not Increase With Age.
Excellence Increases...With Integrity.
Excellence...Has No Color.

1453 Excellence...Is Always Rewarded.
Excellence...Is Addictive.
Excellence...Guarantees Favor.
Few-Get-It.

1454 Excellence...Never Receives Admiration From Mediocrity.

1455 Who Will Experience Your
"Excellence"...Tomorrow?
I Despise...Mediocrity.
I Despise...Mediocrity.
I Despise...Mediocrity.
I Despise...Mediocrity.

1456 It Is Easy...To Find A Job.
But...
Only Excellence...Will "Keep" Your Job.

1457 SUCCESS...Is A Moment of Victory.
I Schedule Them Constantly.
Daily.

1458 Mediocrity...
Never Congratulates Excellence.
That Is How You Recognize It.

1459 Mediocrity...Is Prohibited
In My Environment.
It Will Be Insulted...Not Embraced.
Am Addicted To Excellence.

1460 PRESENTATION~
Same Food In Elite Restaurant Is Served
To Pigs That Night.
Difference Is Simply...Presentation.
Think.

1461 Those Who Truly Learn Honor...Have Mastered
Life.

1462 The Prodigal Son...Found Excellence
Suffocating.

FAILURE

1463 A Failure Is Not Necessary...Just Probable.

1464 Defective Conversation...
Is The Reason Anything Fails.
Anything.

1465 Every Failure Equation...
Includes Dishonor.
Few-Get-It.

1466 Failure...Is A Decision.
Where Have You Decided...To Fail?

1467 If You Fail...It Will Be Because You Refused
Wise Counsel.
(Distrusting The Trustworthy Is Life's
Deadliest Mistake.)

1468 When You Prepare For Failure...
It Will Find You.

1469 Where...Have You Accepted Failure?
Why?

FAITH

1470 Because He Knows My Name..!
...My Faith Outlasts
...The Storms That Pass
Tomorrow Brings...My Gain!
Psalm 91:14

1471 Faith Comes (And Leaves)...
By Hearing.
(i.e. 10 Spies of Doubt)

1472 Faith Is NEVER...Unrewarded.

1473 Faith Without A "Plan"...
Is Really Not Faith At All. Plan 2012.

1474 Faith Is...Confidence In God.

1475 Faith Comes...When You HEAR Something God
Would Say.

1476 Faith Decides...Divine Favor.

1477 Guilt...Is The Thief of Faith.
Sin Creates Discomfort With God.
So, Confess...Forsake...Any Known Sin.

1478 Knees Do Not Make The Difference.
Faith...Would Be The Difference.
(Apprentice..!)

1479 I Fear The Tragedy That Doubt Produces.
That's What Got Me Into Faith.

1480 My Present...Was Produced By My "Past" Faith.
My Future...Will Surpass It.

1481 The Costliest Experience On Earth...Is Doubt.

1482 TRIALS
Your Faith Can Produce Ability:
...To Endure The Storm
or
...To Escape The Storm.
Hebrews 11

1483 With Your Faith...You Can Create Almost Any
Future You Want.

FAMILY

1484 Bloodline...Makes Your Child Lovable.
Training...Makes Them Lovable To Others.

1485 Mothers...Decide What Children REMEMBER.
Fathers...Decide What Children BELIEVE.

1486 Never Leave Any Love-Talk Unused...
At The End of Your Day.
Empty Everything Within You Into Family/
"The Emptied Life."

1487 This Week...Unique Anointing...
"Daniel Week."
Access It.
Please...Embrace It.
Re-visit Past Decisions, Too.

FATHER

1488 Dear Fathers~
Teach Your Child A "Biblical Belief System."
Video Tape Yourself.
Be Repetitious. Mentors.

1489 Fathers~
If Your Presence Makes A Difference...
Your Absence Makes A Difference.

1490 Fathers Only~
...Do Not Wait Too Long...To Discern And
Celebrate The Hidden Greatness of
Your Children.
Honor.

1491 Father-Talk~
On His 93rd Birthday, I Asked Dad His Advice.
Wait A Little Longer...In Prayer...
For Answers.

1492 Father-Talk~
Your Absence...Is An Investment In
The Failure of Your Family.

FAVOR

1493 $10 Hourly With Favor...Is Worth More Than
$50 Hourly Without Favor.
Think.

1494 Every Demand...Diminishes Favor.
In Any Environment.

1495 Everywhere You Find Honor...
You Find Favor.
Everywhere You Find Favor...
You Find Money.

1496 I Prophesy...
...Someone Significant Will Show You Favor
Tomorrow.

1497 Expect Favor...In The Same Measure You Are
Sowing It.

1498 Favor Begins...One Problem
From Now.
When You Solve A Problem For Someone...
You Create Favor Toward You.
(Joseph/David)

1499 Favor Is...A Divine Confirmation You Are Where You Belong. (Naomi/Ruth/Boaz)

1500 Favor...Is A Reaction, Not A Miracle.

1501 Favor Is...A Reward For Pleasure Created. Most Ignored Secret On Earth.

1502 FAVOR Is...Fruit, Not A Miracle.

1503 I SOW Favor...Proportionate To The Favor I Want To Reap.

1504 FAVOR...Is Neither A Miracle Nor Mystery.

1505 FAVOR...Is A Reward For Pleasing Someone. (Pleasure...Favor...Honor...Prosperity)

1506 Favor Is...Usually An Unacknowledged Miracle.

1507 A Little Less Favor...Can Birth Huge Loss. Huge.

1508 Favor Must Become Your Daily Seed...
Before You Can Expect It As A Daily Harvest.

1509 Favor...The Highest Path.
Whose Favor Do You Have?
What Is Proof of Your Gratitude?
Does Keeping It Matter?

1510 I Distrust Anyone...Who Cannot Discern
The Rewards of My Favor.

1511 If My Words Are Unimportant To You...
My Favor Is Unimportant To You.

1512 Mysteries To Me...
Why Favor Is...So Unappreciated And Left
Unprotected.
Fools.

1513 NEVER STAY...
Where There Is The Absence of Favor.

1514 The Absence of Divine Favor...Merely Confirms
The Absence of Divine Approval.
(Linger Only In Fields of Favor/Ruth)

1515 The Experience of Favor...
Reveals The Character of The Giver.
The Continuation of Favor...
Reveals Your Gratitude.

1516 The Favor I Sow Is...As Important As The Favor
I Want To Reap.

1517 Those Who Do Not Treasure Your Favor...
Are Unqualified To Receive It.

1518 Those Who Do Not Treasure Favor...Lose It.

1519 When You Identify Whose Favor Matters MOST
To You...Your Success Is 30 Days Away.
Few-Get-It.

1520 When Your Favor Becomes Unimportant To
Another...So Is Your Presence.
Your Absence Should Be...Your Final Gift.

1521 If You Were My Daughter~
Remember...The Rewards of Agreement.
Your Ingratitude...Will Explain 90% of Your
Losses.

1522 Who Pursues YOUR Favor Most Passionately?
Invest Accordingly.

1523 Whose Favor...Matters MOST?
What Is...The Proof?
~Job.
~Marriage.

1524 You Cannot Earn In A Lifetime...
What Favor Can Give You In A Day.

1525 You Will Never Know...
Most of The Greatest Humans On Earth.
Ever.
So...Lavish Favor On Those You Do Know.
Hourly.

FEAR

1526 Fear And Caution Are Different.
Fear...Refuses To Embrace Opportunity.
Caution...Seeks Validation of Feelings.

1527 Fear Is A Very Tiny Thing...
That Imagination Magnifies.

1528 Fear No Fool.
Rather, Fear Not Discerning Him Soon
Enough.

1529 Fear of God...Produces 5 Personal Rewards.
See Psalm 25:12-14.
It Births Wisdom, Too.

1530 Fear of Woman...
Has Never Kept A Husband Faithful.
Fear of God...Keeps A Husband Faithful.

1531 Fear...Is Not My Greatest Enemy.
DECEPTION...Is My Greatest Enemy.

1532 Fear...No Question.
Fear...The Unwillingness To Accept
The Answer.

1533 Fear...Should Simply Inspire More Research.

1534 Dear Daughter ~
What Is The Proof...That He Makes Good
Decisions?
Does His History...Unleash Your Hope or Fear?

1535 Fearlessness...Is Not A Miracle.
It Is The Fruit...of Obedience.

1536 You Are My Hiding Place.
You Shall Preserve Me From Trouble.
You Shall Compass Me About With Songs...
Psalm 32:7

1537 JEALOUSY...Is The Fear of Being Unimportant
To Someone Important To You.

1538 MY 2 GREATEST FEARS
Fear of Believing A Lie (Deception).
Fear of Not Fully Understanding...
"How To LOVE."

1539 Scrutiny...Dissolves Fear.
...or Justifies It.

1540 Some Fear...Catholics.
Some Fear...Muslims.
Some Fear...Losing Votes.
The Wise...Fear God.

1541 What You HEAR...
Decides What You FEAR.
Faith Comes...By "Hearing."
So Does Doubt.

1542 Where There Is Negotiation...There Is Fear.
Where There Is Fear...There Is No Love.

FEELING

1543 A Feeling...Cannot Kill A Fact.

1544 I Feel So Smart...When I Discover Where I Am Dumb.
:)

1545 Depression Can Often Be Broken...
By Reading Psalm 91 Aloud.

1546 Depression Can Often Be Broken...
By SINGING A Song of Thankfulness
Loudly To God.

1547 Depression Can Often Be Broken With...
Giving A Gift of Gratitude To Someone
Who Has Blessed You.

1548 Depression Can Often Be Broken With...
One Meaningful Conversation.

1549 Depression Is...
A Consequence of Wrong Focus.
Studying People Instead of God.
Personal Weakness.

1550 Depression Is...Anger Without Energy.
Cure: Change Focus To Your Inspirations...
Not Problem-Solving.

1551 DEPRESSION~
...Very Real Place.
...Should Not Be Ignored.
...Has No Clever Solutions.
...Can Be Conquered.
...Needs Listener.

1552 Ecstasy Is...Always One Feeling Away.
Depression Is...Very Defeatable.

1553 Every Feeling You Are Pursuing In Your
Future...Was Hidden In Today.
Did You Find It..?
Think.

1554 Feel Like An Ignited Assassin...
Searching For Stupid.

1555 Feelings...
If Unimportant, Why Do We Pursue...Joy...
Peace...Love...Peace..?

1556 Feelings...Really Do Matter.
Greatly.
So...Learn How To Create "Right" Feelings.
...For Yourself.
...For Others.

1557 Futility Is...A Very Deceptive Feeling.
It Is A Habitual Liar.

1558 I Wish Somebody Would Have Told Me...
That Feelings Can Be Changed...
Instantly...
...Focus.
...Conversation.
...Worship.
...Music.

1559 Never Feel Shame For Having...Feelings.
Be Ashamed of Pride...That Stops You From
Discussing Them.

1560 Nothing On Earth Is Easier To Change...
Than A Feeling.
~Music.
~Focus.
~Conversation.

1561 PICTURES Decide FEELINGS.
Your Mind Is Your Private Collection So You
Can Magnify Your Favorites For Mood Change.

1562 Your Feelings...Are Not You.
Resist Their Tyranny.
Stay Parental Toward Them.
Instruct/Rule Them.
Relentlessly.

1563 Your Feelings...Are Not YOU.
They Are Simply The Fragrance of Your
Thoughts.
(Sometimes Odor...Smile!)

FIGHT

1564 Distraction
A Fight...Always Distracts From A Theft.
In The Ghetto.
In The Government.
Think.
Twice.

1565 Never Run...From Anybody.
Anybody.
Every Bully...Has A Weakness.
Find It.

1566 Their Weapon Is Not A Command To Fight...
It Is An Instruction To Find
A Shield.

FLAWS

1567 Equal To His Gift...Is Every Man's Flaw.
Do Not Ever Forget It.
Humbling.

1568 My Flaws...Make Others Necessary In My Life.
My Lack...Increases Your Importance To
Me.
Kinda Nice.

1569 Unbearable Character Flaws~
Lying.
Disrespect.
Unthankfulness.
Laziness.
Slither.
Know-It-All.
Controlling.

FOCUS

1570 3 Songs That...Inspire You?
3 Friends That...You Trust?
3 Goals That...Excite You?
FOCUS.
Put In Front of You...

1571 Anything That Gets ALL of You...Gets The Best
of You.
~Marriage.
~Job.

1572 DearDaughter~
Somebody In The Field of Boaz...Is Getting His
Attention.

1573 Every Person...Chooses A Focus.
Focus...Is Choosing A Master.

1574 You Do Best...When You Do Less.
The More Narrow Your Focus...The Quicker
Your Success.

1575 Focus...Decides What You Learn.
Passion...Decides How Quickly You Learn.
Honor...Decides Who Teaches You.

1576 Focus Is...Choosing What Will Dominate You.
Freedom Is...The Right To Choose Your
Master.

1577 Focus Is...The Choosing of Your Master.
...For An Hour.
...For A Day.
...For Your Lifetime.

1578 Focus...Is When You Choose What Masters Your
Mind.

1579 Focus On A Happy "Day"...
Instead of A Happy Life.

1580 FOCUS...On Your DIFFERENCE
For One Day.
All Day.
Every Hour.
NOT Your Weakness/Disappointment/
Problem.
DIFFERENCE.

1581 Focus ONLY...On What Has The Ability To
Inspire You.
Nothing Else.

1582 Gaze...At Whatever You Want To Feel.
Focus Is...Choosing What You Want To
Master.

1583 I Let Go~
of Anything That Stops Me.
I Let Go~
of Anything That Slows Me Down.
I Let Go~
of Anything That Breaks My Focus.

1584 If You Stay Focused...You Win.

1585 List Your...
...Top 10 Life Goals.
...Top 10 Investors In Your Life.
...Top 10 Pleasures.
...Top 10 Friendships.
Focus.

1586 POUR INTO DREAM #1....
...All The Energy You Have Been Giving
To Dream #2.
Focus.

1587 So Focused On Planting Flowers In My Garden...I Forgot To Buy Weed Killer.

1588 So Focused On Planting Flowers In My Garden...I Forgot To Kill The Snakes.

1589 So Focused On Planting Flowers In My Garden...I Trusted Others To Water It.

1590 What Do You Feel...Is Worthy of Your TOTAL Attention?
What Has Stopped You...From Giving It?

1591 TV News Is...Their World. Not Yours.
Your Immediate Focus Is...YOUR World.

1592 The World Is A Menu of Ingredients.
You Create The Meal.

1593 What Have You Decided...To Master?
What Is Trying To Master You?

1594 When You Choose A "Focus"...
You Have Chosen Your "Master."

1595 Whose Authority Do You Resist?
Who...Is Positioned To Promote You?

1596 Wherever You Have "Focused"...You Have
Succeeded.

1597 You Will Succeed Wildly...In Anything That
Receives Your TOTAL Focus.
Change...Your Focus.

1598 Your #1 Daily Focus: Keep Yourself Inspired.

1599 Your Season Changes...When Your FOCUS
Changes.

1600 FOCUS.
It Decides...Your Peace of Mind.
It Decides...The Quality of Your Day.
It Decides...The Quality of Your Life.

1601 Do Not Change...Others.
Change...Your Focus.

FOOLS

1602 A Fool Answereth A Matter...
Before He Hears It.

1603 A Fool Is...Someone Who Makes The Same
Mistakes Repeatedly.
Proverbs 26:11

1604 A Fool...Is A Test.
...Not A Task.
A Fool...Made The Decision To Be So.

1605 Be Neither Angry Nor Bitter With Behavior of
Fools.
Be Thankful.
Very.
But For Grace of God~That Could Be You.

1606 Blocking A Fool On Twitter...Is The Easiest
Decision You Will Ever Make.
:)

1607 Do Not Be Concerned...About The Words of Fools.
Be Concerned...That You Willingly Listened To Them.

1608 Dumb...Has An Odor.
Fools Do Not Believe...
The Anointing Is Worth Honoring.
Fear Not...The Fool.

1609 Fools Do Not Believe...Dishonor Is Costly.
...Absalom.
...Judas.
...Others.

1610 FOOLS...Accuse Before They Know.

1611 Fools...Are Not Rare.
(Multitudes Rejected Jesus)

1612 Fools...Are Not Worthy of Your Energy.
Do Not Invest.
:)

1613 Fools...Disdain The Environment of Favor.
(Absalom/Prodigal Son...Look For Greener Grass)
Naomi To Ruth: Stay.

1614 Fools...Do Not Qualify For A Response.

1615 Fools...Instruct Upward.
Only Fools Attempt Withdrawals...
Where They Have Never Made Deposits.

1616 FOOLS...Want Ownership of A Garden...
...Someone Else Planted.
Ahab/Garden

1617 Fortunately For All of Us~
Fools Refuse To Stay Hidden.
"Go From Presence of A Foolish Man, When You
Do Not Perceive In Him The Lips of Knowledge."
Proverbs 14:7
Do Not Correct.

1618 Him: "My Leader Is A Fool."
Me: "So, Why Are You Following Him?"

1619 I Have No Intention To Be A Pleasant
Experience...For Fools.
:)

1620 Logic Is...Always An Unhappy Experience
For Fools.

1621 Never Consider A Fool...Your "Goliath."
God Addresses Fools...Personally.
Never Sue...A Fool.
The Judge May Be One Too. :)

1622 Never Waste Your Energy...On A Fool.
In Thoughts.
In Talk.
In Retaliation.

1623 No Greater Fool Exists...Than He Who Places
Little Value On My Trust.
Position Stated.

1624 Only A Fool...Forgets Who He Is Talking To.

1625 Only A Fool Despises...
Who The King Enjoys.
Think.
Again.
In Every Environment.

1626 Only A Fool...
Permits An Enemy To Explain A Friend.
...Gossip.
...Accusation.
...Abuse.
...Slander.

1627 Only Fools Believe...
Scanning Is For Terrorism.
Do Not Stay Stupid.

~

1628 Only Fools...Would Expect Favor Where They
Created Distrust.

~

1629 Only The Fool...Lives As If He Has No Enemies.

~

1630 The Achievers Demise~
A Fool Is...Attracted To You.
A Fool...Attacks Your Name, Credibility.
Smile.

~

1631 The Fool...Ignores What The Wise Master.
HISTORY...
...of A Leader.
...of A Mate.
...of A Boss.
...of An Environment.
The Fool...Votes Party.
The Wise...Vote Principle.

~

1632 The Hatred From A Fool...Is Not A Crisis To Me.
:)

~

1633 Who Trusts...An Unfaithful Man?
Only A Fool.

FORGIVENESS

1634 Forgiveness...Is A Stress Remover.
Forgiveness Restores Opportunity...
Not Trust.

1635 Forgiveness...Does Not Restore Credibility.

1636 Forgiveness...Is Not Restoration.
Forgiveness...Is Opportunity For Restoration.

1637 Forgiveness...Is Not Trust.
Forgiveness...Is Permitting God To Penalize
Others.

1638 Forgiveness...Is Not Trust.
Forgiveness Is An Invitation...To Rebuild Trust.

1639 Forgiving Someone...
Enables You To Forget About Them.
:)
Kinda Stress-Removal In A Strange Way.

1640 I Said, "I Forgive You."
I Did Not Say, "I Trust You."

1641 If Forgiveness Can Occur Without Confession...
Confession Is Unnecessary.

1642 My Forgiveness...To You Was Swift.
My Recovery...From You Takes A Long Time.
The Absence of Guilt...Is Not Necessarily The
Proof of Forgiveness.

1643 The Instruction To Forgive...
Was Not An Instruction To Trust.

1644 Unforgiveness Is A Decision...To Bond With
Sadness.

1645 Unforgiveness...Makes You Defeatable.

1646 Yes, You Are Forgiven.
So Am I...For Removing Your Knife.

1647 You Have Inspired Me...To Forgive.
I Wish You Inspired Me...To Trust.

1648 I Need...More Than Forgiveness.
I Need...Power To Overcome.

FRIENDSHIP

1649 A Friend...Is Anyone Not Dangerous.
:)

1650 Beware The One Who Cannot...
Stay In Friendship.

1651 Do Your Enemies Get Your Attention...
More Than Your Friends..?
You Need...More Interesting Friends. :)

1652 Every Downfall...Came Through A "Friend."
Judas
Delilah

1653 Every Friendship...Has A Price.
Every Friendship...Has Expectations.
Every Friendship...Can Change.

1654 EVERY FRIENDSHIP...Has Expectations~
Spoken or Unspoken.
(Your Responsibility Is To Discern Them.)

1655 Friends...Accept Your Weakness.
Enemies...Expose Your Weakness.
Mentors...Identify Your Weakness.

~

1656 Friendship Is...An Investment Program Where
Nobody Wants To Discuss The Cost.

~

1657 FRIENDSHIP~
Your Requests...Reveal Your Perception
of Me.

~

1658 I Have Never Lost A Friend.
...Only Impostors.

~

1659 Just Discern The Cage Each Friend Belongs.
Leave No Cage Unchecked. :)

~

1660 Qualify...Friendships.
Identify...Enemies.
Remove Access Quickly.

~

1661 The Unwatered Friendship...Will Die.

~

1662 The Opinions of Others Will Matter...If You Walk
With World-Class Friends.

~

1663 What If..?
The Greatest Friend Possible...
Lived Within Two Miles From You.
What If...Disobedience Sabotaged Opportunity?

1664 When My Friends Cannot Make Me Laugh...
My Enemies Do.
HeHe.
:)

1665 When My Friends Disagree With Me...
I Just Go Make Friends With Smarter People.
:) :)

1666 Your Friends Explain Who You Are...
More Than You Do.

1667 Your Friends Who Enjoy Your Enemies...Are Not
Your Friends.
Read This 3 Times.
True Friends...Have The Same Enemies.

1668 Friends-
Some...Make You Laugh.
Some...Make You Think.
Some...Make You Mad.
Some...Make You Sad.
Some...Make You Change.

FUTURE

1669 Are You Running Away From A Past...
or Toward...
A Spectacular Future?

1670 The Price of Your Present Was...Passion.
The Price of Your Future Is...Credibility.

1671 Are You Racing Toward A Future To
Experience "A FEELING"...
That Is Actually Possible...NOW?

1672 What You Are Willing To Walk Away From...
Determines What God Will Bring To You.
(Joseph/Ruth)

1673 I Put In Front of Me...What I Want INSIDE Me.
God-Facts.
Inspiration.
Past Triumphs.
My Future.

1674 If I Can Wake Up Your Future...
Then I Can Shut Down Your Past.
What FUTURE Do You Want To Be
TRAINED For..?

1675 If You Are Ready For Your Future...
You Are Already In It.
This Is It.
If You Were Prepared For Your Future...
You Would Be In It.

1676 Make Your Future So Big, Yesterday Is
Embarrassed To Show Up.
My Future CANNOT Happen...
Until I Arrive.

1677 Running From Your Past...
Does Not Create A Future.

1678 Something In Your Present Must Stop...Before
Your Future Begins.
What Is It?
What Is Loss/Cost of...This Delay?

1679 The Camel You Are Watering Is...
Your Trip Into Your Future.
Rebekah/Eleazar/Isaac.

1680 The Consistency of Your Disinterest...
Has Helped Me Understand Your Role
In My Future.

1681 The Future of A Relationship Is Revealed
Through Reaction To~
-Correction.
-Greatness.
-Instruction.
-A Gift.
-Weakness.
-Authority.

1682 The Future...Is Not My Creator.
The Future...Is My Creation.

1683 The Future...Is Now Creating Itself
From The Seed I Sent Ahead.
Think.

1684 The Love of God...
Will Not Decide Your Future.
Your Love For God...Decides Your Future.
Few-Get-It.

1685 The More You Discuss Your Future...
The Faster It Moves Toward You.

1686 The Worst Day In Your Future...
Will Be Greater Than The Best Day...of
Your Past.
I Know The Plans I Have/God.

1687 Until You Can SEE Your Future...You Will
Misinterpret Every Conversation God Has
With You.

1688 What Daily Routine...Would Create The Future
You Crave?

1689 What Is The Future...You Are Training For?
WHO...Is Training You?
HOW...Are They Training You?
What Is YOUR Investment?

1690 What Is The "Future"...You Want To Be Trained
For?
Who...Will "Train" You?
When...Will You Make It Your "Only Focus?"

1691 Whatever You Admire Most...Is A Preview of
Your Future.
Admiration Is The Seed
For...Your Next Season.

1692 What "Yesterday" Have You Made...
More Important Than Your Future..?

~

1693 You...Created Your Present.
A Changed You...Can Create A Future.
What Will You Change..?

~

1694 You Must Hate The Present...
Before You Can Create A Different Future.
Sin/Salvation.
Sickness/Healing.
Change.

~

1695 You Will Enter Your Future At The Speed of
Choice.
 ~Crawling.
 ~Walking.
 ~Running.
 ~Car.
 ~Jet.
 ~The Voice You Choose To Trust.

~

1696 You Will Enter Your Future...When You Are
Thoroughly "Trained" For It.

~

1697 Your Future Begins...One Person From Now.
Believe It.
i.e. Joseph/Pharaoh

~

1698 Your Future Depends Entirely On...What You Are Willing To Stop Talking About.
Words Decide What Lives.

1699 Your Future Happens...
At The Speed of Your Learning.
Isaiah 1:17

1700 Your FUTURE Has A Higher Code of Conduct Than Your Present.

1701 Your Future...Has A Price.

1702 Your Future Is Always...
In Someone Who Trusts You.

1703 Your Future Is Crawling Toward You...
At The Speed of Your Decisions. :)

1704 Your Future Is Decided...
By What You Are Willing To Change.
...Your Focus.
...Who You Trust.
...Who You Train.
...Words.

1705 Your Future Is Developing...
At The Speed of Your Faith.

1706 Your Future Will Arrive...At The Speed of Your
Decisions.

1707 Your Future Will Begin...
One Decision From Now.

1708 Your Future Will Happen As Quickly As...
The Questions You Are Willing To Ask.

1709 Your Future Without Pictures...
Is Not A Future.
An Illusion.
An Imposter.

1710 Your Potential...Is Not A Prophecy of Your
Destiny. (Lucifer)
Your Failure Is Not A Prophecy of Your
Future. (Peter)

GENIUS

1711 A Genius Decision...
Does Not Make You A Genius.
Think.

1712 Genius Is Always Accompanied By...
A Great Weakness.

1713 Genius Is Hidden...In
Every Human.
Finding It...Reveals YOUR Genius.

1714 Genius Is...Not An Ability.
Genius Is...An Attitude.
Genius...Is The Willingness To Think Again.

1715 Genius...Is Not A Mystery.
Genius...Is Simply Caring.

1716 The Burden of Genius...Is Impatience.
Patience...Does Not Improve A Fool.

1717 Your Genius Receives...Human Admiration.
Your Obedience Receives...
Divine Admiration.

1718 Your Genius...Was A Divine Decision.
Your Obedience...Is Your Personal Decision.

1719 Nothing Is More Profound...
Than The Ability To Appear Common.

GIFTS

1720 Every Gift...Is An Investment.
Study Well...Your Returns.
God Requires It.
Stewardship.

1721 Gift Giving~
The Greatest Gift...Is Always A Good Book.
...Ageless.
...A Collectible.
...Escape Experience.
...Memorable.

1722 Gifting...Is Not Character.
Never Confuse It.

1723 Gifts...Should Be Sequential.
Give Opportunity...Before You Give Money.

1724 Most of YOUR Gifts From God...
Remain Unopened.
You Are Preoccupied Watching Others
Unwrap Their Gifts.
Think.

1725 Presentation of A Gift...Can Be As Memorable As The Gift.

1726 Some Gifts...Are Hidden Passkeys...
To Create Access Into Your Life.
Careful.

1727 The Greatest Gift You Can Give Someone...
Is A "Happy" You.
Invest Heavily...In Your Own Joy.
FIRST. :)
Think.

1728 The Prettiest Package...
Does Not Always Contain The Greatest Gift.

GOALS

1729 A Sinner With A Goal...Has More Power On The Earth Than A Christian Without A Goal.

1730 Aim...At A Closer Goal.
Pleasure...Happens Quicker.

1731 Big Goals...Create Conversation.
Small Goals...Create Completions.

1732 Discontinue Any Goal...That Has Made You Unkind.

1733 Goals Expose Enemies, Verify Friends, Activate Your Faith.
Until You Set A Goal No Faith Is Needed.
Faith Creates Pleasure In God.

1734 Goals...Decide What You Learn.
Humility...Decides How Fast You Learn.
Passion...Decides The Price You Will Pay.

1735 Hourly Goals...Create Hourly Pleasure.
Daily Goals...Create Daily Pleasure.

1736 If Comfort Is Your Goal...
Stop When You Get There.

1737 It Is Not Your "Goal"...Unless It Has Qualified
For Your Full Attention.

1738 It Is Only When You Establish A Goal...That You
Can Know What You Should Study.

1739 Make Your Goals So Exciting...
Your Past Is Too Ashamed To Be Discussed.

1740 My Goal Is Not...Laying Down My Life.
My Goal Is...My Adversary Laying Down
His Life.

1741 My Goals...Are Not Achieved Because of What
You Do.
My Goals...Are Achieved Because of Who I Am.

1742 Set 3 Small Goals...NOW.
Jump-Starts...Your Pleasure Before 12pm.
The "C-C Factor."
Joy Comes>Creating And Completing.

1743 Set Lower Goals.
You Arrive Quicker. :)

1744 The Destination...Decides The Importance of
The Road.
Many Roads.
One Matters Most.

1745 The Greatness of Your Goal...
Does Not Guarantee Its Success.

1746 The Smaller The Goal...
The Quicker The Pleasure.

1747 Your Goals...Decide Who You Value.

1748 Those Without Your Goals...Despise Your
Passion.

1749 When You Establish A Goal...You Force An
Adversary To Expose Himself...Making Him
Defeatable.

1750 You Choose...A "Dominant" Goal.
Your Goal...Births "Daily" Habits.
Your Habits...Create Your Entire Future.

1751 Your Goals...Create Your Stress.

1752 Your Goals...
Choose The Mentor You Pursue.
Your Discerning...Chooses Who You Trust.

1753 Your Goals Choose Your Mentors.
Until You Establish A Goal...
All Your Knowledge Is Accidental.

1754 Your Goals Decide...
Who Qualifies For Access.

1755 Your Goals...Decide What Is "Unnecessary" In
Your Life.

GOD

1756 A Brilliant God...Does Not Give Crazy Dreams.

1757 Amazing~
...That The God of Others...Seems So
Different Than The Holy Spirit I Fell In
Love With...July 13,1994...7am.

1758 An EXPERIENCE With God...
...Is Not A RELATIONSHIP With God.

1759 EXPECTATION...
My Soul...
Wait Silently For GOD...Alone.
For My Expectation Is...From HIM.
Psalm 62:5
Not Man.

1760 An Unhappy God...
May Explain The Unhappy You.
Think. Again.

1761 Anyone Who Knows God...
Will Recognize Him Instantly In You.
Those Who Do Not Know God...
Will Not Celebrate The God In You.

1762 Avoid Accusatory Tone...When Addressing God.
None of Us Have Qualified For His
Mercy/Goodness.
Ingratitude Is Deadly.

1763 Discouragement Is...What I Feel When God And
I Disagree.

1764 Every Time I Quote God...I Feel Godly.
So I Seize Every Opportunity To Do So.

1765 Find What Excites God Most About You;
Then...Build Your Whole Life Around It.

1766 FYI~
I Am Addicted To...The Presence of God.
I Have A Passion...To Learn From
The Holy Spirit.
I Am A Misfit...Elsewhere.

1767 GOD~
Looking For A Replacement For God..?
Good Luck.

1768 God~
No Enemy...Decides Your Destiny.
Your Enemy...Decides Your Rewards.
David/Goliath
Esther/Haman

1769 GOD~
Stunningly Powerful.
Shockingly Brilliant.
Gentle.
Oh So Gentle.
Speechless...That He Wants Conversation
With Me.

1770 God Always Stands...Close
To "A Door."
The "Door of Favor."

1771 God Can Silence Your Voice In One Accident.

1772 God...DESIGNS Your Future.
You...DECIDE Your Future.

1773 GOD...Did Not Give Without Expectations.
Neither Do I.
(Cross...Love...Time...Counsel...Gratitude.)

1774 God Did Not Instruct Me...To Understand You.
God Did Not Instruct Me...To Change You.
God Instructed Me...To Love You.

1775 God Did Not Predestine...Your Decisions.
God Only Predestined...Consequences of Your
Decisions.
Very Important.

1776 God Discussed Obedience...
Long Before He Discussed Love.

1777 God Does Not Mentor You...Without His Book.

1778 God Does Not Respond To
Needs...
Desires...
Pain...
Concerns.
God Responds Only To Your SPOKEN...
Prayer of Faith.

1779 God Closes Doors...To Wrong Rooms.
Be Thankful.

1780 God Does Not Study...
The Discoveries of Science.
Science Studies...The Creations of God.

1781 God Gave Us Music
...So We Could Change Moods Quickly.

1782 God Gave You A Family...
To Prepare You For Your Enemies.

1783 Everything In Your Future...Is Already At
Your House.
(Judas/Absalom)

1784 God Gave You...A "World Menu."
Your Own Decisions...Created Your Buffet.

1785 God Gives Seed...To Sowers.
God Gives Harvest...To Receivers.

1786 God...
Has Never Created A Common Person.

1787 God Has Never Created A Future...
Only The Plans For It.
Jeremiah 29

1788 God Has Never Given You...
Control Over A Single Person.
Ever.
God Only Gave You...
Authorization To Invest In Them.

1789 God Has Never Invested Time In Those
Resentful of Him.
(Lucifer)

1790 When God Is In The Equation...
Everything Changes.

1791 Pursuers Only...
Qualify For Access, Conversation.

1792 God Has Never Made...A Human Decision.

1793 God Has Never Sponsored...
A Non-Planner.
(Just Planners/Ark/Tabernacle/Temple)

1794 God Has Not Created Your Future.
Your Decisions...Will Create Your Future.
Isaiah 1:17

1795 God Has Predestined Consequences...
Not Decisions.

1796 God Has Pre-Programmed...
The Rewards of Every Right Decision.
Destiny.

1797 God Has Sent You Many Gifts...
You Have Been Unwilling To Receive.

1798 God Has Talked To Me Today.
Through Reactions.
Strangely Strengthened...And Re-focused.
No Fool...Discerns The Wise.

1799 GOD...Has Used Your Mind In Almost Every
Miracle Performed In Your Life.
(Whatsoever Is True...Think...)

1800 GOD Is Fascinated By One Thing~
OBEDIENCE.
Obedience Is The ONLY Proof of Faith.
Faith~Is Confidence In God.
Numbers 23:19

1801 God Is Not Authorized To Open The Door...
You Decided To Close.

1802 GOD...Is Not In Control of Human Decisions;
He Predestined The Consequences...ONLY.
The Difference Is Profound.

1803 "God Is Not Through...Blessing You."
Believe It.
Wake Up The Dreamer...WITHIN You.

1804 God Is...One Conversation Away. 24/7

1805 God Is...Whoever You Think About Most.

1806 God Knows What You Need.
But...
Do YOU...Know What You Need???
God...Leaves No Man Unrewarded.
(Isaiah 1:17-19)

1807 God, Master Investor, Invested His BEST...Into
People.
His Very Best.
They Qualify For OUR Best.

1808 God Never Authorizes A Woman To Marry
A Man...Who Refuses To Lead:
Nor A Man, To Marry A Woman...
Who Refuses To Follow.

1809 God Never Expected You To Solve World Problems.
NEVER.
Just Solve...Your Own.

1810 GOD...Never Ignores Your Decisions.
(Jesus Could Not Do Miracles In The City Because of Unbelief.
God Works With Boundaries.)

1811 God Often Hides His Greatest Gifts In His Most Flawed Vessels...So Only The Most Passionate Can Discover Them.

1812 God Often Hides Something You Need...In Someone You Do Not Enjoy.
:)
Wisdom

1813 God Often Permits People To Disqualify Themselves.
...Through Dishonor.
...Through Abuse.

1814 God...Relaxes Me Incredibly.
You Need At Least One Person In Your Life...Who Requires No Coaxing or Babysitting.
:)

1815 God Rules His World With His Mouth...
He Expects You To Rule Your World With Your
Mouth.

1816 God Should Not Be...
"Part" of The Political Debate.
God Is The "Foundation" of The Political
Debate.

1817 God Talks To Families...Through Their Children.
God Talks To Nations...Through
Their Economy.

1818 God...The Master Conversationalist.
Never Elusive.
Never Evasive.
Intrigued By His Relentless Competence.
I Am...His.

1819 God Talks...In Many Voices.
Which One Have You Decided...To Ignore?
Bible?
Conscience?
Pain?
Loss?
Authority?

1820 God Uses Pain To Teach Fools...
Unwilling To Sit At The Feet of A Mentor.

1821 God Was Not Driving...
The Car You Wrecked.
Blame

1822 God Will Handle...Those You Cannot.

1823 God Will Never Ask You For... Something You Do
Not Have.
But...He Will Always Ask You For...Something
You Want To Keep.

1824 God Will Not Live...
In A Joyless Environment.
Neither Will I.

1825 GOD...Will Not Provide For You
Proportionate To Your Need;
But According To Your FAITH.
(Important Distinction)

1826 God Will Reward A Sinner Who WORKS...
Before He Rewards A Christian Who Will Not.

1827 God's Love...Creates Blessings.
Your Faith...Schedules Them.

1828 God's Mouth...Created The Worlds.
Your Mouth...Is Creating Your World.
Think.

1829 Having More of God...
Does Not Make You Less of A Man.
FYI.

1830 I Could Not Submit To A God...
Who Refused To Perform Miracles.

1831 I Do Not Need Anything Bigger Than God...
To Happen To Me.
He Is Enough.

1832 I Don't Want Anything God Does Not Want To
Give Me.

1833 I Fear Any Man...Who Does Not Have A Fear of
God.

1834 I Know Not The Instructions God Gives...
To Others.
I Barely Grasp His Instructions...To Me.

1835 I Know...God Loves Me.
I Am Concerned That...
God Will ENJOY Me.

1836 I Refuse To Chase Anything...
That God Is Reluctant To Give.

1837 "I Will Do A New Thing.
Now It Shall Spring Forth!
I Will Even Make A Road In The
Wilderness And Rivers In The Desert,"
Isaiah 43:19.

1838 I Will Do The Will of God...At
Any Cost.
ANY Cost.

1839 I Will Walk Through No Door...
God Did Not Open.

1840 If God Does Not Enjoy You...
I Would Not Enjoy You Either.

1841 God Hid His Gold In People...So Only Love Can Discover It.
Think.

~

1842 If God Himself Could Not Stop Stupid...
Why Are You Trying So Hard?
:)

~

1843 If God Ignored You For ONE Day...
You Would Feel It.
You May Be Feeling The Pain...of Ignoring Him.
(1, 2 Days)

~

1844 If God Is In Control of Everything...
Why Are You Praying?
Decisions...Create Destiny.

~

1845 If God Is In Control~
Explain...Rape, Murder, War, Abortion.

~

1846 Why Pursue Wisdom?
What Is The Reward For Obedience?
(Isaiah 1:19)

~

1847 If God Likes Me...No One Else Matters.
:)

~

1848 If God Likes You...He Sponsors You.

1849 IF GOD MADE YOU...The Way You Are-
Why Would You Try To Improve Yourself?
Fact: God Made You The Way You Were;
You BECAME What You Are.

1850 If God Never Spoke To You Again...You Know
Enough To Please Him.

1851 If You Asked God For A Steak...
Stop Eating Sandwiches.

1852 If You Do Not "Enjoy" God...
You Do Not Yet Know God.

1853 If You Ever Really Discover What God Has
Personally Invested In You...You Will Stay
Inspired The Rest of Your Life.

1854 If You Insist On Taking Something God Did Not
Give You...He Will Take Back Something He
Gave You.
Tithe~
Adam/Tree~
Samson/Delilah~
David/Bathsheba~

1855 Islam FAQ~
The Lord Is God.
He Is The Faithful God.
Keeping His Covenant of Love
~To 1,000 Generations.
Deuteronomy 7:9

1856 It Astounds Me That The World
Passionately Pursues Healing~
~Without Any Honoring of The Healer.
Stunning.

1857 It Has Always Been Difficult For Me To Trust
Anyone...
Who Has No Fear of God.

1858 It Is Agitating...
When God Does Not Agree With Me.
:)

1859 It Is Almost Impossible To Trust A Man...That
Refuses To Trust God.

1860 Joel Osteen Does More In One Day...Than Most
of Us Do In Our Lifetime.
I Believe In Men...Who Love My God.

1861 Justice...Is An Absolute Illusion.
God...Is Not.

1862 Never Pick A Fight...With Someone God Likes.

1863 Permit God To Deal With Your Enemies...He Is
Far More Creative.
:)

1864 Permit God To Destroy Your Enemies...In His
Own Creative Way.
I Do.

1865 The Fear of God...
Removes Your Fear of Man.

1866 The Further From God You Are...
The More Unbearable You Become.

1867 The God I Have Experienced Is...
The God I Teach About.
You Should Be Doing The Same.
Might Be The Same God.
Maybe.

1868 THE GOD I KNOW...
"Beloved, I Wish...Above ALL Things
That Thou Mayest Prosper And
Be In Health."
3 John 2

1869 The God I Know...
Leaves Nobody Unrewarded.
Nobody.
And...
Your God?

1870 The God Within Me...Changes Every
Environment I Enter.
~Dramatically.
~Instantly.
~Permanently.

1871 The God Within Me...Creates Instant Stress On
Any Rebel In My Presence.

1872 The God-Within-You Changes Every
Environment You Enter.
Instantly.

1873 The God You Are "Taught" About...May Be Very
Different Than The God You "Experience."

1874 The God You Experience...Is Only A Very Small Part of Him.

1875 The God You Experience...Is Your Message To Men.

1876 The Proof of My God...Is The Change He Created In Me.

1877 The Will of God...Is Always "Immediate."

1878 The Will of God Is Always Verified...By Uncommon Favor.

1879 Those Angry Over God...
Turn One of His Gifts...Into Their Own "god."
Interesting, Huh?

1880 Those Who Do Not Fear God...Despise Those Who Do.

1881 What Part of God...
Are You Willing To Experience NEXT..?
Will You Pay...The Price?

1882 What Part of God...
Are You Willing To Qualify For..?
Sinner...Qualifies For Mercy.
Obedience...Qualifies For Sonship.

1883 What-Would-Happen...
...If You Excelled In Knowing God?

1884 When God Changes A Man...
That Man Can Change A Nation.
~Evangelism.
~Missions.

1885 What The Enemy Has Taken Away God Will
Restore And When He Gives Back He Always
Gives More!

1886 When I Read God's Job Description...
A Great Burden Is Lifted Off Me.
:)

1887 You...Cannot Explain "You."
"You" Were GOD's Idea...

1888 "You Will Seek Me And Find Me, When You Seek
Me With All Your Heart."
Access

1889 Your Best Gift From God...
Is Whoever Brought You To God.
Never Forget It.

1890 Your Experience With God...
Becomes His Message Through You.

1891 Your Experience With God...
Will Become Your Message To Men.
(God Is Much More Than One Experience.)

1892 Your Making God Unimportant In Your World...
Did Not Make You Unimportant In His World.

1893 Your Storm...Is Stopping.
"He Setteth An End To Darkness..."
Job 28:3

1894 If God Agrees With Your Enemies...You Are In Trouble.

:)

1895 I Could Not Submit To A God...I Could Deceive.

1896 If God Is In Control...What Are My Responsibilities?
The Better You Know Yourself...The More You Will Enjoy God.

1897 Some Spend Their Life...Searching For God.
Others Spend Their Life...Avoiding Him.

GOVERNMENT

1898 Government~
Confusion...Is Not An Experience.
Confusion...Is A Strategy.
An Evil One.

1899 Government~
God Did Not Provide You Your Harvest...
To Sponsor Non-Sowers.

1900 Government~
Laws...Do Not Create Morals of A Country.
Laws...Expose Morals of A Country.
(Inspired by Ron Paul)

GRATITUDE

1901 A Thankful Sinner...Will Prosper 1,000 Times
More Than An Unthankful Christian.

1902 Amazing!
The Sound of Gratitude...Creates Contentment.
Instantly.

1903 Exude Gratitude Today.
Focus...On One Important Completion.
Journal...A Divine Thought.
Relax...For 24 Hours.

1904 Gratitude~
Speaking Thanks...And Being Thankful...
Are Two Very Different Worlds.
Very Different.

1905 What Is The Proof of Your Gratitude?
Who Has Benefitted From Your Thankfulness?
Who Should You Thank?
HOW?

1906 Your Greatest Experience On Earth Will
Be...A Thankful Person.
(Next To God.)

1907 Build Your Life Around Them.
Gratitude...Is A Test of Character.
...Makes Loyalty Undoubtable.
...Reveals Hidden Needs.

1908 Gratitude Is...Not A Feeling.
It Is A Fragrance.

1909 Gratitude...Is Test of Character.
Only Cure For Ingratitude
Is...Loss.
Odor of Unthankfulness...Reveals
Disease.

1910 Gratitude...Silences The Roar of Life.
Instantly.

1911 Gratitude...The Leaders Oasis.

1912 Gratitude Unexpressed...Is Ingratitude.

1913 Gratitude Unspoken Is...Gratitude Unknown.

1914 My Addiction?
The Fragrance of Gratitude.
~Stirs Me.
~Lingers In My Mind.
~Awakens Passion To Give.
~Want It Near Me.

1915 Thank You...Is Not Gratitude.
Thank You...Is The Sound of Gratitude.
Gratitude Is A Philosophy...Not A Protocol.

1916 The Proof of Gratitude Is...
The Effort To Repay.

1917 The Scent of Gratitude...
Magnifies The Odor of The Unthankful
For The Rest of Your Life.

1918 Unconfessed Sin...Creates Loss.
Confessed Sin...Creates Gratitude.

GREATNESS

1919 4 Qualities...That Arrest My Attention In A
Person:
Gratitude.
Gentleness.
Goodness.
Graciousness.
That Is "Greatness."

1920 4 Things I Find Irresistible...
Honor.
Kindness.
Thankfulness.
Trustworthiness.

1921 Great Men...Are Not Always Wise.
Founders of America.
Democracy.
Yet, Believed In Slavery.
Astounding.

1922 Great People...Are Not Always Wise.
(Job)

1923 Greatness...Discerns Itself In Another.
Always.

1924 Greatness Is...Permitting Your Weakness To Bond You With God.

1925 Greatness Is...
The Ability To Endure "Average."

1926 Greatness Is...The Ability To Hide Your Response To A Fool.

1927 Greatness Is Simply The Ability To Make A Big Problem...Small.

1928 Greatness Is...Stopping The Pain of Another. Gratitude Is...Celebrating The One Who Stopped Your Pain.

1929 Greatness...Is The Ability To Discern Hidden Rewards.
...In People.
...In Moments.
...In Loss.
...In Pain.

1930 Greatness Is...The Ability To Live With Mediocrity Until It Changes.
Jesus.

1931 Greatness...Is The Ability To Recover From Disappointment.
Re-View.
Re-Set.
Re-Focus.

1932 Greatness Is The Ability To Stay Focused... When You Are Uninspired.

1933 Greatness Is The Willingness To Speak Right Words...When You Have Wrong Feelings.

1934 Greatness...Is The Willingness To Endure The Weaknesses In Others.

1935 The Proof of Greatness...Is The Ability To Discern It In Another.

1936 S.A.P.~
Any Speedbumps And Potholes That Slowed You
Down On Your Journey
To Greatness.
(Or Blocked Your Projects. :-)

1937 The Great...Are Often Denied
The Feeling of It.

1938 "The Proof of Greatness...Is Your Willingness To
Honor It."

1939 Your Greatness Is Not
The Absence of A Flaw,
But Your Ability To Survive It.

HAPPINESS

1940 If Your Money Does Not Make You Happy...You
Have Not Learned What To Do With It.
:)

1941 HAPPINESS...Happens Every Time You Find...
Something You Love.

1942 Happiness Is The Immediate Reward...For
Removing One Wrong Person From Your Life.
Lot/Abraham

1943 Happiness...
Is The Reward For Right Focus.

1944 Happy Is...Always
Just One Feeling Away.
Kinda Remarkable.

1945 Miserable People...Attempt
Many Things.
Happy People...Attempt Right Things.

1946 The Happiest You...Is The Best Gift You Can
Give Those You Love.

1947 The More Thankful I Am...The Happier I
Become.

1948 NOBODY Is...As Happy
As They First Appear.
Wow!
Now, Don't You Feel Strangely Happy
About That..?!
:-)
Sick.

1949 When I Am Happy...
I Feel Unstoppable.
When I Am Unhappy...I AM Unstoppable.
Advised.

1950 When You Become Effective At Creating Your
Own Happiness...We Will Discuss Your
Participating In Mine.
:)

1951 Who Are You So Happy...That You Are Not..?
You Now Have A Lot To Be Happy For,
Don't You..??

1952 Your Happiness Depends...
...On What You Are Willing To LEARN.

1953 Your Happiness Depends...
...On What You Are Willing To Stop Discussing.

1954 Your Happiness Depends...
...On What You Are Willing To Stop Doing.

1955 Your Happiness Depends...
...On Who You Are Willing To Honor.

HARVEST

1956 A DIVINE HARVEST IS...
...ANY OPPORTUNITY...To Reveal
Your Difference From Others.

1957 Everyone Believes...In Sowing Seed.
Some Believe...In Reaping A Harvest.
FEW...Believe In Sowing To Create
A Harvest.

1958 Him: "God Has Never Given Me A Harvest From
My Offerings."
Me: "Then, Hoard Tithe For One Year And
See What Happens."

1959 If Your Entire Harvest Happens Here...
Heaven Is Unnecessary.

1960 No Harvest Arrives...
Without The Seed of Waiting.

1961 NOBODY ELSE...
Has Qualified For Your Harvest.
Nobody.

HATE

1962 David's Family Hated Him...
For His Boldness.
Joseph's Family Hated Him...
For His Dreams.
Hatred...Finds A Reason.

1963 Everywhere You See Hate...
You Will See Chaos.
Everywhere.

1964 Hate...Is Huge Energy.
I Have Not Found A Single Enemy...
Worthy of It.

1965 Hate...Is The Odor of An Evil Heart.

1966 Hater-ade Is...An Addictive Drink.
Contagious, Too.

1967 Haters Could Hurt Your Feelings...
If Their Opinion Mattered. :)

HEAVEN

1968 Heaven Is Probably Like Earth...
Without Dumb, Deception And Doubt.
:)
Smile.

1969 It Only Takes One Idiot...
To Turn Your Heaven Into A Hell.
No Wonder...God Flung Lucifer
Like Lightning.

1970 My Biggest Concern About Heaven Is...
Loneliness. :)

1971 The Closest Thing To Heaven Is...
The Trust of A Good Woman.
Earn It.

1972 The Happiest Thing About Heaven Is...
Only Productive People Will Be There.
No Lazies.

HOLY SPIRIT

1973 5:02am
Spirit Awakened Me:
"I Have Arranged A Life-Altering Event Today.
Prepare For It.
Expect It...Every Moment!!"

1974 Abortion~
Wonder How The Holy Spirit Feels...
About Those Who Killed His Dreams..?

1975 "Holy Spirit...
Give Me The
Mind of A Protégé;
Mouth of A Mentor;
Heart of A Warrior;
Hands of A Servant."

1976 Holy Spirit~
...His Presence Produces...
Unending Clarity.

1977 "I Need You Tonight.
You Are My Voice, My Nest, My Harbor.
Precious Holy Spirit...You Are My Hiding Place."

1978 "Holy Spirit...
I Honor You And
I Listen In Total Obedience.
I Will Not Resist Nor Vex You.
Your Voice Is My Command."

1979 Holy Spirit~
...Is Life Himself.
...Is Aware of Your "Wound" History.
...Is Comfortable With Your Weakness.
...Is Easy To Please.

1980 Holy Spirit~
Singing To Him~Is Master Key.
Master Key.
Few Know It. His Power Fascinates Most.
But, His Presence Fascinates Me.

1981 Holy Spirit...
Thank You...For Escorting Me Today.
Your Advice...Protects Me.
Your Words...Heal Me.
I Am Your Servant.

1982 Holy Spirit...
You Are My Master Mentor...
My Trusted Teacher.
I Am Addicted...To Your Voice.
I Carry Your Presence.

1983 Holy Spirit Is...A Person.
Holy Spirit Is...A Place.
Holy Spirit Is...A Mentor.
Holy Spirit Has...A Language.
Changed Me.
7-13-94.

1984 The Holy Spirit Is...The Only Person Capable of
Being Contented With You.
He Is At Ease With Your History.

1985 Holy Spirit...You Are Enough!
I Won't Look To Another...
I Won't Lean On Any Man.
Holy Spirit You Are Enough!
(Song)

1986 I Never Laugh...About What Angers
The Holy Spirit.
In The World.
In My Church.
In My Staff.
Nor On...Twitter.

1987 If We Do Not Create Passion To KNOW
The Holy Spirit...We Have Failed.
He Is Not The Key To Life.
He IS Life.

1988 Love-Song To The Holy Spirit~
Don't Go Too Far From Me!
Don't Go Too Far From Me!
I Need Your Voice.
I Need Your Touch.
So, Don't Go Too Far From Me.

1989 Meet With The Holy Spirit The First 7 Minutes
of Every Day.
~Enter Singing.
~Be Conversational.
~Document His Words.

1990 My Valentine Is...The Holy Spirit.
Nobody Has Taught Me More About Love.
Nobody.

1991 Oh, I Wish Every Believer Could Fall In Love
With The Holy Spirit..!!!
HE IS LIFE.

1992 Oh, My Dear Family!
Fall In Love With The Holy Spirit..!
Fall In Love With The Holy Spirit..!
He Is My Life.
My Life Focus.

1993 The Holy Spirit Leaves Nobody...Unwarned.

1994 The Holy Spirit Will Not Live...
In A Joyless Environment.

1995 The More You Value The Holy Spirit Who
Designed You...The More Fascinated
You Will Become About Yourself.
Divine Design.

1996 The Secret Place~
...Is Not Where You Give Instructions
To God;
...It Is Where You RECEIVE Instructions
From God.

1997 The Secret Place~
...Stay There Long Enough To Create
A Memory.
...God Talks Differently When Others Are
Not Around.

1998 The Wounded Mind...Cannot Explain Itself.
The Only Healer...Is The Holy Spirit.
Pursue Him.
Relentlessly.

HONOR

1999 Continuous Honor Guarantees...Eventual Access.

2000 Definitions~
Smart...Is Knowing Who To Honor.
Stupid...Is Ignoring Who Should Be Honored.

2001 Dominant Role of Wisdom...
...Is To Recognize Who Qualifies
For HONOR.

2002 When You Learn Honor...
...You Have Learned The Secret of Life.

2003 Everywhere You Honor...You Will Succeed.
Everywhere You Dishonor...You Will Fail.

2004 Never Doubt The Future...
of The Man Who Honors Greatness.
WHO You Honor Reveals...Who YOU Are.

2005 Honor.
Honor.
Honor.
The Way To Do Business With Great Men.
Not Cleverness.

2006 Honor...Creates Access Faster Than Genius.

2007 HONOR...
Creates Instant Access Into Any Environment.
...Advances You Faster Than Genius...
Flourishes In Every Season.

2008 Honor Creates...What Knowledge Cannot.

2009 Honor Does Not Reveal...The Value of Another.
Honor Reveals...YOUR Value of Another.

2010 Honor...Has A Fragrance:
And, It Is Gloriously Addictive.

2011 Honor Is...Attitude Toward Another.
Humility Is...Attitude Toward Yourself.

2012 Honor Is...Earth's Highest Currency.

2013 HONOR...Is Not Celebration of Someone's Character...It Is A Portrait of Your Own Character.

2014 Honor...Is Not Necessarily Agreement.
~Politics
~Leadership

2015 Honor...Is Not What A Culture Defines It To Be. Honor...Is What God Defines It To Be.

2016 Honor Is...Recognizing Who You Are Not Authorized To Correct.

2017 HONOR...Is The Seed That Flourishes In Every Environment or Season.
Honor Creates Access...Before Genius/Relationship.

2018 Honor Is...The Uninvested Price For Every Unexperienced Dream.

2019 Honor Is Unfailing Currency...
In The World of Greatness.

2020 Honor Provides The Fragrance...
Where Love Grows Quickest.

2021 Honor...Turns Every Wall Into A Door.
Few Get It.

2022 Honor Will Qualify You...
When Experience Does Not.
Joseph/Abigail

2023 I Know Your Wisdom...When I Observe Who You
Honor.
I Will Trade 1,000 Geniuses For ONE
Person of Honor...Every Day of My Life.

2024 If I Had Only One Message To
Preach Around The World For The Rest
of My Days-
...I Would Teach "The Law of Honor."

2025 If You Ever Experience True Honor...You Will
Refuse To Live Without It.
If You Have Not Learned Honor...
You Have Learned Nothing.

2026 If You Know Who You Truly Honor...I Can
Predict Your Future.

2027 Honor Is The Seed For Wealth.
Money Is Everywhere There Is Honor.
Everywhere You Show Honor You Birth Favor.

2028 Oh, The Fragrance of Great Servants of God..!
What An Honor...To Host Divine Favorites..!
Invest...In Your Pastor.

2029 Recovery~
Your Healing Can Only Occur...
In An Environment of Honor.

2030 The Cost of Access...Is Honor.

2031 The Fragrance of Honor...Lingers Longer Than
The Memory of Clever.
Nobody Gets It.

2032 The Greatest Tragedy of Life Is...
Not Knowing Who To Honor.

2033 The Most Dangerous Day In Your Life Is...
When You Forget Who To Honor.

2034 The Possibility For Love...
Is Anywhere You Find Honor.

2035 The Truly Confident...Find It Easy
To Lavish Honor Appropriately.

2036 Those Who Know Who To Honor...Cannot Fail.
Those Who Do Not Know Who To Honor...
Cannot Succeed.

2037 True Honor...Is Never Forgotten.
Neither Is...Dishonor.

2038 When You Have Taught Your Children Who To
Honor...You Have Taught Them Enough.

2039 When You Treat Everyone The Same...
No One Is Honored.

2040 We Tithe To Document Honor.
Honor Is The Only Thing On God's Mind.
The 10 Commandments Are Only About Honor.

2041 Where There Is Little Honor...
There Is Little Change.
Protégé.
Fathers.

2042 Where There Is Honor, There Is Favor; And
Where There Is Favor, There Is Currency
(Money, Time, Ideas, Energy).

2043 Genius Will Never Take You To Your Future.
Honor Is The Secret To Your Future.

2044 Teach Your Children WHO TO HONOR.

HOPE

2045 Effective Weapons...Increase Hope.

2046 HOPE...Decides Every Change You Will Make In Your Life.

2047 Your Life Will Not Change Until...You Change Something You Are Doing DAILY. (Habit...Overpowers Desire.)

2048 Hopelessness...Is An Indescribable Whirlpool of Torment Scorned By The Inexperienced. Conquerable ONLY By Divine Words.

2049 Misplaced Hope...Sabotages Your Energy And Creates Endless Depression.

2050 Sleep Is...The Seed For Hope.
:-)

2051 Your Unfaithfulness...Did Not Kill My Love. Your Unfaithfulness...Killed My Hope.

HUMILITY

2052 Humble People...Are Often Incompetent People.
Perhaps, Reason For Their Humility.
:)

2053 Humility...Determines What You Pursue.

2054 Humility Is...Not A Personality Trait.
Humility Is...The Persuasion That
Without God, We Are Nothing.
Nothing.

2055 HUMILITY...Is Recognition of What You Do Not
Have...And Who Your Source Is.

2056 Humility Opens More Doors In One Day...Than
Genius Will Open In Your Lifetime.
Nebuchadnezzar.
Publican.
Paul.

2057 The Rarity of Humility...
Makes It Incredibly Magnetic.

2058 Your Humility...Decides Your Mentorship.
Your Mentorship...Decides Your Faith.
Your Faith...Creates Your Future.

2059 Your Humility...Opened The Door.
Your Arrogance...Closes It.

IGNORANCE

2060 I Am Not Offended At The "Ignorance" In
Others.
But, I Am Daily Appalled...At My Own.

2061 If You Could Accurately Assess Your Own
Ignorance...You Would Not Be Arrogant A Single
Moment of Your Life.

2062 Ignorance...Has Rewards.
...That Is Why So Many Cherish It.
:)

2063 Ignorance...Is Not Knowing.
Stupid...Is Not Desiring To Know.
Ignorance...Is Not Knowing.
Stupid...Is Not Reaching.

2064 Ignorance...Is Not Knowing.
Dumb...Is Not Seeking.
Stupid...Is Not Caring Who Does Know.
Distinguishing Your Ignorant/Dumb/Stupid
Friends.

2065 Ignorance...Is When You Do Not Know.
Stupid...Is When You Will Not Listen To Who
Does Know.

2066 IGNORANCE...Is Not Knowing Who You Need.
STUPID...Is The Unwillingness To Look For
Them.

2067 In What Area...Have You Decided To Remain
Willingly Ignorant?
:)
Peaceful About It?

2068 The Leap From Ignorance To Wisdom Is...
A Question.
:) :)

2069 The Unexplored...Is The Unexperienced.
The Unasked...Remains The Unanswered.
Ignorance...Is A Chosen Lifestyle.

2070 Where Are You Willingly Ignorant..?
Whose Mentorship Have You Chosen...
To Ignore? Why?
What "Inspires" You...Daily?

2071 Where Are You...Willingly Ignorant?
Advice-From-Fools~
"Just Do What You Feel."
Advice That Has Packed Prisons.

2072 Where Have You Chosen To Remain Ignorant..?
...God?
...Love?
...Money?
Can You Handle The Cost?

2073 Where You Are Willingly Ignorant...
You Will Flagrantly Fail.
...Love.
...God.
...$$.
...Health.

2074 Wherever You Are Untaught...
You Are Failing.

2075 Wherever You Are Untaught...
You Remain Unlearned.
Simple.
Yet, Profound.

2076 Where...Do You Want To Be "Brilliant?"
Where...Are You Willingly Ignorant?

IMAGINATION

2077 IMAGINARIUM Is...My New Name For My
Tomorrow Room.
Dream Wall.
Goals...Must Be In Front of You
EVERY Day.

2078 Imagine...
...Discovering The REAL Reason God
Created You And Where You Belong
...Meeting Someone Craving...Your
Difference.

2079 Imagine...
...If You Live Yet Never Discern Your
Unique Greatness.
...If You Live Yet Never Find
Where You Belonged.

2080 Imagine...
...If You Live Yet Never Learn
How To Talk To God.
...If You Live Yet Never Learn
How To Heal Another.

2081 Imagine...
...If You Live Yet Never Learn How
To Overcome Fear.
...If You Live Yet Never Learn How
To Apologize.

2082 Imagine...
...If You Live Yet Never Learn How To
Speak Right Words.
...If You Live Yet Never Learn How To
"Focus."

2083 Imagine...
...If You Live Yet Never Learned Gentleness.
...If You Live Yet Never Learned The Art
of Kindness.

2084 Imagine...
...If You Live Yet Never Learn How To Inspire
Yourself.
...If You Live Yet Never Learn How To Receive
Correction.

2085 Imagine...
...If You Live Yet Never Learn How To Really
Love.
...If You Live Yet Never Learn How To Use Your
Faith.

2086 Imagine...
...If You Live Yet Never Mastered "Listening."
...If You Live But Never Receive True
Mentorship.

2087 Imagine...
...If You Live Yet Never Pursued
Right Things.
...If You Live Yet Never Tasted
"The World-Class" Life.

2088 Imagine~
Is Your Desired Future Really Clear In
Your Mind?
Is That Picture...
On The Walls of Your ROOM?
Why Not?

2089 Imagine~
...The Children You Could Feed If You Really,
Really Prospered.
...The Possibility of Money...If YOU Had It.

2090 Imagine...
...What Your Life Would Be If You Decided To
Only Please God.
Only Him.
For 30 Days.

2091 Imagine…
You Were An Idea…God Had Never Had Before.
Ever.
Absorb.
Absorb.
Absorb.
Rejoice..!

2092 Imagine.
1,000 Puzzle Pieces…
Without A Picture On Box.
Your 1,000 Life Experiences…
Until You Picture A Goal.

2093 Imagine…How Little You Really Know About God.
Imagine.
Now, Allow That To Disturb You…
Into Pursuing Him.

2094 IMAGINE…What You Could Gain By
…Total FOCUS On Your Quest.
…One Apology.
…Asking Questions.
…Exuding Gratitude.

2095 Imagine Where You Would Be...
If You Never Went Backwards.
~Diet.
~Offenses.
Imagine Your World...If You Chose To Master
"Love."

2096 It Is EASY To Distinguish Your Imagination
From The Holy Spirit.
The Spirit Never Produces Confusion,
Nor Worry.

2097 The "Imagination" In A Lonely Man...
Turns A Honda Woman Into A Rolls-Royce.
:)

IMPOSSIBLE

2098 I Have Little Interest In Doing...
The Impossible.
The Possible...Satisfies.
God, Jr. Position Is Too Stressful.

2099 It Is Impossible For Me To Admire Someone
Who Battles My Instructions.
Cleverly...or Secretly.
Now You Know.

2100 The Lesser The Mentorship...
The Harder The Journey.

2101 It Is Impossible To Prove Your Value To...
The Undiscerning.
(Jesus/Pharisee.)
(You Will Lose Your Mind Attempting It.)

2102 It Is Impossible...
...To Help Someone Who Does Not
Trust You.

2103 It Is Impossible...
...To Understand "Stupid."

IMPROVE

2104 If God Cannot Improve You...I Cannot Either.
Goodbye.

2105 Limousine~
A Longer Car...
Does Not Make It A Better Car.
The Length of A Car...Does Not Improve It.
:)

2106 You Cannot Improve Someone...
Who Does Not Care.
You Cannot Improve Someone...
Who Does Not Listen.
You Cannot Improve Someone...
Who Does Not Trust You.

INEXPERIENCE

2107 INEXPERIENCE...Cannot Be Hidden.
Inexperience+Humility=Possibility.

2108 Inexperience...Cannot Stay Hidden.
And...It Is Not A Pleasant Encounter For
The Seasoned.

2109 Inexperience...Is Never Hidden.
But, The Inexperienced Do Not Know It.
:)
Teachability...Is Expected.

2110 Inexperience...Is Not Incompetence.
Inexperience...Is Curable.
Inexperience...Screams.
A Very Painful Experience In The Ears of
The Seasoned.

2111 The Inexperienced...
Always Disagree With Me.
Well...Maybe Not Always.

2112 The Inexperienced...Never Agree.

INFLUENCE

2113 I Am Not A Silent Voice...
In ANY Environment.
Persuaded.

2114 Influence of Anyone Is...By Your Permission.
(Jesus/Pharisees/Woman At Well)

2115 Servants Decide...What Kings Believe.

2116 You Can Be Known For Two Things~
The People...You Inspire...
or...
The People...You Destroy.

2117 Your Position...Does Not Reveal Your Power.
Divine Favor...Is Power.
Haman/Mordecai
God/Lucifer

2118 Know The Weakness...of Those
Who Influence Your Environment.

2119 One Evil Man With A Goal...
Has More Influence Than 10,000 Christians
Without A Goal.

2120 The Only Proof That Jesus Influenced
Zacchaeus...Was His Reimbursement 4
Times What He Stole From Others.
Think.

2121 Eagle-Talk~
Eagles...Do Not Consult Chickens For
Inspiration.

INFORMATION

2122 New Information...
Often Changes Old Beliefs.

2123 Writing...Is The Slowest Way
To Gather Information.

2124 You Cannot Make Right Decisions...
With Wrong Information.

2125 Your "Information-World."
What Will You...Learn?
How Will You...
...Collect Your Knowledge?
...Store It?
...Retrieve It?

INGRATITUDE

2126 Dogs...Don't Bite The Hand
That Feeds Them.
Dogs Bite The Hand...
That STOPS Feeding Them.
Two-Legged Dogs, Too.
 :-)

2127 Every Loss Is Caused By...Ingratitude.
A Humbling Discovery.

2128 Ingratitude...
Makes Decision-Making Very Easy.
~Relationship.
~Gift-Giving.
~Dating.

2129 Ingratitude~
What Does Not Cost You...
Will Not Impress You.

2130 Ingratitude...Is A Divine Alarm.

2131 Ingratitude...Is A Divine Instruction
To Stop All Further Investment.
~Counsel.
~Time.
~Energy.
~Money.
~Gifts.

2132 Ingratitude Is...An Unmistakable Odor
No Amount of Gifts Can Remove.

2133 Ingratitude...Is Never Unnoticed.

2134 Ingratitude...Is The Seed For Loss.
(Gifts/Respect/Access/Friendship)

2135 Ingratitude...Creates Great Unhappiness.
Avoid The Unthankful...
And Your Joy Will Increase.
Amazingly So.

2136 Ingratitude...Stops Favor.

2137 Ingratitude...Talks A Very Long Time.

2138 INGRATITUDE Will Cost You In A Day...More Than Satan Can Steal During Your Lifetime.

2139 Nothing Is More Revealing... Than Ingratitude.

2140 The Quickest Cure For Ingratitude Is...Loss.

INSPIRE

2141 Anything Diminishing Your Motivation Is...
Destroying Your Life.
Move Swiftly On It.
...Person.
...Environment.

2142 Assess Everything...
By Its Ability To INSPIRE You.
Does It Inspire...YOU?
HOW..?
Remove...What Does Not Inspire.

2143 Eliminate Anything...That Diminishes Your
Inspiration.
...From Your Presence.
...From Your Life.
...From Your Mind.

2144 Find The Stream of Inspiration...
And Live There.

2145 I Am Not Responsible...For Inspiring Myself.
I Am Responsible...For Finding Who Does
Inspire Me.
Counsel Delivered.

2146 I Only Place In Front of Me...That Which
Inspires Me Greatly.
That Is My Difference.

2147 I Will Pay ANY Price To Stay Inspired...
Because Without Inspiration I Have No Value.
Few-Get-It.

2148 Identify...WHAT And WHO Inspires You.
Identify...WHO Is Inspired By You.
Two Pillars...For Your Life.
Ignore The Rest.

2149 Identify...What Inspires You.
Identify...What Inspires You.
Identify...What Inspires You.
Identify...What INSPIRES You..!

2150 If You Can Keep Yourself "Inspired"...There Is
Absolutely Nothing You Cannot Do.

2151 Inspiring Yourself...Is Not A Sin.
:)

2152 It Is Impossible To Fail...If You Master The
Secret of Keeping Yourself Inspired.

2153 It Is NOT Your Responsibility...
To Inspire Anyone.
It Is Only Your Responsibility To Find...
What Inspires YOU.
Yea..!

2154 Law of Place~
Where I Do Not Inspire...I Exit.

2155 MAGNIFY...What Inspires You~
...So HUGE In Your Mind...
...That Nothing Else Has A Voice
In Your Life.

2156 Remove From Your Daily View...
Anything That Has Ceased To Inspire You.

2157 REMOVE...Every Picture, Photograph, Glass,
Book...That No Longer Inspires You.
Focus On What Inspires You...NOW.

2158 Romance...Whatever "Inspires" You.
Cuddle It...In The Corners of Your Mind.
Caress It...Smilingly.
It Is A "Fireplace."

2159 Seize The Tiniest Drop of Inspiration...And Hold It Until It Becomes An Ocean Within You.

2160 Staying Inspired...Is Success #1.
Staying Inspired...Makes Every Other Success Possible.

2161 The Unspoken Quest of Life...Is How To Keep Yourself Inspired.

2162 What "Inspires You"...Is Your Difference From Others.
Questions...Identify What Inspires You.

2163 What 3 Sounds...INSPIRE You..?
Now...Saturate Your Environment With Those Sounds.

2164 What Inspires You?
I Never Linger In The Presence of Someone...
...Who Cannot Improve Me.

2165 What Inspires You?
I Never Linger In The Presence of Someone...
...Who Wastes My Time.

2166 What-Inspires-You?
I Never Linger In The Presence of Someone...
...Who Does Not Enjoy Me.

2167 We Have Been Taught To ENDURE...Because
We Have Not Been Taught WHO To Enjoy.
Inspiration.

2168 You Do Not "Decide"...What Inspires You.
You "Discover"...What Inspires You.
So, Have You?
Why Not?

INSTRUCTION

2169 An Instruction...Is The Seed For Rewards.

2170 A Simple Instruction...
Often Exposes The Most Hidden Bitterness.

2171 An Ignored Instruction...
Creates Every Failure.

2172 An Instruction Exposes Everything.
R~Rebellion.
I~Incompetence.
D~Disinterest.

2173 An Instruction...Is A Door.
...That You Walk Through or Slam Shut.

2174 An Instruction Is An Invitation
To Prove Your Passion.

2175 An Instruction Is An Opportunity...
To Birth Favor.

2176 Eagle-Talk~
An Eagle...Cannot "Train" A Chicken.

2177 An Instruction Is An Opportunity...
To Reveal Your Competence.

2178 AN INSTRUCTION...Is The First Proof of Trust.

2179 Every Instruction Is...
An Opportunity For Increased Favor.
...or The Loss of It.

2180 General...Mastered Following Instructions.
Private Is...Learning How To Follow...

2181 Hear-It-Right~
He Re-Painted His Entire House And
Laid Exhausted.
And Heard A Soft Voice, "I Said To Repent...
Not Repaint."

2182 Hunger...Is Not An Instruction To Buy A
Restaurant.
Think.

2183 I Cannot Work With...
Someone I Do Not Admire.
I Am A Painful Experience...
When Someone Ignores My Instruction.

2184 Leadership-Talk~
Those Inspired By Your Words...May Be
Agitated By Your Presence.

2185 If You Refuse To Follow My First Instruction...I
Will Not Burden You With A Second.

2186 Instructions...Excite Servants.
Instructions...Anger Rebels.
Instructions...Expose Fools.

2187 INSTRUCTIONS...Reveal Your Profile.
~The Wise.
~The Fool.
~The Competent.
~The Caring.
~The Rebel.
~The Lazy.
~The Leader.

2188 It Is Ludicrous To Expect Your Boss
To Pay You...Whether You Follow
His Instructions or Not.
Ludicrous.

2189 My Instructions...Always Expose The Uncaring.

2190 The Difference Between An Army General And
A Private Is...An Instruction.

2191 The Smallest Instruction...
Is The Door To A World of Information.

2192 Your $alary I$ Determined...By The In$truction
You Are Willing To Follow.

INTEGRITY

2193 Integrity Has An Unmistakable Sound...And, It Pleasures Me Incredibly.

2194 Integrity...Creates Fearlessness.

2195 Integrity...Invites Inspection. Deception...Acts Insulted By It.

2196 Integrity Is A Spectacular "Find"... Because It Is So Rare.

2197 Integrity...Is Currency. Useable...Anywhere On Earth.

2198 Integrity...Is The Highest Level of Intelligence.

2199 Integrity...Is The Seed For Self-Confidence.

2200 Integrity...Makes Inferiority Impossible.

2201 Integrity: The Ultimate Simplicity That Intrigues Fools.

2202 When Ingratitude Speaks...Listen. When Integrity Enters...Fear Exits.

2203 Integrity Creates Far More Self-Confidence...Than Popularity.

INVESTMENT

2204 Do Not Make A Rolls-Royce Investment...For Honda Benefits.
...of Energy.
...of Time.
...of Money.

2205 Do Not Invest Proportionate To Their Need...
Invest Proportionate To Their Gratitude.

2206 I Am...A Professional Investor.
...My Energy.
...My Thoughts.
...My Moments.
...My Money.

2207 I Am...A Relentless Investor.
...In Conversation.
...In Favor.
...In Mentorship.
And, I Study My Returns...Relentlessly.

2208 I Am...A Serious Investor.
...of Time.
...of Thought.

2209 I Thoroughly Study Those...
Who Invest In Me.
And...Those Who Do Not.

2210 Inventory Thoroughly...
The Divine Investment Within You.
Beyond Calculation.
Invest Accordingly.

2211 Invest As Little As Possible...
In An Enemy.
Energy.
Time.
Attention.

2212 Invest Not...In An Enemy.
...Energy.
...Time.

2213 Invest Nothing...In The Arrogant.
Invest Only...In What INSPIRES You.

2214 Invest Time...In Discerning Others.
Invest No Time...In Destroying Others.

2215 Invest Twice...Where You See Gratitude
Growing.

2216 Invest Your Life...In Watering The Thirsty.
Do Not Invest One Minute...In Critics.
Not One.

2217 Invest...Where You Have Hope.
...The Humble.
...The Repentant.
...The Reacher.
...The Servant.

2218 Investment Advice~
People...
Invest In People.
The God-Book.

2219 Investment-of-Time~
What Would "Time With You"...Produce?

2220 Not Every Enemy Qualifies For Your Time.
Time Is A Valuable Investment.

2221 Rethink...Your Investments.
...of Energy.
...of Mentorship.
...of $$.
...of Time.

2222 Somebody Invested Heavily In You.
What Has Been Their Personal ROI..?
(Return On Investment?)
Theirs. Not Yours.

2223 The Investor~
The One Who Invested 100 Hours In You...Has
Invested More Than He Who Gave You $1,000.

2224 The Size of The Investment...Reveals
The Persuasion.

2225 Those Who Do Not Believe In Love...Are Helpful
To Us Who Can Then Invest Elsewhere.
:)

2226 Tough-Talk~
Somebody Has Invested...In You.
What Has Been Their Return Profit..?
Answer.
Honestly.

2227 Who Have Been Top 10 Investors Into Your Life?
...Time.
...Mentorship.
...$$.
...Love.
...Credibility.
What Has Been THEIR Return?

2228 You Are An Investor...
...Time.
...Information.
...Money.
...Energy.
T.I.M.E.
WHERE...You Invest Reveals Your Wisdom-Ignorance.

2229 You Will Not Get All of Me...
With A Little of You.
I Am An Investor.

2230 Your Investment In Wisdom Reveals Your Passion For It.

2231 Trust...Is An Investment.

JESUS

2232 Anti-Christ...Is Anyone Who Diminishes
The Divinity of Jesus.
Never-Forget-It.
Wolves In Sheep Clothing.

2233 Doctor Said My Blood Problem Was Incurable.
Maybe.
This Jesus Crowd Is Huge.
Wanna Touch His Robe.

2234 Heard Jesus Was Coming Through Town.
Climbed A Tree To See Him.
He Saw Me.
Zacchaeus Diary.

2235 I Love Christmas...
Any Day Celebrating Jesus...Is Glorious.
(Pagans Ideas/Rumors Are Not My Concerns.)

2236 I Often Wonder What Impact Jesus Has
Made...On The Economy $$ of Israel.
American Economy?
During Christmas?

2237 Jesus!
You Are One Breath Away~
That Alone Has Sustained Me Today!
Your Merciful Eyes...Heal Me Inside!
Jesus...You Are One Breath Away.

2238 Jesus~
The Only Person Worthy...
of Your Total Focus.

2239 Jesus Never Invested...In The Unthankful.
The Wise Never Do.
Time.
Energy.
Praise.
$$.
Correction.

2240 Not Every Disciple of Jesus...
Believed Him.
Relax. :)

2241 You Need More...Than One Finger.
You Need More...Than One Tooth.
You Need More...Than One Friend.
But, You Only Need One JESUS.

JOB

2242 A Job Is...Anywhere There Is A Problem.
Anywhere.
Anywhere.
Anywhere.
Anywhere.

2243 Accuracy.
Accuracy.
Accuracy.
Accuracy.
An Encourager...Will Always Have A Job.

2244 Ask Your Boss~
What Do I Need To Improve?
What Concerns You About My Work?
Where Do I Need To Build Credibility?

2245 Everywhere There Is A Problem...
There Is A Job.
Everywhere There Is A Job...There Is Favor.
Everywhere There Is Favor...There Is Money.

2246 I Am Not Amazed At People...Without Jobs.
I Am Amazed At People...Who Keep Their Jobs.
Desperate Employers.

2247 Job-Talk~
An Instruction Is An Opportunity...
To Distinguish Yourself From Those Around You.

2248 Job-Talk~
An Instruction Is An Opportunity...
To Prove Your Trustworthiness.

2249 Job-Talk~
An Instruction Is An Opportunity...
To Stimulate A Desire In Your Leader To
Know You Better.

2250 Job-Talk~
The Passionate...Are Always Stressful To
The Lazy.
Accept it.

2251 New Employees~
The Deadliest Advice You Will Ever Receive Is
Often From...The Person You Are Replacing.
Vashti To Esther.

2252 Osama Bin Laden...Creator of 10 Million Jobs.
Think.

2253 If You Are Out of A Job For 180 Days...
How Many of Those Days...Were You Sowing
Into Your Church or Pastor?

2254 You Hate Your Job?
Quit.
Your Boss...Is Stupid?
Quit.
Satisfied Now?

2255 You Never Forget Someone...
Who Makes Your Life Harder.
(Neither Does Your Boss...Instructions!)

JOSEPH

2256 One Conversation...Can Birth A Lifetime
Change.
Abigail.
Joseph.
Samaritan Woman.

2257 I Have Had Many Disappointments In
Life...But, God Is Not One of Them.

2258 Joseph's Journal~
Prison Is...The Place For Divine Connections.
Joseph/Paul/Onesimus

2259 Joseph's Journal~
Unless You Can Perform In The Prison...
The Palace Will Never Summon You.

2260 Joseph's Journal~
When You Hate Where You Are...Excel.

2261 Authenticity...Has Never Failed.
Unleash...Your "Difference."

2262 Joseph's Diary~
The Problem Nearest You...
Will Be Your Passage To The Palace.
Butler's Dream.

2263 Joseph's Diary~
The History of Your Accusers...
Explains Their Character.

2264 Joseph's Diary~
The Most Difficult Decision You Will Ever
Make Is...Staying Silent When Falsely
Accused.
Joseph/Jesus

2265 Joseph's Diary~
False Accusation...
Begins When You Tell Someone "No."

2266 Joseph's Diary~
The History of Your Accusers...Explains
Their Character.

2267 The Joseph Journal~
Unless You Excel In The Prison...
The Palace Will Never Summon You.

~

2268 The-Joseph-Journal~
Your Family...Is Your First Major Test.

~

2269 Two Prisoners Looked Very Troubled.
I Inquired If I Could Solve Their Problem.
Joseph Diary.

~

JOY

2270 A Small House Brings More Joy...Than A Huge Dump.

2271 Attempting Too Much...Makes You Joyless.
Just Do 2 or 3 Things Well...
Then, Walk Away...From Everything Else.

2272 If Joy Is Your Goal...
...Sit Alone With The Holy Spirit In Your...
Secret Place.
...Sit Long Enough...To Hear.

2273 JOY Is...
Discovering What You Do Not Need.

2274 JOY IS ALWAYS...Just One Feeling Away.

2275 Joy Is...Always One Conversation Away.

2276 Everything From God...
Comes Through A Person.
Believe It.

2277 JOY IS...Discovering Whose Success
Matters Most To You.
SUCCESS IS...Discovering Whose Joy
Matters Most To You.

2278 Joy Is Instant Reaction...When You Enter
The Presence of Someone You Love.
Irreplaceable.

2279 Joy Is...Return On An Investment.

2280 Joy...Is The Door.
Love...Is The Room.
Search For...What Brings You Joy.

2281 JOY Is...The Immediate Reward...
For Making The Right Decision.

2282 Joy Is The Reward...
For Being Where You Belong.

2283 JOY Is...The Reward For Loving Someone.

2284 JOY Is The Unplanned Reaction...
When You Enter The Presence of Someone
You Love/Trust.
Unstoppable

2285 Just Discovered A Profound Thing Today...
Laughlessness Is...A Sin.
Am So Sorry, Father.
Will Change It...Immediately.
Wow.

2286 The First Reward For Overcoming...
Is Instant JOY.

2287 The Goal Is Joy...Not Reality.
:)

2288 The Joy of Others May Be Your Passion...
But, It Is Never Your Responsibility.
Never.

2289 Your Joy Depends On...
Whose Opinion You Value Most.
Think.

2290 Your Joy...Depends On Who You Trust.

2291 Your Joy Is The First Proof...
Your Enemy Lost.
:)

2292 Your Joy Is...Divinely Scheduled.
Tomorrow Morning:)
"Weeping May Endure For A Night,
But Joy Cometh In The Morning," Psalm 30:5.

2293 YOUR JOY...Reveals The Quality of Your
Decision-Making.

KINDNESS

2294 Kind Words...Are Never Inappropriate.
Never.

2295 Kindness Is A Decision, Not A Reaction.
So Is Unkindness.

2296 Kindness Is Currency...Rarely Used.

2297 Kindness Is...Not Availability.

2298 KINDNESS...Is Never Inappropriate.
Ever.
(I Am Addicted To Those Who Exude...
The Fragrance of Kindness.)

2299 Kindness...Is So Addictive.
It Sabotages The Other Relationships.

2300 Kindness...Is Superior To Genius.

KING

2301 Kingly Anointing...Is Staying Poised In
An Environment of Fools.

2302 Kingly Anointing~
Never Exit Your Chariot To Chase...
A Disrespectful Peasant.

2303 KINGS...Do Not Run.
Sip...The Moment.
Savor...The Difference.
Soften...Your Heart.
God Is...Here.
HERE.

2304 Never Leave Your Chariot...
To Chase The Peasants Who Throw Tomatoes.
Kings...Never Run.

KNOWLEDGE

2305 99.99% of Knowledge On The Earth...Is
Unuseable For "Your" Assignment.
So...
Focus.
Focus.
Focus.

2306 All Knowledge Is Accidental...
Until You Ask Questions.

2307 Can You Explain To Me...
...Your Information-System?
...Your Task-Management System?
...Your Search Procedure?

2308 Information-System...For Filing/Retrieving.
Task-Management System...For
Listing Tasks.
Response-System...For Gifts.

2309 It Is Necessary...To Know Yourself.
It Is Unnecessary...To Understand Yourself.

2310 Judging...Is Speaking The Unproven.
Discerning...Is Discovering The Hidden.
Burden of Knowledge Is...When To Use It.

2311 Keep A Knowledge Mind-Map...
...What You Want To Learn.
...Who You Want To Learn From.
...Questions.

2312 Knowledge~
Never Leave A Feeling...Until You Identify
Who Created It.

2313 Knowledge Is...Expensive.
But...Ignorance Is...Costly.

2314 Knowledge...Is What You Know.
Wisdom...Is What You Do.

2315 True Knowledge...Magnifies My Ignorance.
Discovery...Is The Seed For Energy.

2316 Most Knowledge On The Earth...
Is Unnecessary For "Your" Assignment.
Focus...Only On What Truly Matters.

2317 My #1 Mind-Map...Is A Knowledge-Map.
...Questions.
...Mentors.
...What I Wish I Knew.

2318 Never Wait For "Knowledge."
Knowledge...Must Be "Summoned."

2319 Only 2% of What I Know...
Came Voluntarily From Others.
Knowledge...Requires Relentless Battle.

2320 Past Knowledge...Created Your Today.
Future Knowledge...Creates Your
Tomorrow.

2321 REVELATION Is...Instant Knowledge~
Without The Pain of Experience.

2322 The Ignorant...
Are Pleasured By Knowledge.
The Stupid...Are Puzzled By Knowledge.

2323 There Is So Much...I Do Not Yet Know.
But, What I Do Know...I Believe With All My
Heart.

2324 What You Do Not Know...
Explains What You Do Not Have.

2325 WHO...Is Your "Classroom..?"
WHAT...Questions Are You Asking..?
HOW...Do You Store Your Knowledge..?

2326 You Will Not Obtain A "Tomorrow" Dream...
...With "Yesterday" Knowledge.
Journal It.

2327 Your Knowledge-Map...
Is The Hidden Secret.
What...You Already Know.
What...You Want To Know.
Who...You Will Pursue.

2328 Your Present Knowledge...Got You "Here."
Your Future...Requires More.

LEADERSHIP-TALK

2329 Every Leader Has A "Trojan Horse"...Hidden
In His Environment.
The Uncommon Leader...Identifies Them.

2330 It Takes One To Create Unity.

2331 Your Potential Is...
Not A Prophecy of Your Future.
Unrelated.
Completely.
(Lucifer/Absalom/Judas)

2332 Judas...Resents Your Admirers.

2333 Some Staff Have No Plans At All...To Follow
Your Instructions.
None.
Face it.

2334 Beware Those Who Expect Your Favor...
Before They Create Credibility.

2335 Correcting Others...Can Eventually Sabotage
Your Creativity.
Assign Territories.

2336 Do Not Despair Over Vashti's Rebellion.
Esther...Is In The Wings.
Transition Time.

2337 The Fragrance of Thankfulness Is The Only
Cure...For The Stench of The Uncaring.

2338 The Unhappy Disciple...
Becomes Your Judas.

2339 Invest Heavily...In The Most Trainable Who
"Care."

2340 Tolerating Vashti...Delays Your Esther.

2341 The Intensity of Your Love...Should Surpass
The Intensity of Your Instruction.

2342 Your Judas...
Disagrees With Your Financial Decisions.

2343 Your "Judas"...Will Be A Surprise.
Leaders...Do Not Decide To Lead.
Followers Decide...To Follow.

2344 Leaders Who Care...Is God's Greatest Cry.

2345 LEADERS...With Flaws Are Very Reassuring To Me; That God Will Use Me, Also...Even With My Own Weaknesses.

2346 Beware of Workers...Who Want Their Looks And Personality As A Substitute For... Productivity.
Flirtation...Is A Tool.

2347 It Is The Nature of The Peasant...
To Misinterpret The Invitation of The King.
:)

2348 The First Meal Is To Identify...Who Stays To Wash The Dishes.
Meal Two Is For The True Protégé.
:)

2349 Leadership...Is Keeping Yourself Inspired To Do The Next Good Thing.

2350 Slick-Words~
"Working Through Diplomatic Channels."

2351 A Bicycle...Does Not Belong On An Airport Runway.

2352 A Listener...Is Not Always A Receiver.

2353 Humility...Is Recognition of Another's Superiority.

2354 Absence...Is The Seed For Disorder.
...Fathers Away From Children.
...Husband Away From Wife.
Get It.

2355 ACCESS...Does Not Increase Honor.
"For Neither Did His Brethren Believe In Him." (John 7:5)

2356 Adding A New Tire...Does Not Start The Car.
Hiring

2357 Allow Judas To Leave The Supper Table...
And Do His "Thing."
Resurrection Is...72 Hours Away.

2358 An Instruction...Is Not "Training."

2359 At 44...I Confronted Slither...Openly.
At 64...I Discern Slither...Silently.

2360 Attacks Come Hourly.
Establish Human Gates/Walls To Stop
Barbarians And Qualify The Thankful.

2361 Avoid Exhaustion...Where Seed Won't Grow.
"Invest...Where You Trust."

2362 Correction That Demoralizes Is...
An Odor In Any Environment.

2363 Discern Judas...Without Discussing Him.

2364 Discern The Difference Between
A Problem...And A Problem-Person.
The Difference Is Gigantic.

2365 Distinguish Those Around You...
From Those Connected To You.
Judas/John

2366 Elijah Cannot Leave...Until Elisha Is Trained.

2367 Esther Was Never Revealed...
Until Vashti Was Removed.

2368 Every Seed Planted Into The Unthankful...
Was A Loss.
YOUR Loss.
Energy.
Time.
$$.
Advised.

2369 Every Zoo...Requires A Cleanup.
Leave No Cage...Unexamined.
:)

2370 Giving The Incompetent Access...
Is A Huge Mistake.

2371 God Did Not Remove Jonah From Ship.
Sailors Did.

2372 Instructions Expose Rebels On Your Staff...
Quickly.

2373 Judas...Has A Family.

2374 Judas...Is Essential To Your Equation.
Outcome.

2375 Jezebel Never Leaves Voluntarily.
Jehu...Is Anointed For Removing Her.

2376 Move Every Doubter...
Out of Your Environment.

2377 Nobody Listens To Their Dentist...
Until Their Tooth Hurts.
:)
Relax.

2378 No Matter How Long I Yell...The Kitten Refuses
To Bark. :)
You Ain't...What You Ain't.

2379 Only A Fool Invests In...Training A Rebel.
God.
Lucifer.

2380 Parasites...Pursue Your Money.
Protégés...Pursue Your Mentorship.

2381 Permit People To Think Small...
When They Despise Thinking Big.

2382 Pour Yourself Into Those...Who Pursue Your
Personal Training.

2383 Pour Yourself Into Those...Who Follow Your
Counsel.

2384 Pour Yourself Into Those...Who Invest In
Pursuing Your Wisdom.

2385 Pour Yourself Into Those...Who Invest In Your
Comfort.

2386 Pour Yourself Into Those...Who Prove Their
Loyalty.

2387 Pour Yourself Into Those...Who Ask Wise
Questions.

2388 Pour Yourself Into Those...Who Admire How You
Have Invested Your Life.

2389 Pour Yourself Into Those...Who Consistently
Reveal Honor.

2390 Recognize Dishonor.
Do Not Honor...With Continued Access.

2391 Leadership-Talk~
Review.
Remove.
Replace.
Restore.
Remember.
Reward.

2392 Some...Are Teachable.
Some...Are Not.
Invest...In The Teachable.

2393 Some People Are Not...Really Defiant.
They Are Simply...Hopelessly Stupid.

2394 Discomfort Diminishes The Quality of Your
Decisions.

2395 Subtraction...
Is The Divine Seed For Multiplication.
Korah.
Ananias.

2396 Teaching Eagles And Chickens
Simultaneously...Creates Great Stress.
...And Failure.

2397 The Ignorant...Are Trainable.
The Stupid...Are Not.
I Got It...Finally.

2398 The Incompetent...Are Costly.
The Unwilling...Are Even Costlier.

2399 The Most Critical...Are The Easiest To Replace.

2400 The Most Effective Rebels...Are Warm And
Congenial In Your Presence.

2401 The Storm Stopped...
When Jonah "Splashed."
The Peace Begins...One Splash From Now.
:)
Think.

2402 The Uncaring...Will Kill You.
Do Not Keep Them In Your Circle.

2403 Their Disinterest...Is An Instruction To You.

2404 Those Who Desire Your Attention...
Rarely Desire Your Counsel.

2405 Those Who Do Not Admire You...
Are Incapable of Learning From You.
Discern It Early.

2406 Those Who Do Not Know Your Responsibilities...
Do Not Yet Really "Know" You.

2407 Those Who Will Not Follow You...
Are Disqualified For The Destination.

2408 Those Unwilling To Pursue Your Advice...
Would Not Follow It Anyway.
:)

2409 Those Who Need You Most...
Listen To You The Least.
Re-Focus...On The Worthy.

2410 Tolerating Queen Vashti...Creates A
Miserable Palace And Delays The Pleasure
of Esther.

2411 The Inexperienced...
Always Disagree With Your Decisions.

2412 Train...Those You Trust.

2413 Train Your Inner Circle Team THOROUGHLY.
Standardize Your Preferred
Reactions/Requests On Video/DVD.

2414 Turn Every Hint...Into An INSTRUCTION.
Turn Every Hope...Into An INSTRUCTION.
Hints Fail.

2415 When Vashti Refuses The Instruction...
Esther Receives Her Opportunity.

2416 Why Do You Expect The Inexperienced...
To Agree With You..?
:)

2417 Who Fails...
To Improve Under Your Mentorship?
Who...Has Not Been Given Opportunity?

~

2418 You Gave Them Opportunity...To "Talk."
They Made It An Opportunity...
To "Squawk."
Case Closed.

~

2419 Number of Followers...Don't Matter.
Jesus...Had 12.
Hitler...Had Millions.
Relax.

~

2420 The Great Leader...Wins The War.
The Superior Leader...Avoids The War.
"Blessed Are The Peacemakers."

~

2421 Twitter-Talk~
I Will Not Follow You...Until I Know Where You
Are Going.
:)

~

2422 Why Are You Asking Permission...To Lead?

~

2423 You Are Not The Leader...
of Anyone Who Refuses To Follow.

2424 Increased Access May Bring Disappointment...
But A More Accurate Conclusion.

2425 Decide Your...Greatest Need.
Discern Who...Truly Cares.
Give...Instructions.
Assess...After 30 Days.

2426 Your Conversations...Will Not Improve Your
Judas.

2427 First Staff Member God Hired For Moses...
Was His "Voice Replacement." (Aaron)

2428 The Satisfied...Are Ignored.
The Critics...Are Studied.
The Obnoxious...Are Distracting.
Be-Wise.

LEARNER

2429 A Free Puppy...vs...An $18,000 Dog.
Your Training...Determines Your Value.

2430 A Learner Will Never Be Enslaved...By The Opinions of Others.

2431 A Learner Will Never Remain...
In The Present Season.

2432 A Learner...
Will Never Be A Hostage.
...To Opinions.
...To The Present.
...To Fear.
...To His Past.
...To A Memory.
...To Pain.

2433 A Learner...Will Never Live In Fear.

2434 A Learner...Will Outlive His Past Mistakes.

2435 A Regret...Reveals Discovery.
...That You Have Just Learned Something.

2436 Bicycle Training...Does Not Qualify You To Fly A Jet.

2437 Brilliance Without A Teachable Spirit...Is Stupid.

2438 Collecting Boards...
Does Not Build A House.
Collecting Experiences...
Does Not Create A Future.
What Are You TRAINING For?

2439 Experience Is...Not Training.
Collecting Experiences...
Is Not Purposeful Training.
What Future...Are You TRAINING For?

2440 Family-Talk~
Turning-Point Tweets...For Learners.
Sparks...For Scorners.
Love...Is Experienced.
Honor...Is Taught.

2441 How Do You Measure Your "Growth"..?
How? How?

2442 I Am 90% Protégé~
I Am 10% Mentor~
I Wake Up...To LEARN~
302 Books...Are What I Think OTHERS
Should Learn Before We Talk.

2443 I "Learn"...For A Living.
My One Hobby, Too.
:)

2444 I Learn Much...
Observing Non-Learners.

2445 Learning Is Not A Place of Arrival...
But A Place of Beginning.
...of Changes.
...Decision-Making.

2446 Learning Only Matters...If It Improves You.
What Did You Learn Today...
That "Changed" You?

2447 Learning The Art of Receiving...Will Decide The
Future of Your Giving.

2448 Master A Topic...Nobody Else Has.
My Past Is...Not My Project.
It Was My School.

2449 Only Learners...Experience Regrets.
Think.

2450 Passion To Fly...Does Not Make You A Pilot.
The Learner.

2451 Reading...Is Entering The Mind of Another.
What I Do Best: Learning.
:)

2452 Regret?
...Is Delayed Discovery.
...Is Proof of Flawed Decision-Making.
...Is Proof You Have Learned.
...Qualifies You To Teach.

2453 The Learner~
I Do Not Correct Where I See...Disagreement.
I Correct Where I See...A Learner.

2454 The Man Who Keeps Looking...
Has Still Not Learned.
The Price of Change Is...
Simply A Learning Curve.

2455 Those Who Cannot Learn...Argue.
:)

2456 What 3 Things...
Have You Purposed To Learn Tomorrow?
Who...Will Teach You?
How Will It Change You?
Learn.
Isaiah 1:17

2457 What Have You Learned...
From Those You Admire?
Do You Admire Their "Gift" or
Their "Character?"

2458 What Have You Learned...
Through Those Who Failed You?
What Have You Changed...
Because of The Pain?

2459 What I Was Not Taught...
I Still Do Not Know.
It Is A Costly Ignorance.

2460 What You Learned Today Is...Revealed By
Changes You Make Tomorrow.
Wisdom.

2461 Who Are You Refusing...To Learn From..?
Costly Mistake.

2462 You Do Not Need Entire Food Buffet...
To Satisfy You.
Neither Do You Need Everything On Earth...To
Satisfy You.
Learn.

2463 You Have No Idea Where God Would Take You...
If You Knew How To Act When You Got There.

2464 You Only Need One Reason...
To Learn A Different Language.
Ahhh...You Got It..!

2465 Your Learning...Is At The Speed of Your Daily
Questions.
What 3 Questions...Would Make A Difference In
Your Life?

2466 Wherever You Are Struggling...You Are
Untaught.

2467 Those Who Have Something You Do Not
Have...Know Something You Do Not Know.
What?

LEASH-TALK

2468 LEASH-TALK: (Controlling Relationships)
Is To Those Being Controlled By Others
(Dog/Leash).
They Give You The "Illusion" of Freedom.

2469 I Will Never Enter A Cage...Willingly.
Believe It.

2470 I Would Rather Run Free On One Acre...
Than To Wear A Chain On 1,000 Acres.
(Freedom Has No Replacement.)

2471 You Love To Command..?
A Dog Would Love You.

2472 You Will Be A Slave To "Someone" So...
Choose Your Master Well.
(Smile.)

LIAR

2473 Confronted Liars...Simply Become More Skilled.

2474 Confronting A Liar...Is Like Showing A Thief
Where The Cameras Are Hidden.

2475 Do Not Correct Liars.
Replace Them.

2476 Every Liar Becomes Retaliatory...
When Exposed.
Am Learning To Discern Them Only...
Not Discuss Them.

2477 Every Liar...Is A Thief.
He Robbed You...of Information You Needed.

2478 He Is Not The First Liar Who Entered My Life~
But He Has More Ambition...
Than Any I Have Met.
:)

2479 He Is Not The First Liar Who Entered My Life~But He Is The First Liar Captivated By Me.
:)

2480 He Is Not The First Liar Who Entered My Life~But He Is The First Liar... Who Broke Into My Home.
:)

2481 He Is Not The First Liar Who Entered My Life~But His Imagination...Exceeds Them All.
:)

2482 I Do Not Like What I Become...When I Get In The Presence of Liars.
So My Fellowship Is Limited These Days.

2483 Remove Liars...From Every Equation In Your Life.
...Work.
...Home.
...Friendship.
...Dating.

LIFE

2484 4-Fold Purpose~Life On Earth:
Experience Love.
Sow Love.
Reap Love.
Multiply Love.
Nothing Else Makes Sense.

2485 24 Hour Success~
When You Can Manage A Day...
You Have Managed Your Life.

2486 66 Years Old...Where Will I Invest My Life
Next?
...In Those Who Honor.
...In Those Who Pursue.
...In Those Who Change.

2487 A Picture of The Day...Gets Me Out of Bed.
When I Awaken, I Begin Prophesying
My Day.

2488 Life Does Not Happen.
YOU Happen.

2489 A Successful Day...Is A Successful Life.

2490 Change Your "Day"...If You Want To Change Your Life.

2491 Just One 24-Hour Masterpiece... At A Time.

2492 I Only Compete With...Yesterday.

2493 Adult Problems... Are Childhood Problems Unconfronted.

2494 Do Not Burn Down The House...You Chose Not To Buy.

2495 Do Not Ignore...The Thorns of Life. Trample...The Thorns of Life.

2496 Do You Qualify For Anything... That You Are Ashamed To Make Your... QUEST..?

2497 ...Do You Really Discern That Your "Faith" Is Deciding The Quality of Your Life?

2498 Embrace...A "Key"
Unlock...Your Life.

2499 Even Football Is Puzzling...
Until You Read The Rules.
So Is Life...Until You Read The Rules.

2500 Even The Best Medicine On Earth...Was Not
Intended For All.
Diversity.

2501 Every Road...Has More Than One Destination.
(The Path Nearest You...Can Take You
ANYWHERE.)

2502 Everything Believed Is...
Built On Something Unproven.
Think.
Again.

2503 Everything Is...Bought.
Everything.
...The Currency Differs.
Think.

2504 Everything You Are Willing To "Wait" For...Has
Still Never Happened.
Think.

2505 Garden of Life~
A Single Skunk Can Blind You...
To The Beauty of Your Garden.

2506 Garden-of-Life...
Do Not Let The Flowers of Life...
Blind You To The Snakes.

2507 Hello Family...
Well, It's 12:06a...April 18.
The Ole Boy Is...66.
1,001 Thoughts.
The Laws of God Work.
Holy Spirit Is...Life.

2508 Him: "What Do You Do...When Things Happen
To You..?"
Me: "I Happen Back. Twice."

2509 Horoscope~
Only The Traumatized...Believe A Star Is
Deciding The Events of Their Life.

2510 I Am Not Qualified...To Change The World.
I Am Qualified...To Change My Mind.
I Am Not Qualified...To Train The World.
I Am Qualified...To Train My Mind.

2511 I PREDICT-Next 10 Days of Your Life.
~Will Be Incredibly Peaceful.
~A Strange, Glorious Hope Will Rise
Like A Sunrise.

2512 I...Wonder
...IF The Trauma of Killing Your Baby...
Cures The Trauma of Rape.

2513 If "Listening" Is Difficult For You...Life Will Be
Difficult For You.

2514 If You Cannot Walk The First 3 Steps With
Me...You Don't Qualify For The Journey.

2515 If You Had 12 Months Left To Live...
...Who Would You Train?
...What Would You Change?
...Would You Journal It?

2516 If You Let Life Happen...It Will Be Everything
You Did NOT Want.

2517 Life...
Some Decide To Be...The Boat.
Some Decide To Be...The Ocean.

2518 IF YOU...Had ONLY One Year Left To Live...
What Would You Do Differently? Who...Would
You Teach?
Love?
Comfort?
Reach For?
Forgive?
Exits Matter.

2519 Life~
Sometimes, Life Is Too Much To Handle.
So, I Do Not.
I Just Eat A Hotdog...
And Listen To Hillsong.

2520 Life~
Who Shows You The Greatest Favor?
Who Is Patient Enough To "Teach" You?
Who Has A Problem...You Could Solve?

2521 LIFE~
The World...Is A Menu of Ingredients.
YOUR World...Is The Meal You Decided
To Create From It.

2522 Life Is...A 24 Hour MasterPiece.
You Are...The Painter.
Choose Well...Sounds, Colors, Faces,
Moments.

2523 Life Is...A Journey.
Do Not Stop...For A Fool.

2524 LIFE...Is An Investment Program~
What...Do You Have To Invest?
In Whom?
Expectation of Returns: Short/Long Term.

2525 Life Is...Not Creating Your Pain.
Decisions...Are Creating Your Pain.

2526 Life Is Not Full of...Hardships.
Life Is Full of...Difficult People.
Period.

2527 Life...Is Not My Master.
Life...Is My Servant.
It Thrives On My Instructions.
It Sulks...When I Do Not Issue Commands.

2528 LIFE Is...Not Your Boss.
Life Is...Your Child...Doing Whatever
You Allow.
Stay In Dominion.
Hourly.

2529 LIFE...Is Simply The Experiences Your Decisions Created For You.
(Buffet of Choices To Create Your Meal.)

2530 Life Tastes Better...In Smaller Bites.

2531 Life's Greatest Pain...
Is Discovering The Untrustworthy.

2532 Life's Greatest Secret~
Stay Conversational With The Holy Spirit.
Continuously.
And~
Never Argue.
Ever.
Ecstasy.

2533 Life's Greatest Skill:
Keeping Yourself Inspired.

2534 Life's Greatest Habit:
Recording Your Thoughts Relentlessly.

2535 Life-Dance~
Never Wait For Musicians...
To Start Your Dance.
Your Dance...Summons The Musicians.

2536 Life-Journey~
Listen...Carefully.
Confide...In Few.
Focus...Completely.
Think...Again.
Create...Routines.
Assign...Tasks.
Stay...Gentle.

2537 Life-Journey~
Never Travel With Someone Who Does Not Want
To Arrive.

2538 Life-Tips:
Master...Loving.
Stay...Focused.
Listen...Well.
Lavish...Honor.
Tweet...Appropriately.
Speak...Truthfully.

2539 Logic Creates...Order.
Faith Creates...The Miraculous.
Obedience Creates...Favor.
Honor Creates...Access.

2540 Master Focus...You Have Mastered Failure.
Master Questions...You Have Mastered
Wisdom.
Master Love...You Have Mastered Life.

2541 Master...A Day.
Not Life.
Make Your Day...A MasterPiece.
Habitualize It.
Habit? Is...Anything You Do Without Effort.

2542 Mood Changers!
1) A Song (Music)
2) A Phone Call
3) A Scripture
4) A Picture
5) A Tweet
6) A Memory
7) A Decision
8) A Gift

2543 My Life Is About To Experience...
A Glorious Change.
Do You Feel The Same...About Your Life?

2544 My Life Will Change Dramatically
Within 3 Months.
Decided To Work Only With People Who
Care About My Needs/Instructions.
ECSTATIC!

2545 Never Pay A Rolls-Royce Price...
For A Toyota Experience.
(Samson/David)

2546 My Life...Is A Day-Goal.
A 24-Hour MasterPiece.
I Am A Painter.
Today Is...My Canvas.
I Create A New MasterPiece...
Every 24 Hours.

2547 Replace...Is The "Delete Button" In Life.
...Memories.
...Disappointment.

2548 The 24 Hour MasterPiece...
Is The Day You Designed For Yourself.
Faces. Words. Colors. Smile. Moments.
Prayer. Hugs. God.

2549 The Complicated Life~
...Trying To Please Too Many People.
...Ignoring The Law of Order.
...Deceptive In Conversation.

2550 THE EMPTIED LIFE!
That's The Reason I Was Born.
That's The Reason My Heart Is Torn.
With This Burning River of Passion Inside..!

2551 The Essence of Life...
In Whom Will You Invest Your Life...
Love And Your Time..?

2552 The Events In Your "Mind"...Are The Events In
Your Life.

2553 The Greatest Way To Simplify Your Life Is
Simply To...LOVE.

2554 The Hard Road Is...
Not Necessarily The Right Road.
Jesus Said, My Yoke Is Easy.
My Burden Is Light.
Self-Sell?

2555 The Ingredients For A Successful DAY...
Are The Same For A Successful Life.
Powerful.
24 Hour MasterPiece.

2556 Responsibilities Schedule Themselves...So
Master The Art of Scheduling Your Pleasures.

2557 The-Journey~
Movement Is Occurring...Every Hour
of Your Day.
Movement of Miracle-People...Towards You.
God-Thing.

2558 The-Journey~
Treasure Your Own Opinion...
Above The Opinion of Your Critics.

2559 The Longer You Are Willing To Wait...
The More You Will Be Expected To Wait.
Delays.
The Lazy.
The Uncaring.

2560 The Loser Is...Whoever Quits First.

2561 The Only Thing You Really Need To Know In
Life...Is...What To Do NEXT.

2562 The-Journey~
God Will Not Leave You...Unrewarded.
Ever.

2563 The-Journey~
Identify...Your Chief Investors.

2564 The-Journey~
"Listen" For The Divine Opinion...
of Every Person You Meet.

2565 The-Journey~
Success Is A "Daily Fragrance"...Created By
Moments of Excellence.

2566 The-Journey~
Your Life Journey...Has War Zones.
On Every Battlefield...Look For
"The Divine Oasis."

2567 The Size of The Splash...Does Not Reveal The
Size of Fish.
(Apply Where Needed.)

2568 This Will Be The Most Satisfying, Fulfilling,
Happiest Year of My Life.
I Prophesy...Without Reservation.
Journal It.

2569 TWO PHILOSOPHIES:
Self-Worship.
Servanthood.
(Discern Your Friends And You Can Predict
The Future of Your Relationship.)

2570 What Are Your Top 10...
...Pleasures of In Life?
...Scriptures That Changed You?
...Investors In Your Life?
...Goals?

~

2571 What Is Missing In Your Life?
A Need Without Thorns?
A Voice Without Threat?
Love Without Caution?
A Gift Without Motive?

~

2572 What Is The Experience of You
Others Have Had?
What Would Be...
The Very Best Experience of You Possible?
Make It Happen.

~

2573 What Part of Your Life...Is In Disorder?
When Do You Anticipate...
The Consequences?

~

2574 What You Refuse To Celebrate...
Is Already Leaving.

~

2575 What You Respect...Will Move Toward You.
(God...Miracles...Wisdom...Finances...
People)

2576 What You Tolerate...You Authorize To Exist.
What You Tolerate...You "Sponsor."

2577 Whatever Is Unimportant To You...Will Be
Stolen.
Whatever You Look At...Enters You.
Heart Is Filled...With Uninvited Tenants.

2578 When You Watch The News...It Dawns How
Truly Exciting Your Own Life Is.
A Desperate Media.
:)

2579 WHERE...Are You Wanting To Make A REAL
Difference With Your Life..?
For Whom..?
HOW...Would You Make A Difference?
WHEN?

2580 Where Do You Seek..."Increase?"
...Wisdom?
...Money?
...Love?
...Favor?
...Peace?
...Productivity?

2581 Slow Everything Down...Until You Reach "Excellence."

2582 Where Have You Decided...To EXCEL?
What Is The PROOF...of Your Passion?
Where Have You Invested Your ENERGY?
Results?

2583 "Whisper In The Water..."
...Though You Are Going Down
"Whisper In The Water..."
...Your Life Can Turn Around.
Even When Your Mind...
...Is Stained With Pain of Time
Every "Whisper In The Water"
...Brings Healing Deep Inside.

2584 Who Is Scheduling...Your Life Experiences?
Are You Satisfied..?

2585 Who Is...The Bully In Your Life?
Change It.

2586 Whose Opinion And Advice...
Designed Your Present Life..?
Think.

2587 Why Are You Waiting...For Your Life To Change?
Schedule...What You Want To Experience.

2588 YOUR DOUBTS...Will Paralyze Any Benefits of
New Information or Opportunities.
(Unbelief Stopped Miracles of Jesus.)

2589 Your Experiences...
Create Your Persuasions.
Family.
Racism.
Prejudice.

2590 Your Experiences...
Do Not Decide What You Believe.
Your GOALS...Decide What You Believe.
Life-Changing.

2591 Your Life Is A...Feature Movie.
You...Have Chosen "The Characters."
You...Can Change The Plot...Any Day of Your
Life.

2592 YOUR LIFE IS A PICTURE OF
...Your Decisions.
...Mentor You Trusted.
...What You MAGNIFY In Your Mind.
...Your CHOSEN Focus.

2593 Your Life Begins...When You Discover A Cause
More Important Than Your "Living."
Think.
Think.
Life Changing.

2594 YOUR LIFE Is...
Whatever You Decide Is Important.

2595 Your Life Is...
Whatever You Keep Staring At.
Think.
Again.

2596 Never Expect Agreement...From Someone With
Lower Intelligence. :)

2597 Your Life Is...Whatever You Are Unwilling To
Live Without.

2598 Your Life Is...Whatever You Have Decided To
Talk About Most.

2599 Your Life...Reveals What You Will Permit.
Permission...Cancels Every Change.
Think Twice.

2600 Your Life...Reveals Your Skills
At Investing...
...Where?
...Who?
...What?
...When?

2601 Your Life Will Change...When "You" Do.
...Focus.
...Training.
...Honor.
...Servanthood.
...Faith.

2602 Your Only Problem In Life...Is Knowing Who To
Trust.

2603 Do Not Listen To Anything...
You Will Need To Forget.

2604 YOUR QUEST Decides...
~What You Avoid.
~Who Sees You.
~What You Overcome.
~What You Ignore.
~Changes You Make.
~Who You Honor.

2605 The Dance of Life...Requires Two.
Sometimes, You Are The Only One Investing In
"The Music..."

2606 Some Do..."What They Can."
I Do..."What Others Won't."
:)

LIFESTYLE

2607 3 Daily Pleasures!
~Birthing.
~Progress.
~Completions.
All 3 Should Occur...Continuously.

2608 4 LIFE-CHANGERS:
Invest First 7 Minutes In The Secret Place
Every Morning.
Create A Dream-Wall.
Turn One Desire Into A...Quest.
Ask Questions.

2609 A Routine...
Is A "Road" To Where You Want To Be.
Birth One New Routine...A Week.
Health.
Bible.
Planning.

2610 A "Routine"...Is A Road To Where You Want
To Be.
You Can Birth A New One...In 21 Days.

2611 A "Routine"...Is Creating Your Future.

2612 A Specific "Routine"...Is The Road To The Future You Desire.
What Is It?

2613 Blessing Is Not...An Experience.
Blessing Is...A Lifestyle.

2614 Anything You Endure...Will Continue.
~Abuse.
~Dishonor.

2615 Are You Training For An Experience...or A Lifestyle?
Esther
Joseph
Daniel

2616 Cheetos...The Poor Man's Cocaine.
:)
Addiction

2617 Do You...HAPPEN?
Or, Simply Criticize Those Who Do..?

2618 Create "The Top 10 Lifestyle."
...Top 10 Daily Goals.
...Top 10 Life Goals.
...Top 10 Investors (Friends).
...Top 10 Pleasures.

2619 Do Right Things.
They Are...The Great Things.

2620 Find 3 Things...That "INSPIRE" You. YOU.
Keep Them...In Front of You...All Day Long.
...A Picture.
...A Song.

2621 Habits...Have A Future.
Anticipate.

2622 HAPPEN...First.
If Not...Happen...Second.
But, Whatever You Do...Make Sure You
HAPPEN.
Everywhere You Are.
@100%.

2623 I Do Not Love..."Back."
I Love..."First."
Think.

2624 I Do Not Wait...For Something To "Pass."
I Move It.

2625 I Only Surround Myself Daily...
With People Who Know How To Talk To Me.
...Clearly.
...Truthfully.
...Concisely.

2626 Journal~
Cannot Remember A Day...That I Did Not
Empty My Very Best Into It.
Insatiable Hunger...To Learn.
Laws of God/Life.

2627 Journal...Every Day.
Something...You Learned.
Someone...You Love.
Something...That Made You Laugh.

2628 Journal...Next 365 Days.
Daily.
List 3 Harvests Received...Daily.
Will Release...Paralyzed Harvests.

2629 Morning Habit...
Alone With The Word of God...
That Is The Voice of God.

2630 Lifestyle~
AVOID...ALL Victim Talk.
~ADDRESS...Dishonor In Your Environment.
~CREATE...24 Hour MasterPiece...Daily.

2631 Lifestyle~
Do Not Cast Pearls Before Swine.
Shake Dust Off Feet.
Answer Not A Fool.
Remove...Strife Ceases.
Blessed Are Peacemakers.

2632 MasterPiece 24
...Focus On A 24 Hour MasterPiece DAY.
Not A Life.
A DAY.
A Beginning.
Sounds.
Colors.
Faces.
A DAY.

2633 My 10-10-10 Program
...My Top 10 Goals of My Life.
...My Top 10 Life Circle (People).
...My Top 10 Questions (of The Day).

2634 My Conscience Is 1,000 Times More
Important...Than My "Culture."

2635 My Favorites~
Scripture...Isaiah 43:2.
Chapter...Psalm 119.
Mentor...Mother.
Song..."I Love Sitting At Your Feet."
Place...Home.

2636 "Routine"...Is The Road To Where You Want To Go.

2637 EVERYTHING...Is The Size I Want It To Be.
Profound. Via My Mouth or My Imagination.
An Offense...or My Victories.

2638 Stop Waiting For The Disinterested...
To Rush To Your Aid.
Happen...To Yourself. :)

2639 "The Top 10 Life"
10...You Trust.
10...You Enjoy Most.
10...You Sponsor.
10...Whose Trust You Cherish.
10...You Pray For.

2640 Things...Do Not Happen To Me.
I Happen...To Things.
I Have Decided..."To Happen."
:)
THINK.

LONELINESS

2641 Aloneness Is...Your Choice;
Loneliness Is...Not.
(Jesus-Gethsemane)

2642 LONELINESS...Is Emotional Emptiness
Created When You Focus On Something
ABSENT.
(Focus Decides A Feeling.)

2643 Loneliness...Is Not The Absence of People.
Loneliness...Is The Absence of
Meaningful Conversation.

2644 Loneliness Is Not...The Absence of People.
Loneliness Is...The Wrong People Present.

2645 LONELINESS...Is When You Feel Unimportant
To Someone Who Is
Important To You.

2646 Loneliness Is...When You Have No One To Pleasure.

⌇

2647 Loneliness...Makes Average Fascinating.

⌇

2648 Somebody Is Pushing Their Way Through The Crowds...To Get To You. Never Doubt It.

⌇

2649 You Know You Are Lonely...
...When You Slow Down For A Stalker.
:)

⌇

2650 Pain.
Storms.
Loneliness.
Emptiness.

Places...God Likes To Hide.
:)

⌇

LOSS

2651 Every Loss Studied...
Will Avoid 100 Future Losses.
Theft.
Loss of Trust.
Loss of Favor.

2652 Everywhere There Is Disorder...There Is Loss.

2653 Losing Does Not Begin...Until You Stop.

2654 Loss Is An Explanation...of Character, Misplaced
Trust...Etc.
LOSS...Does Not Need An Explanation.

2655 LOSS...Is The Most Effective Cure
For Unthankfulness.

LOVE

2656 4 Proofs of Love~
...Relentless Desire To Give.
...Obsession To Protect.
...Passion To Pleasure.
...Instinctive Honor.

2657 5 Proofs of Love:
1~Willingness To Listen.
2~Relentless Honor.
3~Passion To Pleasure.
4~Need To Protect.
5~Passion To Give.

2658 A Limitation of My Time...
Is Not A Limitation of My Love. Ever.

2659 Admiration...Is Not Love.
Admirers...Are Spectators.
Lovers...Are Servants.

2660 I Don't Love..."Back."
I Love..."First."
Think.

2661 Assassins-of-Love...
Fear.
Silence.
Deception.
Memories.
Fatigue.

2662 Assignment Is...To Create
Unforgettable Love-Moments...
When Someone Will Feel Loved.
Completely.
Wow! Think On This.

2663 Disinterest Dismantles Love.

2664 Cheerfulness...Is Not Love.

2665 Every Love Circle Has...A Judas.

2666 Explainable Love Is...Not Love.

2667 I Can Survive...Without Money.
I Cannot Survive...Without Love.

2668 I Do Not Need Your Approval...
To LOVE You.

2669 I Do Not Think Love Is A Decision.
Love Is...A Reaction.
I Am Incapable of Deciding Not To Love.
I Have Tried. :)

2670 I Do Not Want To Leave The Earth...Before
Finding Every Possible Way To Show You
My Love.

2671 I Greatly Admire...People Who Communicate
Their Love Effectively.
An Ability Worthy of Our Total Focus.

2672 I Have Never Heard A Love Song...To
Mohammed.
I Have Never Heard A Love Song...To Buddha.
But, Thousands To Jesus.

2673 I Owe You...Love.
The Proof of Love Is...An Opportunity.
Opportunity To~
...Learn.
...Change.
...Give.
...Invest.
...Listen.

2674 If Love Was Enough...Lucifer Would Still Be Heaven's Worship Leader.
(God Himself Is Love.)

2675 If You Ever Find True Love...
Do Not Ever Let It Go.
Never.
Never.
Never.

2676 If You Ever Find...Where You Are Loved.
You Will Not Go Back...
To Where You Are Not.

2677 If You Excel In Love...
You Will Excel In Life.

2678 If You Fail At "Love"...Where Else Could You Succeed?

2679 Leave No Love...
Unspoken And Unused Inside You.

2680 If You Sense Danger...It Is Not Love.

2681 Love~
...Comes In 1,000 Sizes.

2682 Love~
Ignorance...Is Not Knowing Who You Need.
Stupid...Is Not Reaching For Them.

2683 Love...Is More Relentless Than Evil.
God...Is A Forever Force.
Satan-An Ex-Employee of Heaven.

2684 Love...Is When You Find Your Rightful Owner.
:)

2685 It Is Easy To Impress...
Someone Who Loves You.
It Is Impossible To Impress...
Someone Who Does Not Love You.

2686 Live Slow Enough...To Love Well.
Really, Really...Well.
Fast...Usually Fails.

2687 The Ability To Attract...
Is Not The Ability To Love.

2688 When You Master Love...You Have
Mastered Life.
It Must Become...Your Lifestyle.
Source: The Holy Spirit IN You.

2689 Who God Has Authorized You...To Love...
...He Will Empower You...To Understand.

2690 Love? Taste Before Swallowing.
Anger? Re-focus. Good Energy.
Business Offer?
Secure ALL In Writing...Then Discuss.

2691 Love Analyzed...Dies.
Love Spoken...Lives.

2692 Love And Caution...Always Compete.
Caution...Always Loses.
Always.

2693 Love...As If This Will Be Your Last Christmas
With Your Family.
It Could Be.
One...Could Be Gone Next Year.

2694 Love...Calculates Not.

2695 LOVE...Births Expectations.
Expectations...Birth Stress.
Stress...Births Conversations.
Conversations...Birth Understanding.

2696 Love...Can Be Learned.
Fruit...of Divine Presence.

2697 Love...Cannot Stay Silent.

2698 Love Chooses...Whose Pain Matters To You.

2699 LOVE...Creates Opportunity.
Honor...Creates Access.
Obedience...Creates Miracles.

2700 Love...Creates Strength.

2701 Love...Discerns A Need Quickly.

2702 Love...Does Not Die.
Love...Is Killed.

2703 Love Explained...Becomes Love Lost.

2704 Love Does Not Die...It Just Goes To Another Address.

:)

2705 Love...Finds Temperance Impossible.

2706 Love Grows Faster...
In The Environment of Honor.

2707 Love Happens...Without Your Permission.

2708 Love...Has Great Expectations.
Most...Unspoken.

2709 Love Increases Peace...Not Agitation.
Love Creates A Rest In Your Heart...
Not Fear.
Love Is...Energizing...Not A Burden.

2710 Love Is...
Wanting Her To Be Your Confidante.
Loneliness Is...Knowing She Cannot Keep
A Confidence.

2711 Love Is...
The Unexplainable Need To Protect.
...From Pain.
...From Loss.
...From Lack.
...From Fear.
...From Loneliness.

2712 LOVE Is...
Whatever You Can Not Walk Away From.
~Mentally.
~Emotionally.

2713 Love Is...
When Someone Services Your Heart.

2714 Love Is...
When You Wished She Wanted You.
Loneliness Is...Knowing She Does Not.

2715 Love Is...
Whoever You Cannot Walk Away From.

2716 LOVE...Is A Choice.
But, Not Yours.

2717 Love Is...A Current.
People Love...At Different Speeds.

2718 Love...Is A Divine Implant.

2719 Love...Is A Most Pleasurable Chain.

2720 Love Is A Passion...
To Be "OWNED" By Someone.
Lust Is...A Passion To "OWN" Someone.

2721 Love Is...A Passion To Buy Her Gifts.
Loneliness Is...Knowing She Thinks You Are
Trying To "Buy" Her.

2722 Love Is...A Reaction.

2723 Love Is...A Relentless Passion To Pleasure
Another.

2724 Love Is...A Relentless Reacher.

2725 LOVE Is...An Investment.
That Is Why...Love...Has Great Expectations.

2726 LOVE Is...Accomplishment Enough.
ENOUGH.
...Not Fame.
...Not $$.
...Not College.
...Not Influence.
...Not Productivity.

2727 LOVE Is An Invitation...
To Establish Credibility.
Your Unwillingness To Establish
Trustworthiness...Unlinks Us.

2728 Love Is...An Unexplainable Need To Share Your
Pain.
Loneliness Is...
Knowing She Does Not Really Care.

2729 Love Is...Discovering Where To
Invest The Rest of Your Life.
The Unthankful Do Not Qualify.

2730 Love Is...Having A Passion To Give To Her.
Loneliness Is...Knowing She Expects It.

2731 LOVE IS...Having A Passion To Please Her.
Loneliness Is...Knowing You Cannot.

2732 Love Is...Having An Uncontrollable Urge To Tell Her Your Secrets.
Loneliness Is...
Knowing She Will Not Tell You Hers.

2733 Love Is...KIND.
(Further Commentary/Conversation/ Exploration Is Unnecessary.)

2734 Love Is...Longing To Tell Her Your Vision.
Loneliness Is...Knowing Your Vision Is Unimportant To Her.

2735 Love...Is My Greatest Daily Goal.
Moments...Are Love-Deposits.
People...Are Banks Where I Make My Daily Deposits.

2736 Love...Is Never Frugal.
Never.

2737 Love Is...Not A Mere Decision;
Love Is...An Unstoppable Reaction.
Unplanned.

2738 Love...Is Not A Product.
Love Is A Master...

2739 Love Is...Not A Word.
Love Is...A Reaction.
...To Presence.
...To Need.
...To Request.
...To Difference.
...To Pain.

2740 Love Is...Not Complicated.
Explaining It Is...Complicated.

2741 Love Is...Passion To Pleasure Another.
Lust Is...Passion To Be Pleasured.

2742 Love Is...Placing Her Needs Before Your Own.
Loneliness Is...Knowing She, Too, Will Place Her
Needs Ahead of Yours.

2743 Love...Is Reproductive.
So Thankful.

2744 Love Is...Simply You At Your Very Best.

2745 Love Is Something You..."Build."

2746 Love Is...The Ability To Discern Their Pain.

2747 Love Is...The Opposite of Logic.
The Heart...And The Mind Are Usually
Enemies, Who Rarely Agree.

2748 LOVE...Is The Seed For Happiness.
Doing...The Work/Job You Love.
Talking...About Passion You Love.
Giving...To Someone You Love.

2749 Love Is...The Willingness To Reach Again And
Again.
Relentlessly.

2750 Love Is Too Glorious...To Leave Unmastered.
...Too Complex To Trivialize.

2751 Heart-Talk~
Love...Is Too Glorious To Leave...Unmastered.
Singleness...May Be Unnatural.

2752 Love Is Too Glorious To Leave...Unmastered.
You Have Mastered Love...
When You Become Its Servant.

2753 Love Is...Unwilling To Leave.

2754 Love Is...Wanting To Phone Her.
Loneliness Is...Knowing What Her Reaction
Will Be.

2755 Love...Is What Life Is About.
I Study Love...Intensely.

2756 LOVE Is...When His Exit Creates Emptiness.

2757 LOVE...Is When The Needs of Another Matter
More Than Your Own.

2758 Love Is...When Their Absence Makes You Feel
Empty.

2759 Love Is...When Their Approval Ignites An
Unexplainable Energy Within You.

2760 Love Is...When Their Exit Makes You Empty
Inside.

2761 Love Is...When Their Opinion Matters More
Than Yours.
Ain't There Yet.

2762 Love Is...When You Cannot Walk Away.

2763 Love Is...When You Find Your Owner.

2764 Love...Is When You Greatly Value What Is Important To Another.

2765 Love Is When You Want Them To Own You.

2766 LOVE...Is When Your Passion To Give Far Exceeds Your Desire To Receive.

2767 Love Is...Wherever You Want To Invest The Rest of Your Life.

2768 LOVE...Makes You Listen Longer. Again And Again.

2769 Love...Never Considers Price. Never.

2770 Love...Never Dies Willingly. It Is...Assassinated. Love Never Negotiates. Never.

2771 Love...On Your Enemies.
It Will Prevent Your Embarrassment...
When They Become Your Friends. :)

2772 Love Removes The Robe of Limitation...From
Your Imagination.
Think.

2773 Love Solves...An Unexplainable Problem.
Think.

2774 Love Stays...
Without Any Need For A Leash.

2775 Love That Stops...Is Not Love At All.

2776 Love Unfelt...Is Unneeded.

2777 LOVE...Without Approval Is Often
Condescending.
Approval...Generates Energy.
(Think Strong On This. Very Powerful.)

2778 Love Without Rules Is...A Fantasy.

2779 Love Words...Are Not Proof of Love.

2780 Love-Talk~
Arguing Is A Glorious Thing...
If You Are A Lawyer.

2781 Love-Talk~
...Is Learned.
...Is Taught.
...Is Different To Different People.
...Contains Sound of Honor.
...Silences Fear.

2782 Love-Talk~
My Ears...Have Heard Your Words.
My Heart...Has Heard Your Tone.

2783 Love-Talk...Is Not Love.

2784 Love Has Happened...When You Want To Be
Owned.
:)

2785 Loving Me Is...Not Enough.
Loving What I Love...Matters Too Much.

2786 "Loving Someone...Does Not Necessarily Make Them Happy."
-God

2787 Lust...Has Never Been Comfortable Around Love.

2788 Master Love...
Nothing Else Comes Even Close.

2789 Millions Loved By God...
Remain Unchanged.
So, Love Is Only Effective...When Received.

2790 My Love...Does Not Guarantee My Trust.
My Trust...Does Guarantee My Love.

2791 My Love For You...
Does Not Depend On Your Love For Me.
Power.

2792 My Love For You Is...
Not Agreement With You.
Love Is Not...Agreement.
And, You Must Know That.

2793 Needing Love Is...
Very Different Than Giving Love.
Two Different Worlds.

2794 Never Permit Humor...
To Substitute For Love.
Humor...Is A Moment.
Love...Is Oxygen.

2795 No Love...Is Better Than False Love.

2796 Over-Loving Is...Not Possible.
Under-Receiving...Is.
Think.

2797 Sometimes...
...Those Who Know You Least...Love You Most.
:) :)

2798 The "Love Fantasy" Never Dies.
Meanwhile...God Does Not Either.
:)

2799 The Decision To "Love"...
Solves About 80% of Our Problems In Life.

2800 The Ability To Talk...Is Not Proof of Love.

2801 The Loveless Life...Is Not A Life.

2802 The Mysterious Power of Love Is...
That You Cannot Stop It.
Forever Mastered.

2803 The Proof of Love...
Is The Willingness To Teach.

2804 The Proof of Love Is...The Pain.
If You Did Not Care...You Would Not Hurt.

2805 The Unspoken...Remains The Unknown.
Love-Talk...Really, Really, Really Matters.

2806 There Is Nothing More Glorious Than
Believable Love.

2807 "Undoubtable" Love...Is Rare.
Give It...Opportunity.
Toward You...or, Within You.

2808 What You Truly Love...You Cannot Ignore.

2809 Unspoken Love...Becomes Unknown Love.
Unknown Love...Is Not Love At All.

2810 Valentine~
It Is Wonderful...
When Someone Says, I Love You.
It Is Life-Changing...
When You Can Believe Them.

2811 WHAT IF...
...You Lived A Lifetime And Never
Mastered...Love?
...A Hidden Prejudice Sabotaged
Your Love-Experience?

2812 What Would Happen...
If You Decided To Master Love..?
Daily.
Relentlessly.
One Priority.
MASTER Love.

2813 Whatever You Love...Will Reveal Its Secrets To
You.

2814 When Love "Hits" You...The Opinions of Others
Do Not Matter At All.
:)
Unfortunately.

2815 When You Learn How To Love...
You Have Learned How To Live.

2816 Where You Find Strategy...You Will Not Find
Love.
You Heard It Here.

2817 Who "Taught" You...How To Really Love?
What Is The "Proof"...That You Actually
"Learned?"

2818 Who Mentored You...On How To Love?
Has It Really Worked For You?
What Is Your Passion Level...
For Learning To Love?

2819 Who Taught You..."How To Love?"
Was It...Effective?
Was It..."Enough?"
Is There "More"...You Should Learn?
When..?

2820 Why Are People Always Telling Me To Love
People...They Do Not Even Know..?
(Smile)

2821 Would Your Life Change...
If You Pursued LOVE...
With The Same Passion You Pursue Truth..?

2822 You Do Not Have To Change...
For Me To Love You.
You Have To Change...
For Me To ENJOY You.

2823 You Will Lose...
Whatever You Refuse To Love.

2824 Of All Human Emotions...Love Is Least Truthful
of All.

LOYALTY

2825 Admiration...Does Not Guarantee Loyalty.
I Would Trade The Genius of 1,000...
For The Loyalty of One.

2826 Loyalty Is Not A Decision...But,
The Inevitable Fruit of Character.
Judas...Is Judas.

2827 Loyalty To A Good Person...Is Never A Wrong
Decision.

2828 What Special Quality In You...Is Rare To Find In
Others?

2829 Lust...Is Never Loyal.

2830 Never Permit The Unknown To Stain Your
Loyalty To A Proven Friend.

2831 The Jealous...Cannot Sustain Their Loyalty.

MAN-TALK

2832 2 Reasons Men Marry~
How He Feels...In Her Presence.
How He Feels...In Her Absence.

2833 3 Things Men Expect~
~Interesting Questions About My Work.
~Sound of Honor/Admiration.
~Appreciation For My Time Invested.

2834 3 THINGS MEN HATE IN A WOMAN
Correction.
Correction.
Correction.

2835 8 Things Men Want In A Woman:
1~Admiration.
2~Conversation.
3~Energy.
4~Entertainment.
5~Fear of God.
6~Kindness.
7~Trustworthiness.
8~WOW Factor..!

2836 A Man Does Not Want A Lot...But, What He DOES Want, He Will Not Wait For.
(Abigail-David)

2837 A Man Is Driven By One Delusion: That He Can Please A Woman.
:)
A Major Genetic Flaw.

2838 A Man of Permission...
Permits What Should Be Penalized.
A Man of Order...Promotes Integrity.

2839 A Man Reacts To A Woman...According To How He Feels In Her Presence.
A Fool.
A King.

2840 A Man Who Sneers At Men of God...Is A Fool.
A Man Who Speaks Evil of Men of God...Is Evil.

2841 An Evil Man. No, Sir.
You Are Not A Mystery.
You Are...A Fool.

2842 A Man Without Goals...
Has No Need To Prosper.

2843 Are Her Answers...Evasive?
Is Her Past...Unclear?
Are Her Requests...Inappropriate?
Is Her Mood...Unpredictable?

2844 Choosing A Woman~
Are You Comforted or Troubled By...
Her History?

2845 Choosing A Woman~
Are You Pleasured or Puzzled By Her...
Choice of Friends?

2846 Choosing A Woman~
Who...Trained Her..?
For What?
Who...Admires Her?
Why?

2847 Curvy Straws On Love Basket Weaved...
She Was Confident I...Was Deceived~
Her Mastery of Words Cleverly Sown
Made Me More Willing To Go It Alone.

2848 Do You Really Want A Woman...
Who Has No Conversations With God..?
Really..?

2849 Every Man Has A King...
And A Fool Within Him.
The One You Address Is...
The One That Responds.
Abigail/David

2850 Every Man Is The Creation of...
The Woman He Trusts.
...His Heart.
...His Decisions.
...His $$.
...His Beliefs.

2851 Every Man Is Trained...Through The Reactions
of The Woman He Trusts.

2852 Every Man Is...Trusting A Woman:
The Woman You Trust...
Decides Your Future.

2853 Every Man Needs...A Different Woman.
Nobody Gets It.

2854 Every Man Secretly Wants The Woman...
He Secretly Admires.
A Man.

2855 Every Man...Is Chasing A "Picture."

2856 Manhood~
When Your Need For Trust...
Exceeds Your Need For Beauty.

2857 Never Set A Goal...That Diminishes Your
Energy For Love.
Counsel Completed.

2858 The Single Most Important Quality
In A Woman Is...Gratitude.
When You Find It, Linger.
When You Do Not, Flee.

2859 Her Needing You...Is Very Different Than
Her Caring For You.
Advised.

2860 Her Reactions To Your Responsibilities...
Explained The Depth of Her Caring.

2861 MAN-TO-MAN:
90% of Knowledge Comes From Passionate,
Relentless Questioning.
Questions To Your Boss Reveal Passion To
Excel.

2862 MAN-TO-MAN:
Are You A SERIOUS Learner?
What Proves It?
Is Your Passion~
1) "Survival"...
2) Escape...or
3) Mastery of Life..?

2863 Many Men...Love Well.
Few Men...Think Well.

2864 Men of Mercy Deteriorate Into...
Men of Permission.
Men of Order...
Thrust Weak Men Into Excellence.

2865 The Difference In Men...Is In The Weakness
They Overcome.

2866 Mother's Day.
#1 Priority of Every Son.
Do It Right.
(Dad Won't.)

2867 No Girl Has Ever Admired Her Sugar Daddy.
She Admires Herself...For Mastering Him
Through Words.

2868 Real Man~
Even Dogs Do Not Feel A Need...
To "Announce" What They Are.
Macho World.

2869 She Is Erratic In Her Reaching?
Are You Her Toy For Moods?
She Is Clingy?
Her Last Loss Shocked Her.

2870 She Is Forcing You...To Chase?
You Are Her Amusement.
She Is Forcing Your Decision?
You Are Delaying Her Next Fishing Trip.

2871 She Is Not...Your Weakness.
Your Desire For Her...Is Your Weakness.

2872 She Offered...A Trickle~
You Imagined...A Wave.
:)

2873 Sometimes...
A Man...Is Simply A Woman's Zoo.
Entertainment...Not Maintenance.
:)

2874 The Man Who Asks The Questions...Controls
The Quality of The Conversation.

2875 The Man Who Honors...Is Teachable.
The Man Who Honors...Is Protective.
The Man Who Honors...Prospers.

2876 The Man Who Permits His Chains...May
Secretly Fear
The Responsibility of Freedom.
Slavery By Consent.

2877 The Most Stupid Woman...Can Out-Talk The
Smartest Man.

2878 The REAL Difference In Men Is...
What They Use To Get The Attention of
A Woman.

2879 The Wiser You Become...
The Fewer Your Choices.
Men.

2880 The Woman Comfortable Without You...
Is Often Uncomfortable...With You.
Need Is Necessary...For Reaching.

2881 The Woman Who Enjoys Your Presents...May
Not Enjoy Your Presence.

2882 TO BROTHERS ONLY...
Successful?
Remember Your Sisters Who Loved You
Before Your $$.
Invest...In Their JOY.
Relentlessly.

MARRIAGE

2883 A Trained Bride...Will Choose A Different Groom.

2884 Dear-Husbands~
If She Understands Your Days...
She Will Treasure Your Minutes.

2885 Dear-Wife~
Wisdom Is...Simply Sharing Your
Opinion...During A Foot Massage.
:)

2886 Every Thinking Man Craves Improvement...
Wife...Must Know What He Wants
To Improve.

2887 Excited Servants Always...
Build A Good Marriage.

2888 Gay-Marriage~
A Dangerous Decision...
Contrary To Scripture.

2889 Hiring A Professional Arguer For Your
Mate...Could Save Your Marriage.
or, At Least Your Mind.

2890 Husband: "Yes, I Admit She Is Trustworthy."
Me: "Then, What Is Your Complaint?
Ohhh...You Are Not..!"

2891 Husband-Talk~
She Is...Your Greatest Investment.
Protect It With Your Life.
Infidelity...Is A Killer.
Re-Focus.

2892 If One Is Complete...Why Did God Bring Eve
Into The Equation?
(Genesis 2:18)

2893 If You Prayed Aloud For Your Mate The First 7
Minutes Every Morning...
...The Change Would Make You Speechless.

2894 In Every Broken Marriage...Was A Poor
Receiver.

2895 Every Love Garden...Has A Snake
To Be Discerned...And Killed.

2896 Integrity Builds...A Palace.
Lust Creates...A Tent.
Storms Are...Inevitable.

2897 Only Those Who Water The Camels...
Are Qualified To Ride Them.
Rebekah/Isaac

2898 Submission Does Not Begin...
Until Agreement Ends.
Submission Is...Authorization To Protect.

2899 The One To Whom You Are Assigned...
Is The Only One Qualified To Train You.

2900 When Two Servants Decide To Master
Servanthood...In The Same House.

2901 The Difference In Men...Is In The Woman They
Trust.

2902 Marriage Does Not Document...
Your Wisdom.
Marriage Documents...Your Hope.

2903 Marriage Is...A Daily Investment Program~
With A Lifetime Reward System.
...Words.
...Honor.
...Comfort.
...Trust.

2904 Marriage Is A Decision...To Learn "Love."

2905 Marriage Is A Garden...Where You Are
Sometimes The Only Gardener.

2906 Marriage Is...An Unexplainable Obsession To
Pleasure One Person.
For The Rest of Your Life.

2907 Marriage Is...Hosting Someone On The Earth.

2908 Marriage Is...Like Buying A Restaurant...
When All You Wanted Was...A Pancake.
Smile :)

2909 Marriage Is Two Excited Servants...In The Same
House.

2910 Marriage Mysteries~
The Desire To Be A Slave...Is Equal To The
Passion To Dominate.

2911 Marriage Solves Problems~
Confidante.
Sex Without Guilt.
Soil To Sow Your Hospitality.
Satisfies Passion To Protect.

2912 Marriage...Two Excited Slaves.
:)
Proverbs 5:18-19.

2913 Marriage-Talk~
Distrust...Dissolves Passion.

2914 Mate-Talk~
The Unspoken, Hidden Longing In Every
Man...Is Entertainment.
:)

2915 I WOULD RATHER LOVE...
Too Much...Than Too Little.
Too Many...Than Too Few.
Too Quickly...Than Too Slow.

2916 Men Will Trade Anything They Can Live Without...For Something They Cannot Live Without.
Think

2917 Never Marry Someone...Until You Have Watched Them Work.

2918 No Woman Stays Fascinated...With The Man Who Will Not Lead.

2919 No Woman Stays Submissive...
To The Husband She Can Deceive.
Marriage.
Dating.
Workplace.

2920 Not Every Marriage That Stays Together...IS Together.

2921 Sarah Was Too Tired, But I Was Not.
Closest Thing To Heaven Is A Loving Woman.
Abraham Diary.

2922 Schizophrenia Is...When She Dresses For The Bedroom While Giving You Talks On Holiness.

2923 Sexual Feelings...Desire FOR Pleasure.
Romantic Feelings...Desire TO Pleasure.

2924 SEX...Is Too Glorious...To Originate With A
Man.
God-Stuff.

2925 Sex Without Love...Produces Contempt.

2926 She Screams Uncontrollably, "I Have Married A
Fool!"
He Murmurs Agreement. "Yes, I Have Been A
Fool...For Marrying You."

2927 The Greater The Honor...
The Longer The Romance.

2928 The Most Painful Burden In Marriage...Is
An Uninteresting Mate.

2929 The Smile On Your Husband's Face...Explains
The World You Are Creating For Him.

2930 There Is Only One Thing Uglier...
Than A Lazy Woman.
Her Lazy Husband.
:)

2931 The-Vashti-Diary~
Familiarity...Is More Costly Than I Ever
Dreamed.

2932 What Excites You Today...
May Bore You Tomorrow.
~Does Their Presence Improve You?
~Marriage Bonds You With Their Weakness.

2933 What Future Paradise Will You Permit
Disobedience To Sabotage..?
Adam/Eve/Garden

2934 Your Mate...May Be Your Most Effective
Marriage Mentor.
...If You Willingly Become The Protégé.

2935 Your Performance...Does Not Keep Her Faithful.
Her Character...Keeps Her Faithful.

MEMORIES

2936 Discussing Your Past...
Makes It Last Longer.

2937 It Is Your Own Memory That Has Made A Past
Injustice...Permanent.

2938 You Have Already Been In Your Past;
You Did Not Like It or You Would Have
Stayed There.

2939 What You Choose To Keep Alive...
Cannot Die.
(Love-An Offense-Romance-Hurt-Disloyalty)

2940 Miss My Mother Greatly.
Try To Avoid Thinking of Her~
Because Tears Come So Quickly.
Advice: Pour ALL Into Your Mother.

2941 No Kiss...Erases The Memory of A Slap.
Physical. Emotional.

2942 To Be Unforgotten...You Must Do Something Unforgettable.

2943 What Trash Can of Past Memories...
Have You Decided To Carry With You On The Journey of Life?
...To Share With New Friends?

2944 You Cannot Walk Away From A Memory.
You Can Only Walk Toward...A Different Memory.

2945 Your Memory...Makes Pleasure "Endless."
"Thanks, Precious Holy Spirit."

2946 Your Memory...Re-Experiences.
Your Imagination...Pre-Experiences.

2947 Your Past...Is Only In Your Mind.

2948 Your Past Only Happened Once...
...Your Memory Has Kept It Alive.

MENTORSHIP

2949 A MENTOR Is...The Quickest Exit Out of A Crisis.
(David-Samuel...Mordecai-Esther)

2950 All Believing Is...Based On Believing Someone Else.

2951 Believing...Is Not The Key To Life.
Believing The Right Person...
Is The Key To Life.

2952 GET CLOSE...To Whatever You Admire.

2953 Honda Mentorship...Will Not Produce A Rolls-Royce Future.

2954 I Have Nothing To Say...To Those Who Do Not Listen To Me.
Absolutely...Nothing.

2955 I Hire "Trainers"...To Mentor Me.
Some People Even Reject..."Free" Mentorship.
:)

2956 I Will Invest My Life...
In Teaching The Thirsty.
I Will Not Invest A Minute...
In Arguing With Critics.

2957 Many Who Receive From You...
Have Not Received You.
Painful Discoveries.

2958 Access Is The Costliest Investment
A Mentor Can Make Into A Protégé.
But, The Insights Are Priceless.

2959 Mentors~
~Protégés...Differ Greatly.
~Identify Your Heart-Circle.
~Assess Them By Passion, Not Potential.
~They Find You.

2960 The Protégé Without Questions...
Is The Protégé Without Interest.

2961 Anything The Student Cannot PICTURE...
Will Remain Confusing.
Secrets-of-Jesus.
Teaching.

2962 Elijah Never Requested...
Opportunity To Teach.
Elisha Requested...Opportunity To LEARN.

2963 Judas And John...Received The Same
Mentorship.
You Are Assigned To Sow Seed...Not Upgrade
The Soil.

2964 Sometimes, I Teach...To END Your Search.
Sometimes, I Teach...To BEGIN Your Search.

2965 Who Trained You...For Today?
Who Will Train You...For Tomorrow?
What Price...Will You Pay?

2966 Mentorship...Does Not Create Success. (Judas)
Obedience To The Mentorship...Decides It.
(John)

2967 Mentorship From Paul~
Consider...What I Say.
"The Lord (Will) Give Thee Understanding
In All Things."
2 Timothy 2:7

2968 Mentorship Is...
The Rose Without The Thorn.
Pleasure of Knowledge...
Without The Pain of Experience.

2969 Mentorship...Should Be The Reward For
Admiration.

2970 Your Presence...
Is The Greatest Investment In Another.
Evaluate...For Your Impact.

2971 Those Who Do Not Heed You...Do Not Believe
You.

2972 What A Financial Deliverer Begins...A Financial Mentor Completes.

2973 When I Know Who You Admire...I Can Predict What You Will Become.
When I See Who You Admire...I Understand Why We Are Still Apart.
:)

2974 Where You Are...Shows Who You Chose To Follow.

2975 Who Mentored You...On "Love?"
Has It Satisfied You?
Does Learning How To Love...
Matter To You?
What Is The Proof?

MERCY

2976 10% More Mercy...Will Double Your Friendships
In A Single Week.

2977 Assassins~
My Message To Anointed Assassins...
Let Us Hope You Never Have A Need
For Mercy.
Blessed Are The Merciful.

2978 I Believe In Pardons.
I Am Alive...Because of It.

2979 If You Have Reached 40 Years Old Without
Learning To Apologize...
I Would Classify You As An Imbecile...
Living On Mercy.

2980 Mercy...
Is Simply An Opportunity To Repent.

2981 Mercy...Has A Pay-Off. :-)

2982 Mercy Is...The Factory For Your Future.

2983 Mercy...Is A Divine Investment.
Favor...Is A Divine Reward.

2984 Mercy...Is When You Give Someone
An Opportunity To Dishonor You...Again.

2985 The Mercy of God...Is Eternal.
Mine...Is Not.
Advised.

2986 The Secret of Every Failure In My Life Has
Been...Misplaced Mercy.

MILLIONAIRE 300

2987 Money...Is Unimportant To You..?
...That Explains Its Absence.

2988 Insanity...
Nobody Admires The Labors/Toil of
The Millionaire.
They Only Admire Him...
When He Gives It Away.

2989 FINDING A Job...IS Your New Job.
Presenting Yourself As A Problem-Solver.
9a-6p.

2990 Solve Problems...For A "Problem-Solver"
Close To You.
~Joseph.
~Daniel.
~Rebekah.
~Money-Secrets.

MINISTRY-TALK

2991 Dear Pastor~
Delilah...Views You As A Mountain
To Be Conquered.
Proverbs 31...Views You As A Jewel
To Be Protected.

2992 For-Preachers-Only~
The Anointing Increases...Proportionate To
The Enemies You Survive And Overcome.

2993 For-Preachers-Only~
Preach...Until Disease Is Destroyed.
Preach...Until Conviction Enters.
Preach...Until Hope Comes.

2994 For-Preachers-Only~
Preach...Because You Are Accountable To God
For The Souls of Men And Women.
(1 Corinthians 4:1-4)

2995 For-Preachers-Only~
Preach With Gratitude...
Because You Have Been Chosen By God Himself
To Represent Him On The Earth.

2996 Ministry~
Those Who Empty Themselves
Into Others...Cannot Refill Themselves.

2997 Ministry Choice...
Touch Many...
Embrace A Few.

2998 Inspirational Preaching...Is What Could
Happen.
Prophetic Preaching...Is What Will Happen.

2999 MINISTRY OF MEMORY
...To Remember Goodness of God.
...To Revisits Places of Pleasure.
...To Know Who To Reward.

3000 Ministry-Mistakes~
Not Memorializing Your Ministry Journey
Through Celebrations, Pictures And
Journalizing.

3001 Go...Where They Listen.

3002 The Call of God Does Not Qualify You;
It Is The Divine Invitation To "Qualify."
Paul/Disciples

3003 Pastoral-Talk~
50% of Your Giving Could Enter...
Wrong Soil.
Qualify For Seed.
(Energy/Time/$$)
Now You Know.

3004 Pastoral-Talk~
A Judas Must Merely Be Discerned...Not
Confronted.

3005 Pastoral-Talk~
Absalom Is Not Persuaded By An Invitation To
The Palace.
Judas Is Not Affected By Your Anointing.

3006 Pastoral-Talk~
Entertainment Is...Not Impartation.
(Is 90 Minutes An Overdose of Divine Presence?
Really?)

3007 Pastoral-Talk~
Every Body Part Has...Different Function,
Hence, The Divine Design.
Likewise, The Body of Christ.
Accept.

3008 Pastoral-Talk~
Everyone Wants...The God In You.
Nobody Wants...The Humanity In You.
Never-Forget-It.

3009 Pastoral-Talk~
"One True Protégé Is Worth 1,000
Pharisees."
"We Teach The Masses To Find The Protégé."

3010 Pastoral-Talk~
Staff~
If They Are Not Eating The Food In The
Kitchen...Do Not Serve It In The Dining Room.

3011 Pastoral-Talk~
You Are...Deceivable.
Never-Forget-It.
We All Are.
Unfortunately.
So...Invest What It Takes.

3012 Pastoral-Talk~
You Sowed...The Seed of Wise Counsel.
It Was Rejected.

3013 Your Role Is...Completed.
Accept It.
Without Guilt.

3014 Pastoral-Talk~
Your Judas Is Not Hidden...
Just Undiscerned.

3015 Pastors~
An Instruction Is The Quickest Way...To
Expose Flawed Character.

3016 Pastors~
Sometimes...
Your Church Is...A Place of Laughter.
Your Church Is...A Place of Tears.
Always...A Place of "Learning."

3017 Pastor's Life...
"Pastor, I Did Not Go To Church Yesterday;
God Told Me To Stay Home,
So He Could Talk To Me."
Growth?

3018 Pastors Only~
Never Confuse Human Expectations...
With Divine Duty. Never.

3019 Representing God On The Earth...
Can Become Stressful.
Like A Perfume Salesman...
To Hogs In The Pig Pen.
Yep. :)

3020 So Much of The Ministry...Is Not Ministry.
Lotta Devils.

3021 The Gospel Not Believed...
Is The Gospel Not Experienced.
Healing.
Holy Spirit.
Prosperity.

MIRACLES

3022 A Miracle Is A "Seed" In The Opinion of God.
("Harvest" To You.)
Is Your "Ground" Prepared...For Seed..?

3023 A Miracle...Is Simply A Divine Reaction To A
Human Mistake.

3024 Every Miracle...Has A Price.
The Currency...Is Obedience.

3025 Every Time...God Wants To Create
A Miracle In Your Life...
There Will Be A Conversation.

3026 I Am A Miracle...
Deciding Where To Happen Next.
I Will Happen...At 100%.

3027 Map To Miracles~
Picture Your Desire...Habakkuk 2:2.
Pick Intercessor...Matthew 18:18-19.
Plant Seed...Luke 6:38.
Persist...Matthew 7:7.

3028 Maturity...Is When Your Miracles Happen More Often Than Your Mistakes.

3029 Miracle Season Is Always War Season.

3030 Miracles...Are Merely Planned Surprises.

3031 Miracle-Lize...Your Mind.
Miracle-Lize...Your Mouth.
Miracle-Lize...Your Home.
(My New Word!)
Make Miracles A Lifestyle.

3032 When You Ask God...For A Miracle-He Will Ask You...For A Decision.

MISTAKES

3033 Delilah Was Not Samson's Deadliest Mistake.
Rejecting His Father's Counsel Was.
Rebellion Is...An Act of Fools.

3034 Greatest Mistake of Your Life Will Be...
Misplaced Trust.

3035 It Is A Mistake To Treat A Man...
Like A Boy.

3036 It Is A Mistake...To Mistreat A Kind Man.

3037 Mistakes Women Make:
...Misjudging Longevity of Beauty Impact.
...Ignoring Rewards of Timing.
...Magnifying Sex Appeal.

3038 My Deadliest Mistake...Has Been Sowing Seed Into...The Soil of Ingratitude.

~

3039 My-Greatest-Mistake~
Sowing My Favor...
Where It Was Not Valued.

~

3040 MY GREATEST MISTAKES:
~Misplaced Mercy In Disrespectful People.
~Permitting Contentious People To
Stay/Sow Discord.

~

3041 Accepting 1st Bid...Because of Likeability.
...or Smooth Talk.
...or Impatience.

~

3042 Confrontation...Without A Predictable
Outcome Is A Mistake.

~

3043 I Have Overestimated 1,000 Times More...
Than I Have Underestimated.
Stay Cautious.

~

3044 Those Who Need You...Do Not Always Love You.

3045 There Is Someone You Have Decided To
Ignore...And It Is A Costly Mistake.

3046 Your Biggest Mistake This Year~
Shutting Your Dominant Door of Favor
Through Ingratitude.
Advised.

3047 Your Mistakes Proved...Your Willingness To
Insult To Your Own Conscience.
God Warns.
Always.

3048 Your Most Costly Mistake...
Will Be...Forgetting Who You Are Talking To.

MOMENTS

3049 A Moment of Access...Can Remove The Confusion of 1,000 Love Letters.

3050 A Moment of Dishonor...
Can Cost A Lifetime of Favor.

3051 A Moment of Loneliness...Can Birth A Lifetime of Pain.

3052 A New Experience Is...Not
A Change.
Remember.

3053 A Single Moment...Usually Decides
The Loss of A Relationship.

3054 DIGNIFY A MOMENT:
Stay In It.
Do Not Hurry. Ever.
S-i-p It. Inhale. Exhale.
Habitually.
NOW Is...The Seed For Next.

3055 Dignify Moments.
Sculpture Environment.
Exude Gratitude.
Lavish Honor.
Honor Difference.
Question Relentlessly.

3056 Dignify...The Immediate Moment.
Relentlessly.
With Total Attention.
Honor.
Focus.
Discern Its Divine Difference.

3057 Drink Deeply From The Present Moment: It
Took You A Lifetime To Get Here.

3058 EVERY MOMENT...
Has A Divine Distinction.
JOY Is...
The Immediate Reward For Discerning It.

3059 Extraordinary Secrets...
Are Always Hidden In Ordinary Moments.

3060 Intelligence...Is The Ability To Read The
Moment.

3061 Greatest Inventor On Earth Is...
The One Who Can Create...
...Unforgettable Love Moments.
Daily.
Hourly.
Habitually.

3062 I Consider A Moment...
A Serious Investment.
...In People.
...A Tweet.
...Listening.
...Mentorship.
A Moment...Is Life.

3063 I Put All of Me Into A Moment To Prevent
Regretting That Moment.
I Don't Listen At 50 or 80%.
Create Moments of Excellence.

3064 Meaningful.
Meaningful.
Meaning-FULL.
Every Moment.
Every Hour.
Every Day.
Life...Moments...Impactful.

3065 "Moments"...Are Serious Gifts From God.
I Do Not Squander Them...Nor Visit With
Those Who Do.

3066 Moments Matter~
...Joseph Had 1 Conversation...
To Persuade Pharaoh.
...Esther Had 2 Meals...To Persuade A King.

3067 Most Moments...Are Never Unwrapped To
Discern The Divine Deposit?
Why?
Addiction...To The Future Blinds You
To The Present.

3068 Perfect...Moments of Excellence.
...Until They Are Continuous.

3069 Sad Moments...Produce Profound Wisdom.

3070 Savor The Moment...It Took You A Lifetime To
Get Here.

3071 The Importance of A Moment...
Is Decided By Your Own Discerning of It.
Divine Distinctions.

3072 Unwrap...Unwrap...Unwrap A Moment.
...Until You Find The Divine Difference In It.

3073 Will A Moment With You...
Be "Memorable?"
How?

3074 Excel In "Moments"...To Excel In Life.

MONEY

3075 Everywhere You Sow Honor...You Will Reap Favor.
Everywhere You Find Favor...You Will Find $.

3076 Human Zoo Facts:
Humans Invest 8 Hours Daily Working For Money.
Then, "Tweet" 8 Hours Daily On How Unimportant Money Is.

3077 IF MONEY IS EVIL...
...Why Are You Looking For A Job?
Duh.

3078 IF MONEY IS EVIL...
...Why Are You Working 40 Hours Weekly?

3079 IF MONEY IS EVIL...
...Why Did God Make Money A Reward For Obedience? (Psalm 112:1-3)
Duh.

3080 IF MONEY IS EVIL...
...Why Did Jesus Allow Judas To Carry A Bag of
It Around When They Travelled?
Duh.

3081 IF MONEY IS EVIL...
...Why Do You Allow It To Be Discussed Around
Your Children?

3082 IF MONEY IS EVIL...
...Why Don't You Work For Free,
As A Volunteer?

3083 IF MONEY IS EVIL...
...Why Did You Give Your Financial Testimony
About That "The Lord Blessed Me!?"
Duh.

3084 IF MONEY IS EVIL...
...Why Didn't You Refuse The Raise Your Boss
Gave You?
Duh.

3085 IF MONEY IS EVIL...
...Why Do You Carry It Around Every Day In
Your Pocket?
Duh.

3086 IF MONEY IS EVIL...
...Why Do You Give It To People You Love??
Duh.

3087 IF MONEY IS EVIL...
...Why Do You Hug The People Who Give It To You?
Duh.

3088 IF MONEY IS EVIL...
...Why Do You Pick It Up...When You Find It On The Street??
Duh.

3089 IF MONEY IS EVIL...
...Why Do You Protect It So Passionately?
Duh.

3090 IF MONEY IS EVIL...
...Why Get Excited And Happy When Someone Gives It To You On Your Birthday?

3091 IF MONEY IS EVIL...
...Why Hasn't Satan Doubled Your Income?
Duh.
(Satan Did Not Double Job's Income.)

3092 IF MONEY IS EVIL...
...Why Haven't You Burned Yours Up?
Duh.

3093 IF MONEY IS EVIL...
...Why Is Your Wife Working On A Second Job?
Duh.

3094 IF MONEY WAS EVIL...Satan Would Double
Your Salary Weekly.

3095 A Problem...Is The Golden Door To An
Opportunity.
...Relationship.
...$$ Reward.
...Change.
...Significance.

3096 If Your Money Created A Good Memory For
Someone Today...You Succeeded Again.

3097 Insanity~
Working 40 Hours A Week To Get Money...
Yet...Angry When The Minister Says,
"God Wants You To Have It."
Duh.

3098 Is Your Guilt Over Money About...
...Having Too Much of It or...
...Not Having Enough?

3099 Money~
...Decides What You Can Experience.
Cruise.
Travel.

3100 MONEY...
~Feeds Children.
~Prints Bibles.
~Destroys Poverty.
~Evangelizes World.
Now, Explain Again Your Anger About
Money?

3101 Money~
...Is A Reaction.
Not...A Miracle.
Money Grows...
Wherever You Planted Honor.
Few-Get-It.

3102 Money Grows...On The "Tree of Honor."
Few-Get-It.

3103 Money I$ Not A Miracle.
Money Is A Reward...For Obedience.
"If They Obey/Serve Him, They Shall Spend
Their Days In Prosperity," (Job 36:11).

3104 Money Is More Important Than Anyone Will Tell
You.
Money Is For...Creating Experiences.

3105 Money Is...Not A Miracle.
Money...Is A Divine Reward For Solving A
Problem.
Simple, Really.

3106 MONEY Is Not A Miracle, A Mystery, Luck, Sin,
Nor Destiny.
~Is Simply The Reward System For Those
Who Solve Problems.

3107 Money Is Not The Destination;
It Is The BRIDGE To Your Destination.
(A Tool...Weapon...Key...)

3108 Money Is What You Receive...When You Help
Someone Else Achieve Their Goal.

3109 Money Is Not The "Only" Reward For Solving A
Problem:
Favor.
Worthiness.
Commendation.
Promotion.
Recognition.
Honor.

3110 Money~
Romance...The "Moment."

3111 Money: Something You Need To Create What
You Love.

3112 Money...Will Not Make You Happy.
Ahhh...But, How You Spend It...May.
:)

3113 Money Is...The Seed For New Experiences.

3114 Parasite...Someone Who Likes Your Money But
Ignores Your Advice.

3115 Parasite...Those Who Spend Money They Did
Not Earn.

3116 PUZZLING...How Those Hostile Toward Money
Still Work 8 Hours A Day To Get It.

3117 The More Important People Are To You...The
More Money Will Become.

3118 Money Is...A Pain-Remover.
Marvelously So.

3119 Those Critical of Money...
Disqualify Themselves For It.

3120 Those Hostile Toward Money...
Rarely Attract It.

3121 Two Ways People Make Money:
...Helping People. Or,
...Hurting People.
...Discern.

3122 There Is A Huge Difference Between Someone
Who Wants Your Money...And Someone Who
Wants An Opportunity To Earn It.
Parasites

MOOD

3123 Music...Controls Moods.
The-David-Secret

3124 Music Changes Your Mood...
In A Single Moment.
Learn.

3125 Sounds...Decide Your Moods.
65 Years To Learn This.
:)

3126 Your Next Mood...Begins One Song From Now.

My-Feelings-Changed

3127 My-Feelings-Changed...When I Discovered She Preferred Giggling Playfulness Over Completed Tasks.

3128 My-Feelings-Changed...When I Heard Sarcastic Tone of Dishonor As I Attempted To Explain My Side of The Story.

3129 My Feelings Changed...When I Realized Her Belief Was That Beauty Was Her Credibility.

3130 My Feelings Changed...When I Realized My Instructions And Counsel Would Be Continually Ignored.

3131 My-Feelings-Changed...When I Realized She Had No Admiration For Productivity.

3132 My-Feelings-Changed...When I Realized She Had No Interest In My Daily Responsibilities.

3133 My-Feelings-Changed...When I Realized She Wanted To Trade Her Presence For Financial "Sponsorship."

3134 My-Feelings-Changed...When I Saw A Pattern In Her Attempts To Mislead Me.

3135 My-Feelings-Changed...When I Saw Her Insatiable Need For Male Attention.

3136 My-Feelings-Changed...When I Saw The Others Who Excited Her.

3137 My-Feelings-Changed...When I Watched Her Skillfully Evade My Questions.

NEED

3138 Despising Your Needs...
Does Not Remove Them.

3139 The Need For You...
Decides The Value of You To Another.
...Comfort.
...Inspiration.
...Mentorship.
...Association.

3140 The Need To Be Loved...Never Leaves.

3141 The Need To Love...Surpasses The Need To Be
Loved.
Takes A Lifetime To Discover This.

3142 The Needs of The World Are My Opportunities.
NEVER My Responsibility.
No Guilt Trip.

3143 Your Need...Does Not Qualify You.
Your Seed...Qualifies You.

3144 Your Need Is...My Opportunity,
Not An Instruction.

3145 I Am Not Responsible...For The Pain of Your
Decisions.

3146 Your Need...Is The Seed For Your Humility.
Humility Makes You Attentive.

3147 Your Needs...Determine
What You See.
They Also Determine...
What You Are Willing To Ignore.

NON-REACHER

3148 A Non-Reacher...Is Not A Non-Receiver.
Non-Reachers Just Receive...
What Nobody Else Wants Anymore.
Leftovers.

3149 Anything Unexplored Is...Unexperienced.
Non-Reachers...Forfeit 99% of Life.

3150 Many Hungry People...
Have Ignored The Chef.

3151 Non-Reachers...
Lose More Than Anyone On Earth.
...Opportunities.
...Friendships.
...Promotions.
...New.
...Experiences.

3152 Non-Seekers...Are The Unknowing.
Non-Reachers...Are The Uninterested.
Non-Attentive...Are The Unfeeling.

3153 The Fewer Your Questions...
The Longer Your Journey.
(Pride of The Non-Reacher Is A Tragedy.)

3154 The Most Powerless Person On Earth Is...A
Non-Reacher.
~Miracles.
~Prayer.
~Love.
~Relationship.
~Marriage.

3155 The Weakest Person On Earth Is...
The Non-Reacher.
He Is Forever Limited To...
Accidental Discoveries.

OBEDIENCE

3156 Delayed Obedience Is... Disobedience.

3157 Disobedience...Cancels Out Every Other Worthy
Quality In You.
(Korah/Ananias)
Even On Job...Startling Truth.

3158 ERROR:
Any Teaching That Obedience Is
Unnecessary...Unrewarded And
Unimportant To Your Salvation.

3159 Every Act of Obedience...
Increases The Anointing On Your Life.
Anointing...Destroys Yokes. (Chains)

3160 IF THEY OBEY HIM~
They Shall Spend~
Their DAYS...In Prosperity And
Their YEARS...In Pleasures.
God-Talk.
Job 36:11

3161 Instant Obedience Creates...
Instant Confidence.

3162 It Is So Difficult...To Admire "Stupid."
It Is Even More Difficult...To Admire
"Rebellion."

3163 No Mind of Man...
Can Explain The Logic of God.
Obedience...Is Never Logical.
Never.

3164 Obedience~
Focus On 7 Days of Absolute Obedience To
Whispers of The Holy Spirit.
Require Obedience From Those Under Your
Authority.

3165 Obedience...Authorizes Divine Rewards of Our
God-Relationship.
(Launches The Full Reward System.)

3166 Obeying One Divine Instruction...Produces
1,000 Times More Joy Than All Your Dreams
And Goals Combined.

3167 Obedience Is A Seed...God Never Ignores.
Obedience...Makes Faith Easy.
Obedience...Simplifies Your Entire Life.
...To Holy Spirit.
...To Authority.
...To Conscience.

3168 "Slick"...Is The Attempt To Substitute Affection
For Obedience.

3169 The Love of God...
Does Not Guarantee Benefits.
Obedience...Guarantees Benefits.

3170 Your Obedience...
Creates A Higher Reward...
Than Mercy.
Think.

3171 Your Obedience...
Does Not Reveal Submission.
Your Obedience...Reveals Honor.

OFFENSE

3172 A Forgotten Offense...Is Now Powerless.

3173 An Ignored Offense...
Is Instantly Powerless.
An Imagined Offense...
Needs No "Forgiveness."

3174 An Offense...
Contains Irreplaceable Knowledge.

3175 Every OFFENSE...Requires One of 3 Reactions:
Dialogue, Discipline or Disconnect.

3176 I Decide The Future...of Every Offense.
Kinda Powerful.

3177 YOU Have Decided...
The Size of Every Offense.

3178 Ignoring An Offense...Often Makes It Powerless.
My Mind...Resizes Offenses.
Downsizes.

3179 Never Ignore An Offense;
It Contains Too Much Information.
Never Permit An Offense...Unexamined.

3180 Nobody Else Chooses...How Big An Offense
Becomes To You.
Just You.
So, Shrink It. :)

3181 The Impact of Every Offense...
Is Your Personal Decision.
Remember This.

3182 What-Would-Happen...
...If You Made One Serious Apology To An
Offended Friend?

OPINION

3183 An Opinion Is Mature...
When It Becomes Your Persuasion.

3184 An Opinion...Does Not Create Credibility.

3185 An Opinion...Is Not A Persuasion.
Too Often, Christians...Have An Opinion.
That's All.

3186 Find...
Where Your Opinion Does Not Matter.
Rename It..."Never Never Land."
Move On To Place Called..."Next."
:)

3187 I Consider My Own Opinion More Valid...Than
Any Critic I Have Experienced.
Hence, My Peace.

3188 Nothing Is More Lifeless...
Than The Opinions of My Enemies.

3189 I Consider My Own Opinion...
More Valuable Than The Opinions of 1,000
Enemies Combined.

3190 I Surround Myself With People Whose Opinion
Matters To Me.
Greatly.

3191 If You Don't Like My Opinion...
...Quit Reading It.
:)

3192 IS IT TRUE....
...That You Value The Opinion of Your
Critic Above Your Own..?

3193 LISTENING:
I Listen Well To The Opinions of...
Those I TRUST.

3194 My Opinion...Did Not Anger You.
The Possibility You Are Wrong...Angered You.
Atheist.

3195 Sipping...From A Cereal Bowl Was Simply...An
Opinion.
Now...You Have Accepted Etiquette As...
Your Prison.
Think.

3196 The Gift of Your Opinion...Is Received, If You Do
Not Mind What I Do With It.

3197 The Opinions of Friends I Admire...
Always Matter.
Always.

3198 When He Is Determined To Be A Big Problem...
Determine To Make Him A Little Problem.
Your Opinion Matters, Too.

3199 When Your Opinion Does Not Matter...Stop
Paying Their Bills.

3200 Your Opinion Is A Seed...So, Beware The Soil.

OPPORTUNITY

3201 An Opportunity Is A Gift...Most People Do Not Accept.
That Has Been..."My Daily Experience."

3202 An Opportunity...Is An Invitation To An Experience.

3203 ANY Opportunity...Is Your Harvest.
Believe This And You Will Never Be Broke Another Day In Your Life.
I Promise.

3204 Arrogance...Assassinates Opportunities.
Every Opportunity...Has An Expiration Date.

3205 Everything God Promised Arrived...
Disguised As An Opportunity.

3206 Everything You Ever Wanted...Arrived:
Disguised As An Opportunity.
Think.

3207 Everything You SEE Is...Simply The
Beginning...of What You Have NEVER Seen.
Think.
(The Door Is Not The Building.)

3208 Everything You Want...
Has A Hidden Path To It.
The Path Is Called...Opportunity.

3209 I Do Not Wait...For Opportunity.
I "Discern"...Opportunity.
Think.

3210 I Will Give You Opportunity...
Long Before I Give You My Heart.
...To Learn.
...To Discern.
...To Honor.
...To Adapt.

3211 Never...Give Your Heart Away.
Give People...An Opportunity To Know It.
Assess Their Reaction To...The Opportunity.

3212 Opportunities...
Often Change My Priorities.

3213 OPPORTUNITY Is...
Simply An Invitation To An Experience.
...Embraced or Ignored.

3214 Opportunity Is...
The Only Product Created By Time.
Time Does Not Teach.
Time Does Not Change You.
Time Provides Opportunity.

3215 Opportunity...Is A Divine Disguise.

3216 Opportunity...Is An Intelligence Test.

3217 Opportunity...Is The Only Harvest You Really
Need.
Opportunity To: Learn...Sow...Serve...Heal...
Solve Problems.

3218 Opportunity...Is Your Harvest.
The Door To Every Other Harvest!!
...To Learn.
...To Serve.
...To Solve A Problem.

3219 OPPORTUNITY:
Currency:
...$$.
...Credibility.
...Integrity.
...Knowledge.
...Energy.
...Time.
...Favor.
...Cheerfulness.
What Are You Not Using?

3220 Opportunity~
An Open Door...Can Close.
Quickly.

3221 Some Opportunities...Are Once-In-A-Lifetime.
Even Teenager David Understood This. (Goliath)
Some Opportunities...Happen Once.

3222 The Greater The Opportunity...
The More Important Your Decisions.

3223 The Opportunity I Offer You...Is My Seed Into
Your Life.
Your Reaction...Was My Harvest.
"Soil Quality" Revealed.

3224 The Only Thing God Owes You
Is...OPPORTUNITY.
~To Learn.
~To Serve.
~To Repent.
~To Obey.
~To Change.
~To Honor.
~To Reach.

3225 The Opportunity Offered You...Is A Test.
...of Your Adaptability.
...of Your Discerning.
...of Your Gratitude.

3226 Vashti...Has Left The Palace.
Somewhere...Today...A Rebel Created
An Opportunity For Esther.

3227 Whatever Is Missing In Your Life Has Already
Arrived...Disguised As An Opportunity.

ORDER

3228 4 PROOFS OF ORDER~
...Absence of Strife.
...Completion of Tasks.
...Honoring of Instructions.
...Joy In Leadership.

3229 7 Systems-Order~
1. Information-System.
2. Task-Management.
3. Time-Management.
4. Energy Management.
5. Investment.
6. Appreciation.
7. Mentorship.

3230 12 Zones of Order~
Life.
Day.
Delegations.
Response Systems.
Finances.
Opportunities.
Mentorship.
Protégés.
Etc.

3231 A 24-Hour MasterPiece Day...
...Is When I Take Many Tiny Steps Toward
Order.
Continuously.

3232 Any Disorder In My Life...
Greatly Diminishes The Joy of
Every Other Achievement.
(Order...Is Life's One Pleasure.)

3233 Disorder...Is The Birthplace For Deadly
Decisions.
Operation Order.

3234 Every Conflict...Is A Defiance of Order.
...Marriage.
...Job.
...Government.

3235 O...R...D...E...R.
7 Days...of Divine Adjustments
In Your Life.
Expect It.
Listen...For Divine Whispers.
"Whispers."

3236 ORDER...Is My Hourly Obsession.
Order...Is The Accurate Arrangement of Things.
Order...Is The Divine Goal of Every
Biblical Instruction.

3237 Outside "Order"...Increases Internal Peace.
Every Step Towards Order...Generates Pleasure.

3238 Steps Towards Order...
Step 1 Is...A Goal.
Step 2 Is...A Plan.
Step 3 Is...Divine Approval.

3239 You Will Move Dramatically...And Gloriously
TODAY...
Towards ORDER.
Order..!
Order..!
The Proof Is...Peace.

PAIN

3240 48 Hours of Pain...Can Produce A Lifetime of Wisdom.

3241 99% of My Pain...
Has Come From Trusting Wrong People.

3242 Fame...Does Not Cure Pain.
It Multiplies It.

3243 Lack of Pain...Creates Arrogance.

3244 Nothing Is More Pleasurable...
Than The Absence of Pain.
...Marriage.
...Conversation.
...Health.

3245 Only The Wounded Dog Returns To A Painful Experience.

3246 Pain Begins...When Wrong Voices Are Given The Gift of Access.

3247 Pain Is A Divine Instruction..."Make Changes."

3248 Pain Is A Divine Invitation...
To Make A Change.
...In Focus.
...In Your Words.
...In Relationships.

3249 PAIN Is...Discomfort Created By Disorder.

3250 PAIN Is Not Your Enemy...
Merely, It Is The Proof You Have One.

3251 PAIN Is...A Message.

3252 Pain...Is More Persuasive Than Any Mentor.

3253 PAIN Is...The Announcement That Something
Wrong Is Exiting Your Life.

3254 PAIN Is...When A Protégé Tells The Mentor He
Has Learned All He Can From You.
Which of Us Is...The Fool?

3255 Pain...Always Makes Decision-Making Easier.

3256 Pain...Births Distrust.
Distrust...Births Searching.
Searching...Births Wisdom.
Wisdom...Births Order.

3257 Pain...Does Not Make You Reach.
Hope...Makes You Reach.

3258 Pain...Has Been My Irreplaceable Mentor.

3259 PAIN...Is How We Discern What Is Most
Important To Us.
Emotional Emptiness.
Loneliness.
Physical.

3260 Pain...Is Merely Concentrated Knowledge.

3261 Pain Unleashes The Genius In Your
Imagination.
Think.

3262 Stay By The Well of Pain...
Long Enough...
To Extract The Wisdom It Contains.

3263 Stay In The Pain Long Enough...
Until It Becomes Your Place of Wisdom.
Will Not Happen The Second Time.

3264 Stay Long Enough In Your Present...To Strike
Oil.

3265 The Greater The Pain...
The Closer The Palace.
The-Joseph-Journal.

3266 The Pain of Rebellion...Is A Delayed
Consequence.

3267 The Pain You Create In Me...Makes You
Memorable.
...Not Pursued.

3268 The Painful...Are Often Your Temporaries.

3269 Those Who Cannot Feel Your Pain...Will Never
Agree With Your Decisions.

3270 Those Who Cannot Feel Your Pain...Will Never
Understand Your Goals.

3271 Uncommon Pain...Produces Uncommon Ideas.

3272 Until You Feel Their Pain...You Will Not Understand Their Decisions.

3273 What Percent of Your Pain Is...From Satan? What Percent of Your Pain Is...From Your Decisions?
(Humility Relentlessly Pursues Counsel.)

3274 You Are NOT A Father...If You Do Not Feel The Pain of Your Children.
Those Who DO Feel It...Respond To It.

3275 You Are NOT A Husband...If You Do Not Feel The Pain of Your Wife.
Those Who DO Feel It...Respond To It.

3276 You Are NOT A Leader...If You Do Not Feel The Pain of Your People.
Those Who DO Feel It...Respond To It.

3277 You Are NOT A Servant...If You Do Not Feel The Pain of Your Leader.
Those Who DO Feel It...Respond To It.

3278 You Are NOT A Wife...If You Do Not Feel The Pain of Your Husband.
Those Who DO Feel It...Respond To It.

3279 You May Experience Much Pain In Your Life.
I Purpose That NONE of It...
Will Come From Me.

3280 Your Greatest Pain Will Come Through...Misplaced Mercy.

3281 Your Knowledge Will Determine...The Pain You Avoid.

3282 Your Pain...
Is The Divine Seed For Your Ministry.

3283 Your Pain...Chooses Your Doctor.

3284 Your Pain Is Determined...By The Voice You Have Chosen To Ignore.
(Prodigal Son)

PARENT-TALK

3285 Verbal Correction...Should Be Accompanied By Verbal Love.

3286 The Wise Stay Close...To Their First Investors.

3287 Your Absence...Empowers Someone Who Is Present.

3288 Parents...Never Argue With A Child.
Only Argue...With Equals.

3289 Today's Burden Is...Tomorrow's Reward.
God Is Very Partial To Parents.
He Is A Father.

3290 Uncommon Mother...Trains Her Children
Through Her Reactions.
Thank You, Mother.

PASSION

3291 3 Levels of Passion~
Ask.
Seek.
Knock.

3292 Few...
Few...
Few...
...Have One Passionate QUEST.
Do You?
What "Proves" It?

3293 Hunger...Creates Your Energy.
...For God.
...For Change.
...For Wisdom.
...For Future.
...For Companionship.
(Ruth/Elijah, Etc.)

3294 I Think About R.O.M.I...Every Single Day.
Return...On...My...Investment.
...My Time. Energy. Money. Counsel.

3295 If It Is Not Your Life "Quest"...It Will Not Happen.

3296 If It Is Not Your True QUEST...
It Will Never Be Your Experience.

3297 Loud Is...Not Always Proof of Passion.
Loud Is...Simply The Unwillingness To Listen.

3298 Passion Is...Energizing.
Intelligence Is...Fascinating.
Integrity Is...Comforting.
Kindness Is..."Addictive."

3299 Passion...Finds The Shortest Path To Any Goal.

3300 Passion...That Is Scornful of Authority And Protocol Is No Longer Passion; It Is Insanity.

3301 Passion...To Pursue A Relationship With The Holy Spirit.

3302 Somewhere...Your Passion Will Be Treasured.
Somewhere.
Stay Strong.

3303 The "Best"...Is Always Hidden.
Only The Most Passionate...Qualify.

3304 The Cost of Access...Is Passion.

3305 The Passionless...Have No Need
To Speak.

3306 TIME Is...Not Your
Decision-Maker.
Passion Is.

3307 Whatever You Are Willing To Live Without...
You Will.

3308 Your Passion To Argue...
Birthed My Passion To Exit.
Decision-Makers.

3309 Your Passion To Correct Is...Intense.
Let's Pray...You Attract A Student.

PATIENCE

3310 Patience...Cannot Make A Cat Bark.
I Can Help You Become What You Really Are.
I Cannot Make You What You Are Not.

3311 Patience...Forces Your Enemy To Reveal His
Weaknesses.

3312 Patience...Has Forced Many Enemies To Make
Fatal Mistakes.

3313 Patience Is A Sign of Trust.

3314 Patience...Is Ability To Silently Entertain
Yourself While Someone You
Love Is Learning...Very S-L-O-W-L-Y.

3315 Patience Is...Camouflaged Passion.
Never Forget It.
Advised. :)

3316 PATIENCE...Is Not A Forever Seed.
It Is Seasonal.
(Israel/Korah/Ananias)

3317 Patience...Is Often The Explanation For Delaying A Decision.

3318 Patience Is...Providing Your Enemy Time To Create His Deadliest Mistake.

3319 Patience...Is Simply Waiting For Your Enemy To Make His Next Mistake.

3320 Patience Is...The Ability To "Endure" An Irritation.
Wisdom Is...The Ability To "Avoid" An Irritation.

3321 Patience...Is The Ability To Pressure An Enemy Into Making A Fatal Mistake.

3322 Patience...Is The Weapon That Forces Deception To Reveal Itself.

3323 Patience Is...Very Stressful On A Deceiver.
Maturity Is...The Ability To Out Wait Them.

3324 Your Patience Is The Greatest Stress...Your Enemy Can Experience.
Increases Their Opportunities For Mistakes.
:)

PEACE

3325 Delusions~
God Himself...Could Not Keep Peace
In Heaven.
But, Man Is Persuaded That He Can Keep
Peace...On Earth.

3326 If You Ever Experience One Single Day of Total
Peace...You Will Invest The Rest of Your Life To
Reproduce It.

3327 Jonah Papers~
Someone's Exit...Is The Seed For Peace.

3328 Peace...BE. (Within Thy Walls)
And Prosperity...Within Thy Palaces.
(NOT Tents And More Than One!)
Psalm 122:7

3329 Peace...Is Created.

3330 Peace Is Merely...The Absence of The Rebel.
~Family.
~Government.
~Church.

PEOPLE

3331 2 Classes:
2 Different Searches~
#1...
~Acceptance.
~Affection.
~Approval.
#2...
~Excellence.
~Accuracy.
~Achievement.

3332 2 Classes of People:
Pro-Choice.
Pro-Child.

3333 4 Kinds of People...
~Never.
~Occasional.
~Often.
~Always.
N.O.O.A.

3334 A Jealous Person...Is A Dangerous Person.
Saul/David

3335 4 PEOPLE I DISTRUST:
Those...
Who Distrust Me.
Slither Around My Questions.
Who Justify My Enemies.
Disinterested In My Favor.

3336 5 Kinds of People Who Fail:
1~The Undecided.
2~The Untaught.
3~The Unfocused.
4~The Unexcited.
5~The Unthankful.

3337 A Quality Person...
Is Not Always A Qualified Person.
My Mother Was "Quality" But Not
Qualified As Heart Surgeon.

3338 A Quiet Snake...Is Still A Snake.

3339 A Right Person...Becomes Tormenting To The
Conscience of A Wrong Person.
Absalom/David
Judas/Jesus
Jezebel/Elisha

3340 Affection Is...Not Proof of Trustworthiness.
Affection Is A Reaction...or A Diversion.

3341 Almost Every Problem In My Life...
...Has Turned Out To Be...A Person.

3342 Amazed...At Difference In People.
Some...Love Excellence.
Some...Despise It.
Some...Love Accuracy.
Some...Battle It.

3343 Bad Dreams Come Because...
Your Name Is Belshazzar...or Daniel.
Your Name Is Joseph...or You Are A Baker.
(Smile..!)

3344 Bad People...Do Not Change.
Repentant People...Change.

3345 Clever Arrives...In Many Different Packages.
Comedians~
Appearing Stress-Free Is...
Extremely Stressful, I Am Told.

3346 Comedians Who Despise Christians/The Beauty of The Bottle...Must Never Distract You From The Poison It Contains.

3347 Crazy...Never Makes Me Angry.
It Simply Makes Me...Sad.
And...Very Thankful For The Grace of God.

3348 Cruel People...Have Been The Most Mystifying Part of Life For Me.
And, There Are Many.

3349 Depression...Is The Absence of Someone Who Can Inspire You.

3350 Destructive People...Are Very Sick People.

3351 Do Not Limit Your Life...To People You Understand.

3352 Enjoying~
Never Assume The Tormenting Chore of...
Enjoying The Unenjoyable.

3353 Every Hour With A "Judas" Creates Distrust Toward "John."

3354 Every Hour With Judas Is A Lost Hour With John.

3355 Every Thief...Loses Far More Than He Ever Steals.

3356 Everyone Belongs...In Your Life.
Some...For One Conversation.
Some...For One Hour.
Some...For A Memory.
Some...For A Seed.

3357 Everyone Is Qualified...For Love.
Few Are Qualified...For Access.
Trust Qualifies For...Every Gift.

3358 Everyone Loves...Love.
One Will Love...You.
Test It.

3359 Family~
~Today The Seasons Changed.
~People Are...Who They Are.
~What They Do...Is Who They Are.
~Float...Another Boat.

3360 Good Men In Wrong Places...
Create Stormy Experiences.
(Jonah)

3361 Good People In Wrong Places...
Are A Bad Experience.
(Advice From Jonah On The Ship With The
Sailors Who Threw Jonah Off The Ship.)

3362 Good People...
Are Not Always Good Workers.
Good Workers...
Are Not Always Good People.

3363 Have You Noticed That 90% of Your Problems...
...Are With 3 People?
Make A Move.

3364 Have You Noticed...
...All Unbiased People Are Critical?
:)

3365 I Am Unimpressed...By Anyone Who Does Not
Want To Impress Me.
I Am Not Going To Change.

3366 I Despise...Bullies.
...In Government.
...In Schools.
...In Families.
...In Business.
...In Life.

3367 I Do Not Do Well...With Someone I Do Not
Trust.

3368 I Do Not Enjoy Someone...Who Does Not Verify
Facts For Accuracy.

3369 I Do Not Enjoy...Someone Who Ignores
My Instructions.

3370 I Do Not Trust Anyone...
Who Does Not Enjoy Me.

3371 I Do Not Trust Unkind People.

3372 I Do Not Work Well...
With Those Who Do Not Work.

3373 It Is Easy To Find...The Lovable.
It Is Difficult To Find...The Trustworthy.

3374 It Is Not Stressful...To Love Them.
It Is Stressful...To Change Them.
So, Do Not.
Just..."Love Them."

3375 Name 3 People...
...Who Inspire You?
...Who Invest In You?
...Who Improve You?

3376 Needy People~
Always Give Opportunity...Before You Give $.
...To Learn.
...To Earn.
...To Serve.
...To Qualify.

3377 News...Is A Horror Trip Into The
"Problem-World" of People I Have Not Met. :)

3378 NEWS~
A Presentation of Problems Others Have
Created...That You Cannot Solve.
(Explains Inner Agitation In You.)

3379 No Right Person...Has Ever Left Your Life.
I Believe This With My Whole Heart.

3380 NOBODY IS EQUAL
In IQ/Discerning/Skills/Wisdom/
Opportunities.
SOW...Into Those With Less.
LEARN...From Those With More.

3381 Nobody Is...Ever As They First Appear.
Nobody.

3382 Nobody Matters But Jesus!
My Best Friend And My King.
Nobody Matters But Jesus!
He Is The Only Song I Sing..!

3383 Nobody Who Gets Into My Face...
Ever Gets Into My Heart.
Now...Why Would I Want To Have A Meal With
A Faceless Person..?
:)

3384 Parasites:
~Those Who Want Your Money...
But Not Your Message.
~Those Who Want Your Sympathy...
But Not Your Advice.

3385 People Are Different...Around Different People.
Some Manipulate...Via Affection.
Few Love Enough...To Put Another "First."

3386 People Can Only Experience What You
Teach...REPETITIOUSLY.

3387 People Do Not Always Like..."You."
People Like The You "They Have Imagined."

3388 People...Do Not Change Much.
"Discoveries" About Them...Change.

3389 People Hard To Know...
Do Not Want To Be Known.

3390 People Who Argue...Do Not "Entertain" Me.

3391 People...Who Heal.
People...Who Kill.
People...Who Steal.
I Want To Be #1.

3392 Presentation Is...Their Gift, or Their Trap.

3393 REASONS PEOPLE ARE IGNORED
~Tone of Disrespect.
~Desire For Useless Argument.
~A Distorted Perception of Relationship.

3394 Right People...Increase Order In Your Life.
Wrong People...Increase Disorder In Your Life.

3395 Some...Allow Their Loneliness To Choose Their
Mate.
The Wise...Allow Their JOY To Choose
Their Mate.

3396 Some Are Gifted...To Think.
Some Are Gifted...To Talk.
Some Are Gifted...At Neither.

3397 SOME...Awaken The Worst In You.
Make A Decision.
Quickly.

3398 Some Become Memorable...
Through Their Honor.
Some Become Memorable...
Through Their Dishonor.

3399 Some Belong...For One Conversation.
Some Belong...In Your Day.
Some Belong...In Your Life.
Distinguish.

3400 Some Choose...What To Birth.
Some Choose...What To Change.
Some Choose...Who To Destroy.
I Will Choose...What To Heal.

3401 Some...Empty You.
Some...Empower You.
~Distinguishing Their Difference Is Critical.
~Love Does Not Change That.

3402 Some...Get Your Attention.
Some...Get Your Admiration.
Some Invest...In An Experience.
Some Invest...In A Lifestyle.
The Difference Is Profound.

3403 Some...Look For A "Party."
Some...Never Find A "Party."
Some...Do Not Believe There Is A "Party."
I Decided To Be "The Party."

3404 Some Lose Favor...Faster Than God Can Give It.

3405 Some Love...How You Look.
Some Love...What You Say.
Some Love...What You Buy.
One Loves...Who You Are.

3406 Some Love...Your Words.
Some Love...Your Look.
Some Love...Your Gifts.
Some Love...Your Money.
Just Know What.

3407 Some Marry...To Escape Their Past.
Some Marry...To Enter Their Future.

3408 Some Men Speak...To Closed Doors.
I Do Not.
I Let Closed Doors...Speak To Me.

3409 Some People...Are A Fragrance.
Some People...Are An Odor.
Some People...Are Nothing At All.
:)

3410 Some People Are Dark Experiences...That
Launch New Days.
Never Waste Pain.
Make A Change.
Quickly.

3411 Some People Are Important...
And Do Not Know It.
Some People Are Unnecessary...
And Do Not Know It.
Some People Are Replaceable...
And Do Not Know It.

3412 Some People Are More Comfortable Around Old
Error...Than Around A New Truth.

3413 Some People Claim They Came From Monkeys.
I Really Cannot Disagree.
A Strong Possibility...They Did.

3414 Some People Deteriorate...In The Very Presence
of God.
Lucifer.
Absalom.
Judas.
Demas.

3415 Some People Have Mental Problems...And You
Are Not Their Healer.
Let-Go-Let-God.

3416 Some People Speak...Words That Hurt.
Some People Speak...Words That Heal.
Their Decision...Exposes Their Character.

3417 Some People Think...Yesterday.
Some People Think...Big.
Some People Think...Why?
I Think...NEXT.

3418 Some People...Care.
Some People...Do Not.
Wisdom...Is Recognizing The Difference.

3419 Some Received From God...
The Gift of A Mate.
Some Received From God...
The Gift of Singleness.

3420 Some Respond...To The God Within You.
Some Do Not.
Learn From It.
Stephen/Stoned.

3421 Some See...The Web.
Others See...The Spider.
The Wise See...Both.
The Fool Sees...Neither.
Egypt.
Politics.
Poems.

3422 Some...Speak To Be Heard.
The Wise...Speak To Be Understood.

3423 Some...Think.
Some...Talk.
Some...Tempt.
Some...Tease.
Delilah Does All 4...Very Well.

3424 Some Use Their Faith...
To "Endure" Their Life.
Some Use Their Faith...
To "Change" Their Life.
Both Are Admirable.

3425 Some Use Words...
To Reveal Their Feelings.
Some Use Words...To Hide Their Feelings.

3426 Some Want...To "Change" Their Life.
Others Want...To "Improve" Their Life.
There Is A Difference.

3427 Some Want...To Do What Pleases You.
Some Want...You To Be Pleased With What They
Do.
Worlds Apart.

3428 Some Want To Move God...
With Their Needs.
God Wants Men To Move Him...
With Their Faith.

3429 Some You Love...Are Not Trustworthy.
Some You Trust...Are Not Enjoyable.
Some You Desire...Do Not Desire You.

3430 SOMEBODY...
Somewhere...
...Wants To Take Care of You. And
...They Are Capable.
Prophetic.

3431 Somebody Is Looking For You...
Are You Subconsciously...Hiding..?
Be Honest.

3432 Someone "Experienced" You Today.
What Made You...Memorable?

3433 Someone Is Always Observing You...Who Is
Capable of Greatly Blessing You.
(Boaz And Ruth...Rebekah And Eleazar)

3434 SOMEONE...Somewhere...
Does Not Want To Live Without You.
They Will Find You.

3435 Someone You Are Trusting Today...
Is Trusting Someone Else You Would Not.

3436 Sometimes The Removal of One Person In Your
Life Equation...Turns A Tragedy Into A Miracle.
Judas.
Absalom.
Delilah.

3437 SOMETIMES...
Those Who Hurt You Most...Have Taught You
The Most.

3438 Sometimes...When I See The Other People God
Loves...
I Do Not Feel So Special.
:) :)

3439 SOMEWHERE...
Someone...Is Out of Place~
...Because Their Place Is...Next To You.

3440 Strife Is Proof...A Talebearer Is Present.
Remove Him...Strife Ceases.

3441 The Smartest People In Your Life...Are Often
Those Who Admire You The Most.

3442 The Unpredictable...Is The Unreliable.

3443 An Interesting Person...Is Not Always Easy
To Love.

3444 The Young...Want To Be Heard.
The Old...Want To Be Believed.

3445 The-Daniel-Formula~
Do Not Ask People...To Trust You.
Ask People...To Test You.

3446 Those Who Can Be Bought...
Will Be Bought...By Another.

3447 Those Who Do Not Want To Earn
Admiration...Seem Quite Satisfied With
Attention.

3448 Those Who Entertain Us...Rarely Satisfy Us.

3449 Those Who Excel In Christianity...
Excel In Love.

3450 Those Who Excel In Remembering...Will Excel
In Testing.

3451 Those Who Follow Instructions...
Will Never Be Without A Job.

3452 Those Who Hate People...Always Hate Life.
Learned This Reading Twitter. :-)

3453 Those Who Hate You Without A Reason...
Simply Cannot Handle Their Infatuation With
You.

3454 Those Who Have Invested In Your Life...Should
Get A Return.
Have They?
Were They Right...or Wrong?

3455 Those Who Have Not Heard Your Heart...Have
Not Listened.
Noted.

3456 Those Who Ignore The Invisible...
Live The Smallest Life.
God.
Imagination.

3457 Those Who Ignore Your Counsel...Disqualify For
Your Presence.

3458 Those Who Ignore Your Words...Have Already
Ignored Your Feelings.

3459 Those Who Increase My Caution...
Kill My Creativity.

3460 Those Who Know How To Talk...
May Not Know How To Love.
Those Who Know How To Love...
May Not Know How To Talk.

3461 Those Who Labor Hard To Find Your
Weakness...Are Disappointed When They Do.
:)

3462 Those Who Lost Love...
May Know Most About It.
Mystery of Love Is...Its Fragility.

3463 Those Who Love You...May Not Enjoy You.
Those Who Enjoy You...May Not Love You.

3464 Those Who Love Your Presents...
Do Not Necessarily Love Your Presence.
Be Wise.

3465 Those Who Master Words...
Have Mastered Words.
Those Who Master Love...
Have Mastered Life.
Words Are Doors...Not Destinations.

3466 Those Who Refuse To Solve Their Own
Problems...Will Rarely Solve Yours.

3467 Those Who Reject You...Often Birth Your
Greatest Improvements.

3468 Those Who Remain Passionless In My
Presence...Are Disqualified For It.
Bye-Bye Talk.

3469 Those Who Remind You of Your Past...
Resent Your Future.

3470 Those Who Request Your Time...Have Asked You For Your Greatest Investment.
What Is Your Return?

3471 Those Who Require Little...Are Rarely Influenced By Those Who Have Achieved Much.
~Influence.
~Dating.

3472 Those Who Resent Another Man's Harvest... Are Called Thieves.
(In Court Every Day.)

3473 Those Who Sabotage Your Sowing...Have Destroyed Your Harvest.

3474 Those Who See Only Good...Create Few Changes.

3475 Those Who Sow Doubt In God...Are Satanic Assassins of Your Future.

3476 Those Who Speak Well...Do Not Always Love Well.
Advised.

3477 Those Who Stay In The Presence of
God...Cannot Stop Caring.
Those Who Do Not...Cannot.
Kinda Simple.

3478 Those Who Teach Us To "Enjoy The
Journey"...Seem Incapable of Choosing A
Destination.

3479 Those Who Work...Easily Recognize OTHERS
Who Work.
...And, Those Who Do Not.

3480 Those With A Disdain For My Favor...Stop
Receiving It.

3481 Those Without Goals...Use Their Energy To
Attack Others.

3482 Those Without Your Experiences...Will Never
Agree With Your Persuasions.

3483 Someone Can Love You...And You Not Feel It.
But...
You Cannot Love Someone...And Not Feel It.

3484 Those You Can Trust...Have Given You
The Highest Pleasure Known.
Never Leave Them Unrewarded.

3485 Those You Love The Most...
May Seem The Least Interested.
Focus...Magnifies It...Not Improves It.

3486 To Some...You Are A Passing Wave.
To Some...You Are A Mere Drop.
To Someone...You Are "The Ocean."
Discern.

3487 To Some...You Are Simply An Experience.
To Some...You Are An Escape.
To Someone...You Are "The World."

3488 Two Classes of People...
Producers.
Protestors.
:)

3489 Team-Talk~
Two Kinds:
~Those Who Want To Walk On The Beach.
~Those Who Want To Walk On Water.
Both Ask The $ame $alary.

3490 Two Kinds of Humans On Earth:
Those Pleasured By...Building.
Those Pleasured By...Destroying.
Religion. Government. Family.

3491 Two Kinds of People In My Life:
Those Who Enjoy...My Presence.
Those Who Enjoy...My Absence.
Both...Are Easily Discerned. :)

3492 Two Kinds of People On Earth:
Those Who...Live Life.
Those Who...Take Pictures of Them.

3493 Two People Control Your Future:
The Person You Trust.
The Person Who Trusts You.

3494 Wasted Lives~
Some People Invest Their Entire Life...
In Fighting Someone They Do Not Like.

3495 When I Hear Your Music,
I Know How You Feel.
When I Hear You Talk,
I Know Who You Honor.
When I See Your Friends,
I Know Who You Trust.

3496 When I Know What You LOVE...I Know What You Require.

3497 When I Know Who You Honor...I Can Predict Your Future.

3498 When I See How Little It Takes To Interest You...I May Be Over-Qualified.

3499 When I See Who You Honor~
I Know Your Measure of Wisdom.
Wisdom Knows...Who Qualifies For Honor.
Always.

3500 When I Understand What You Require...I Understand My Role In Your Life.

3501 When One Wrong Person Leaves Your Life...
10 Right People Will Enter.

3502 When You Are Lonely...Nobody Is Ugly.
:)

3503 Why Are Super-Intelligent People...Usually Dangerous?

3504 Whitney Houston...
Users.
Accusers.
Abusers.
Misusers.
Excusers.
Confusers.
You Have Them In Your Life, Too.

3505 Loving Someone...Is More Exciting Than Being
Loved.

3506 Wrong People...
Want Your Money, Not Your Counsel.

3507 Wrong People...Are Costly And Deadly
Experiences.

3508 Wrong People...Are Different When You Are Not
Present.

3509 Wrong People...Are Highly Skilled
At Re-Entering Your Life.

3510 Wrong People...Are Very Comfortable With Your
Enemies.

3511 Wrong People...Are Not Always Easy To Discern.
Wrong People...Are Those Who Expect Your
Approval...Before They Provide Credibility.
(Require Their Qualification.)

3512 Wrong People...Attract Wrong Experiences.

3513 WRONG People...Birth Sad Seasons.
Wrong People...Can Last A Lifetime.

3514 Wrong People...Cannot Be Upgraded.

3515 Wrong People...Come In Many Shapes, Sizes,
Ages And Disguises.

3516 Wrong People...Do Not Leave Voluntarily.
"So They Picked Up Jonah And Threw Him Into
The Sea, And The Sea Ceased From Its Raging."
Jonah 1:15

3517 Wrong People...Do Not Respect Your
Accomplishments, Desires, Needs, Preferences
Nor Territory.

3518 Wrong People...Do Not Place Value On Building
Their Own Credibility.

3519 Wrong People...Do Not Want Who You Are.

3520 Wrong People...Want What You Give.

3521 Wrong People...Evade Answering Your Questions.

3522 Wrong People...Expect Their Simple Apology To Restore Trust.
It Doesn't.

3523 Wrong People...Feel Like You Owe Them Time And Attention.

3524 Wrong People...Have No Idea How Quickly They Can Be Replaced.

3525 Wrong People...Last A Long Time.
Their History...Explains Their Conduct.

3526 Wrong People...Last A Long Time.
Stay Guarded.

3527 Wrong People Never Leave Your Life
Voluntarily.
Their Success Depends On Your Undeserved
Mercy.

3528 Wrong People Never Leave Your Life
Voluntarily.
Their Survival Depends On Your Patience.

3529 Wrong People Never Leave Your Life
Voluntarily.
Your Misplaced Mercy Sustains Them.
(Jonah/Sailors...Samson/Delilah)

3530 Wrong People...Never Really Believe They Have
Been Discovered.

3531 Wrong People...Often Enter Your Life With
Flattering Words.

3532 Wrong People...Place No Value On Your
Integrity.

3533 Wrong-People...Should Be Discerned, Not
Discussed With Everyone.

3534 Wrong People...Sometimes Enter As Right People, But "Become" Wrong People After Access.
Judas.
Lucifer.

3535 Wrong People...Sneer At Your Standards And Expectations.

3536 Wrong People Stay Anywhere Change...
Is Not Required.
Single-Talk.
Government.
Terrorists.

3537 Wrong People...Think They Are Really Clever, And That You Are Stupid.

3538 Wrong People...View You As An "Opportunity"...Not A Divine Gift To Be Treasured.

3539 You Are Not Commanded...To Change Fools. You Are Commanded...To Identify Them.

3540 Wrong-People...View Your Integrity And Accuracy As Eccentric, Quirky And Problematic.

3541 Wrong People...Want You To Make Them An Exception To Your Relationship-Rules.

3542 Wrong People...Want You To Pay "Their" Bills.

3543 Wrong People...Want Your Attention Without Qualifying For Your Trust.

3544 Wrong People...View Your Favor To Be Their Bridge... Not Your "Gift" To Them.

3545 You Are A Different "Experience"...
To Different People.
Think.
Think.

3546 You Do Not Know Anyone...Until You Know What Matters To Them "Most."

3547 You Will Never Really "Know" Someone Until...
...You Hire Them.
...Fire Them.
...Marry Them.
...or, Tell Them "NO."
:)

3548 YOUR WORLD Is...A Collection of People.
Circles.
You Need.
You Trust.
Problem-Solvers/Etc.
Identify.
Then. LAVISH Honor.

3549 YOUR World Is...The World God Has Assigned
You To.

3550 It Is Very Difficult To Admire...
The Scorner.
TV Commentators.
I Guess Comedy Can Hide Ignorance
Magnificently.

3551 SEARCHING...
Will Find What Waiting Cannot.
(Eleazar/Rebekah...Shepherd/Lost Sheep...
Jesus-Ask/Seek/Knock)

PLANNING

3552 Ideas...Do Not Succeed.
Plans...Succeed.

3553 If Pain Can Happen Without ANY Planning
Whatsoever...
Imagine The Success That Can Happen With A
Little Planning.

3554 Planning...Makes Your Future Gloriously
Predictable.
Planning...Eliminates Pain.

PLEASURE

3555 Downsize...Your Problems.
Supersize...Your Pleasures.

3556 Every Pleasure...Has A Price.
The Debt...Often Outlasts The Pleasure.
(Samson/Prodigal Son/Jonah)

3557 Every Pleasure...Has A Season.
Every Pleasure...Has A Price.
Every Pleasure...Has An End.

3558 Small Steps In The Right Direction...
Create As Much Pleasure As...The Big Steps.

3559 Schedule Your Pleasures...
Because Pain Schedules Itself.

3560 Those Who Pleasure You The Most...Are
Remembered The Longest.

3561 You Liking "You"...Will Bring You More Pleasure
Than 10,000 Others Liking You.

POLITICS

3562 3 DANGER SIGNALS-USA...
~Disrespect For Israel.
~Contempt For Christianity.
~Cowardice Toward Confrontation.

3563 Amazing...
~Those Who Hate Slavery...
Still Vote For Control.
Government Control.
Change The World~Change The Vote.

3564 America?
A Child Praying In School...Infuriated Judges.
A Football Player...Kneeling On A Field...
Infuriates Media.

3565 America...Has Some Very Dangerous Leaders.
Christians...Pray. Vote. Persuade.

3566 America Is...Being Bullied.
Brilliant, Articulate And Skilled In Deception.
Hope...Is Not A Weapon.

3567 America...Is Wise To Choose Beatable Enemies. It Will Be A Mistake...To Think God Is One of Them.

3568 America~
Some See...An Economic Problem.
I See...A God-Problem.

3569 Egypt...Destroying Your Country.
Rioters...Cutting Off Your Own Arm To Get The Attention of A Doctor.

3570 Egypt~
Chaos In The Heart...Creates Chaos In The Street.

3571 Egypt~
An Evil Heart...Resents Peace.

3572 Egypt~
If You Have Nothing You Love...You Find A Reason To Hate.

3573 Egypt~
Hate Is The Seed...For Tragedy.
Politics~

3574 Egypt~
The Reason For Authority Is...Order.
The Fruit of Legitimate Authority Is:
~Protection.
~Provision.
~Promotion.

3575 I Don't Want A President..."Who Can Win."
I Want A President..."Who Can Pray."

3576 I Don't Want A President..."Who Has Money."
I Want A President..."Who Has A Conscience."

3577 I Have No Confidence In Anyone...
Who Doubts The Divinity of Jesus.
Integrity Is More Important Than Votes.

3578 I Would Not Vote For A President Who Does Not
Believe Jesus Is The Only Way.

3579 If You Disagree With God...I Assure You That I
Will Disagree With You.

3580 Is Race...More Important Than Principle?

3581 Message To Politicians~
Be Very Careful...In Your Dishonoring
of Israel.
Advised.

3582 Mr. Politician~
God Is Here...To Stay.
You...Are Not.
FYI.

3583 My-Dear-President~
Divine Favor...Is On Israel.
Those Who Favor Israel...Receive Favor.
Compelling-Argument.

3584 Only Thieves...Believe In
The Re-Distribution of Wealth.
Stealing From Producers And Investing In Non-
Producers.

3585 Beware The Man...Who Cannot Speak Without
Sarcasm.

3586 Clever Manipulation of Words...
Sickens My Heart.
Caution.

3587 Clever Men Use Right Words...
To Hide Wrong Hearts.
Examine All Things.

3588 Condescension Is...An Unmistakable Odor.

3589 Deceivers Defend...Deceivers.
Don't Stay Stupid.

3590 Deception...Cannot Be Understood,
Only Discerned.

3591 Elections Are Choices of Philosophies...
Not Men.

3592 Fear...Creates Silence.
Silence...Conveys Cowardice.
Cowardice...Produces Tyrants.

3593 I Am Not A Silent Partner...
In ANY Environment.

3594 I Don't Listen For...The Sound of Clever.
I Listen For...The Sound of "Real."

3595 I Do Not Trust Any Politician...
Who Resents Successful People.

3596 I Do Not Want A President...
"Who Argues Well."
I Want A President..."Who Listens Well."

3597 I Do Not Want A President Who Gets Along
With People...I Want A Leader Who Gets Along
With God.

3598 "I Have Seen Servants Upon Horses...
And Princes Walking As Servants Upon The
Earth."
Ecclesiastes 10:7

3599 It Is My Persuasion...That Dictatorship
Will Not Succeed In America.

3600 Only Fools...Honor Fools.

3601 Prejudice...Chooses Who You Vote Against.
Conscience...Chooses Who You Vote For.
No Baby Assassins Receive My Vote.

3602 Sarcasm...Is A Skill That Increases Distrust.

3603 Scorn...Is An Attitude, Not An Argument.

3604 Some Make Decisions...According To Votes.
Some Make Decisions...According To Bible.

3605 The Attempts To Improve America Without
Including God...Is Ludicrous.

3606 The Flawless Candidate...Remains Hidden.
May Just Vote For A Man...Who Actually
Believes In The Bible.

3607 The Politician Who Ignores Scriptural Laws...Is
A Fool.

3608 The "Sound" of Authority...Is Not Authority.

3609 The Wolf Pack Is Devouring...The Kill.
Each Other.

3610 Those With Faith...Always Infuriate
Those Without It.

3611 To Some, Jesus Is...A Drop.
To Others, Jesus Is...A Trickle.
To Me, Jesus Is...My Ocean.

3612 Who Believes Votes...Are More Important
Than The Word of God..?
Homosexuality

3613 You Must Learn To Live With An Enemy...
You Are Not Authorized To Destroy.

3614 Politics And Religion~
Jesus Has Not Stopped My Anger.
He Changed What I Do With It.

3615 Presidential-Debates~
Debates...Reveal The "Little Boy" Hidden In
Grown Men.
:)

3616 Presidential-Election~
Dishonoring Others...Is The Quickest Way To
Lose.

3617 Presidential Politics~
Disagreement...Does Not Authorize Dishonor.
Dishonor...Does Expose Your Character.

3618 Taxes!!!
Those Who Pay The Bills...Should Make
The Rules.

3619 The Answer For America...
Is Neither Democrat Nor Republican.
The Answer...Is A Return To The Word of God.

3620 Voting For Baby Assassins...
Insults My Conscience.

3621 You Want To Represent America...As President.
But, You Are Ashamed To Represent God...In
A Debate?
Joke Time.

3622 Position Does Not Give You Power,
It Gives The Illusion of Power.
God Can Silence Your Voice In One Accident.

PRAYER

3623 2012-Year of Answered Prayers.
Write Your List.
Unleash Gratitude.
Focus...Your Faith.
Agree...With An Intercessor.

3624 An Unspoken Prayer...
Is An Unheard Prayer.
An Unheard Prayer...
Is An Unanswered Prayer.

3625 Distractions Do Not Qualify For...Prayer.

3626 Father~
Birth A Militant Spirit In Christians.
For...
Obedience.
Evangelism.
Government That Honors You.
I Am Yours.

3627 Father~
Birth In Me~
...Touch of A Shepherd.
...Mind of A Protégé.
...Will of A Warrior.
...Eye of An Eagle.
...Heart of A Father.

3628 Father~
Forgive...America~of Its Arrogance.
Inspire...Our Ministers~To Boldness.
Heal~The Broken Through Us.

3629 Father~
I Decree~
Truth Will Emerge In Cairo.
That Advocates of Your Laws Will Move Into
Position of Authority.
Amen.

3630 Father~
My Follower Will Walk In Indescribable
Peace...All Day.
The Hidden Will Become Known.
Future...Is Clearer.

3631 If You Know How To Pray...Nothing Else Really
Matters.

3632 Father~
You Are My Rock. My ROCK.
I Will Not Be Shaken Nor Moved.
I Rest.
I Listen.
Love On Me.
I Receive.
Total Peace.

3633 If You Wait For Inspiration To Pray...
You Will Have A Prayerless Life.
Establish A Prayer Routine.

3634 Master Key To Prayer Life...Is "Unceasing
Mutterings To The Holy Spirit."
Unending Conversation...About Tasks, People.

3635 My Prayer...For You.
Authority...To Destroy Chaos.
Peace-Making.
Passion...To Solve Problems.

3636 Next 7 Days...Will Unlock The Most Glorious
Answers God Has Ever Given You.
Journal It.
I Decree It.
You Agree With It.

3637 No Amount of Prayer...Can Displace A Divine
Principle.
Think. Again.

3638 No Prayer..."Removes" Your Humanity.

3639 Players...Are Not Prayers.
Prayers...Are Not Players.

3640 Pray For My Government...
But I Enjoy Praying With "Faith" A Lot More.
:(

3641 PRAYER~
"Jesus~
YOU Are My Whole World.
Your Opinion Is My Instruction.
You Talk. I Obey.
No Arguments From Me.
None."

3642 PRAYER~
"Precious Holy Spirit,
Please Kill Anything In Me That Is Stopping
Others From Experiencing The Jesus In Me."

3643 Prayer For Israel...Is Seed For Prosperity.
"Pray For Peace of Jerusalem: May They Prosper
Who Love You."
Psalm 122:6

3644 Prayer For Pastors...
"Father, As We Sow Our Persuasions
~Enable Us To FOCUS On The Crushed...Not
Critics,
Reachers...Not Rebels."

3645 Prayer For Pastors...
"Father, Keep Us Focused/Bold/
Kind...As We Pour Your Healing
Wisdom Into Wounded Hearts of
Our People."

3646 PRAYER Is Important...
Because It Is Your Channel For RECEIVING.
If You Are Not Receiving...
You Know Your Prayer-Life Is Flawed.
(My Father)

3647 PRAYER...Is SPOKEN Conversation With God.

3648 Prayer...Produces Nothing.
Prayer With Faith...Produces Everything.

3649 Prayer To The Holy Spirit~
World Class Me.
...My Mind.
...My Mouth.
...My Reactions.
...My Caring.
...My Conversations.
...My Life.

3650 Prayerlessness...Is The Habit of Fools.

3651 The Fruit of Prayer Is Different Than...The
Rewards of Principle.

3652 The Prayers of Jesus...
Did Not Change Judas.

3653 Thoughts...Are Not Prayers.
Hope...Is Not Prayer.
Worry...Is Not Prayer.
Prayer...Is SPOKEN Conversation With God.

3654 THOUGHTS...Are Not Prayers.
NEEDS...Are Not Prayers.
WORRY...Is Not A Prayer.
DISCUSSIONS...Are Not Prayers.
Think.

3655 What-Would-Happen...
...If You Entered Your Prayer Place For 30 Consecutive Days?

3656 When You Intercede For Someone In Prayer...You Will Become Very Protective Toward Them.

3657 Worry...Is Not Prayer.
Anger...Is Not Prayer.
Pain...Is Not Prayer.
Prayer...Is Conversation With God.

PREJUDICE

3658 Are You Openly Against Something...You Have Never Yet Even Researched..? This...Is Prejudice.

3659 I WONDER...What Hidden Prejudice Lies Undetected Within Me... Poisoning My Decisions And Sabotaging Significant Relationships?

3660 Prejudice~ Chains...Are Contagious.

3661 PREJUDICE...Is A Thief...of Pleasure, Change And New. (Whether Against Race/Gender/ Wealth/Religion)

3662 PREJUDICE...Is Embracing An Opinion Before You Have The Experience.

3663 Prejudice...Is Relentless, Unending Abortion.
...of Change.
...of Relationships.
...of Impartation.
...of Possibilities.

3664 Prejudice...Is The Invisible Assassin Who Aborts Your Greatest Experiences.

3665 Racism...Is Demonic.
Nobody Can Become That Stupid Naturally.

3666 Racism...Is Not An Attitude, But A Spirit.
You Do Not Need More Tolerance;
You Need A Deliverance.

3667 Racism...Is Rejection of Divine Authority.

3668 Those Who Are The Most Outraged About Prejudice...Seem To Have It Themselves.

PREPARATION

3669 Honda Preparation...Will Not Produce A Rolls-Royce Future.

3670 Preparation Zone...
Is Not A "Wasted Season" In Your Life.
Jesus Invested 30 Years...
For 42 Months of Ministry.

3671 Preparation...
Multiplies Self-Confidence.
...Job.
...Performance.
...Crisis.
Self-Confidence Is...Transferable.

3672 Preparation...Is The Proof of Humility.

3673 The Proud...Refuse To Prepare.

3674 Preparation...Removes Fear.
...Job Interviews.
...Marriage.
...Public Speaking.

3675 The Greater Your Future...The Longer Your Preparation.

3676 Those Who Assume Winning...
Never Prepare.

3677 Your PREPARATION...Reveals Your True Passion For Your Future.

PRESENCE

3678 Celebrate...Completions of Tasks.
Whisper Praise...Incessantly.
Absorb...Holy Presence.
Lavish...Love.

3679 I Never Linger In The Presence of Someone...
...Who Has The Tone of Dishonor.

3680 I Never Linger In The Presence of Someone...
...Who I Cannot Inspire.

3681 I Never Linger In The Presence of Someone...
...Who Is A Non-Learner.

3682 I Never Linger In The Presence of Someone...
...Who Wants To Be Somewhere Else.

3683 I Never Linger In The Presence of
Someone...Who Tires Me.

3684 I Never Reach...For The Disinterested.
Presence Is...The Ultimate Investment.
Why Invest...Where I Do Not Inspire?

3685 Many People Are Happier...Without My
Presence.
A Marvelous Time-Saver.
:)

3686 Men Do Not Marry A Woman Because of Her
Beauty; They Marry A Woman Because of How
They Feel In Her Presence.

3687 Never Linger In The Presence...of
A Non-Receiver.

3688 Presence~
Your Entry...Changes The Equation.
ANY Equation.

3689 PRESENCE...Can Change Any Equation.
Any.
So...ENTER.
With Expectation.

3690 PRESENCE...Changes The Equation of Every
Environment.
When The Rebel Is Removed, The Storm
Will Cease.
(Jonah)

3691 Presence Ignites...Energy, Honor, Guilt or Fear
And A Host of Invisible Emotions.
Sow Your Presence Carefully.
Analyze Your Harvest.

3692 PRESENCE...Is A Seed.
Assess Reactions of "Soil" (Environment)
You Enter.

3693 Are You Ignored? Discerned? Embraced?
Reactions Reveal Discerning.

3694 Presence...Is Your Greatest Investment.
Identify...Dividends.
Honestly.

3695 Presence-of-God
..."Prince of Peace" Is Honored.
..."Pace of Peace" Is Established.
...Passion For God Is Restored.
...Patience Toward People Is Installed.

3696 The Impact of "Presence"...
Is Immeasurable.
...Comforting.
...Healing.
...Stabilizing.

3697 The Presence of Jesus...Did Not Improve Judas.
Assess Your Impact...To Identify Your Judas.

3698 The Presence of Teachable...
Produces Passion In Me To Teach.
The Presence of Unteachable...
Kills My Appetite To Teach.

3699 Those Who Do Not Improve In My
Presence...Are Unqualified For It.

3700 Your Presence...Is A Seed.
Assess Reactions To You Relentlessly.
Ignored?
Discerned?
Interest?
Tension?

PROBLEM-SOLVING

3701 A Problem Is...
An Invitation To A Relationship.

3702 A Problem Is...
The Golden Invitation of Life.
...To $$$.
...To Honor.
...To Relationship.
...To Reward.
Don't Stay Stupid.

3703 A Problem Is The Hidden Door...To Favor.
A Problem-World...Is A Champion's Paradise.
(Problems Magnify Your Difference.)

3704 A True Problem-Solver...
Will Always Have A Job.

3705 Every Problem Around You...Is A Door To Favor.

3706 Every Problem Is Solved The Same Way...Asking
Enough Questions.

3707 EVERY PROBLEM...
Is Simply A WISDOM Problem.

3708 Every Problem...Has A Divine Explanation.

3709 Every Time You Solve A Problem For
Someone...You Increase A Divine Debt To You.
Isaiah 58...Ephesians 6:8

3710 I Wonder Who "Hears" Me.
Master Solving "Present" Problems.
Then, Train...For The Problems In Your Future.

3711 Problems...
...Are Invitations To Relationship.
...Are Seeds For Favor.
...Decide Your Salary.
...Reveal Your Difference.

3712 Problems...
Are Invitations To A Reward System.
Your Wealth Begins...
When You Solve The Problem Nearest You.
Believe Me.

3713 SOMETHING...God Has Already Given
You...Will Solve Any Problem He Has Allowed.
(David's Slingshot/Moses' Rod)

3714 Problems...Are DOORS...
To Life's Reward System.

3715 Problems...Are Everywhere.
So...
Jobs...Are Everywhere.
A Job Exists...Anywhere There Is A Problem.
Think.

3716 Problems...Are Glorious Invitations To
Relationship.
Problems...Create Introductions To The Palace.

3717 PROBLEMS...Are Invitations.
...To Favor.
...To Rewards.
...To Relationship.
...To Show Honor.
...To Reveal Your Heart.

3718 Problems...Are Seeds For Divine Rewards.
Joseph/Pharaoh
Esther/Haman

3719 Problems Are Solved...
At The Speed of Your Questions.
Simple, Yet Profound.

3720 Problems...Determine Who Thinks You Are
Important.

3721 Problems Do Not Always...Require Prayer.
Problems Always...Require A Decision.

3722 Every Mountain Requires...
A Different Command.

3723 If You Are Not Solving Problems...
You Are A Problem.

3724 Rebekah's-Diary~
It All Started When I Offered To Solve A
Problem...For An Old Man.
He Made Me A Wealth Manager.

3725 The Problem God Created You To Solve Is
Called...Your "Assignment."

3726 Wall-Street-Protestors~
When You "Happen"...Do You Solve A Problem,
or Create One?

3727 The Problem You See...
Reveals Your Opportunity.
Your Reaction To It...
Reveals Your Character.

3728 Until Someone Has A Problem...
You Are Unnecessary.
Think.
Twice.

3729 When You Solve A Problem For Me...You Create
Favor.
When You Create A Problem For Me...You
Create A Memory.

3730 When You Solve A Problem...You Birth A
Reward.
When You Ignore A Problem...You Lose Access.

3731 Wherever There Is A Problem...
There Is A Future.

3732 Wherever There Is A Problem...
There Is A Job.
Wherever There Is A Job...There Is
Opportunity To Create Credibility.

3733 Who Has The Problem...
You Are Qualified To Solve?
Do They Know You Can Solve It?

3734 Whose Problems...Have You Decided To Solve?
The Key To Life.

3735 WHOSE Problems...Matter Most To You?
What Is The Proof...That You Care?
What Has Been Your Investment...To Solve
Them?

3736 Your Problem...Has A Solution.
Your Problem...Will Birth A Good Change.
Your Problem...Contains A Hidden Reward.

3737 Your Problem...Is A Wisdom Problem.
Your Problem...Should Inspire Questions.
Your Problem...Will Be A Turning-Point.

3738 Your Problem...Is Actually A Seed For
Financial Increase.
Every Problem...Has A Scriptural Exit.

PRODUCTIVITY

3739 I Despise...Laziness.
I Despise...Laziness.
I Despise...Laziness.
I Despise...Laziness.

3740 Increasing Speed Does Not Increase...Accuracy.

3741 If You Are Willing To Follow A Checklist...You
Can Succeed Anywhere.
If You Refuse...Nobody Needs You.

3742 Productivity~
The More Frequent Your "No"...The More
Powerful Your "Yes" Will Be.

3743 Productivity~
What You Stop Doing...
Determines What You Will Complete.

3744 The Harvest of Favor Grows Best...
In The Field of Productivity.

3745 The Productive Man...Never Forgets
A Slow~Moving Woman.
Lazy.

3746 The Unproductive...Qualify For A Reaction.
"Every Tree That Bringeth Not Forth Good
Fruit Is Hewn Down/Cast/Fire."

3747 There Are 10 Ways...To Get Anything Done.
Do Not Stop Thinking...On #1.

3748 Your Productivity...Has Explained Your Life
Philosophy.

PROMOTION

3749 You Can Only Be Promoted By
The Person...Authorized To Instruct You.
Few-Get-It.

3750 Promotion Is A Reward...Not A Miracle.

3751 You Can Only Be Promoted By The Person You
Serve.

3752 Since You Despise "Authority"...Who Have You
Arranged To Promote You..?

PROSPERITY

3753 Anti-Prosperity Often Attacks Those Teaching...
"Blessing."
I Wonder...
"Do You Really Love...POVERTY?"
Why?

3754 Do Not Criticize Prosperity...
Then Ask Me For Mine.
:)

3755 Him: "I Am Anti-Prosperity Christian."
Me: "So...Do You Hate Having Money...or Angry
Because Someone Else Has It?"

3756 I Am Trying Hard...To Understand Why The
Anti-Prosperity Christian Does Not Have The
Same Anger Toward Poverty...Drugs...Liquor.

3757 Name 3 Proofs...That You Have A True Passion
For Prosperity.
...or Shut Up.
:)

3758 Persuasion: Embrace Scriptures
On The Blessing.
Purpose: Tool For Influence.
Problem-Solving: $ Is Reward.

3759 Prosperity Always Begins...With A Problem.

3760 Prosperity...Is A Feeling.
Few-Get-It.

3761 Prosperity Is...Having Enough Provision To
Complete Your Assignment.

3762 Prosperity Is Merely A Weapon For Warriors.

3763 Prosperity Tips~
The Quickest Path To Prosperity Is...
Frugality.
Requires Ruthless, Unbiased Decisions.
Just Do It.

3764 The One Who Unlocks Your Giving...Has
Created Your Prosperity.

3765 Wealth Is Not A Money Word, It Is A Supply
Word.

3766 The Prosperity Gospel...Is The Belief That
Partnering With God Has A Financial Reward.
Malachi 3...Luke 6:38...Mark 10:28

3767 The-Journey-From-Poverty-To-Prosperity~
Put Great Value On Your Time.
~Make Every Moment...Important.
~Read.
~Question.

3768 The-Journey-From-Poverty-To-Prosperity~
Find What Makes You Happy...Then Build Your
Day Around It.

3769 The-Journey-From-Poverty-To-Prosperity~
EXCEL...At One Thing.
...What Do You Want To Know A Lot About?
...Focus.

3770 The-Journey-From-Poverty-To-Prosperity~
Keep A Knowledge Mind-Map...
...What You Want To Learn.
...Questions.
...People.

3771 Your Prosperity Reveals...Who You Trusted.
"...Believe His Prophets, So Shall Ye Prosper."
2 Chronicles 20:20

PROTECT

3772 Anything Unprotected...Can Be Stolen.
Anything.

***

3773 Caution Is...A Divine Fragrance Usually
Scorned By The Inexperienced.

***

3774 "No Weapon Forged Against You...Will Prevail.
This Is The Heritage of...The Servants of The
Lord."

***

3775 You Are Unqualified To Keep...What You Are
Unwilling To Protect.

***

3776 You Will Lose Everything...
You Refuse To Protect.
Think.

***

3777 Your Unwillingness To Submit...Removes You
From The Umbrella of Divine Protection.

***

PROTÉGÉ-TALK

3778 A Disinterested Protégé Is...Not A Protégé.

3779 A Parasite Wants...A Check.
A Protégé Wants...Correction.
Identify.

3780 Admiring Someone...Is Very Different Than
Admiring Their "Gift."

3781 Dear Protégé~
I Do Not Keep Speaking...If You Have
Chosen To Listen To Another.

3782 Dear Protégé~
When You Alter The Equation...You Alter
The Outcome.

3783 Dear Protégé~
Your Demands...Will Diminish Your Access.

3784 Every Protégé...Has The Freedom To Choose
Another Mentor. Always.

3785 FYI...To Protégés.
I Fly Across The USA And The World.
Have Never Met A Single "Protester" Nor Seen
Them.
Only On "TV."
:)

3786 Know Your Mentor.
Do Not Substitute Affection...For Obedience.
An Ignored Instruction...Destroys Credibility.

3787 No Rebellious Protégé...Ever Succeeds.

3788 Do Not Read And Absorb Deadly Poison of
Your Critics.
It Is Almost Impossible To Rid It From
Your Spirit.

3789 Protégés~
Some...You Coax.
Some...You Endure.
Some...You Trust.
Some...You Enjoy.
Some...You Study.
ALL...You Love.

3790 A Protégé Will Receive More In A Day...
Than An Employee Will Receive In A Year.

3791 A Protégé...Is Not Someone Who Should Learn From You.
A Protégé...Is Someone Who YEARNS To Learn From You.

3792 Abuse of Access...Diminishes Favor.

3793 ACCESS Is Opportunity
~Joseph...Had One Conversation To Impress Pharaoh.
~Esther...Had Two Meals To Change A King.

3794 Always Study The Qualifications of:
Accusers.
Abusers.
Critics.
Enemies.
It Is Very Comforting.

3795 Attention Given To A Fool...
Merely Builds Their Credibility.

3796 Choose Friends...Whose Opinions Matter.

3797 Confusion Is...A Strategy, Not A Mistake.

3798 Continuously Examine Your Heart For...
Hidden Prejudice.
Errors In Childhood Training.
Flawed Mentorship.

3799 Develop An Addiction...
To The Voice of The Holy Spirit.
Savor...His Presence.
Honor...The Access.

3800 Dishonor...Will Close Every Door Favor Opened.
Never-Forget-It.

3801 An Inappropriate Request...Can Destroy Access
In One Moment.

3802 Do Not Let Any Environment...
Exist Without Your Presence Strongly Felt.
Strongly.
Integrity.
Clarity.

3803 Every Failure In Your Life Will Occur...
Because of Dishonor.
...Marriage.
...Money.
...Ministry.
Advised.

3804 Everyone Is...Memorable.
As A...Giver.
~or~
As A...Taker.

3805 Focus...On 3 Inspiring Images Today If
Exhilaration Is Your Goal.
It Just Works.

3806 I Relentlessly Evaluate...Profit From
Every Single Investment.
~Time.
~$$.
~Energy.
~Advice.
It Is Startling.

3807 If ANYONE Attempts To Read Your Private
Emails/Tweets...You Would Be A Fool To Trust
Them With ANYTHING.

3808 If Everyone Is Equal...Who Will You
Learn From..?

3809 If You Are Forced To Fight...Fight To Win.
Leave No Weapon...Unused.
None.

3810 If You Dream of Helping Many People...
Money Will Become Very Important To You.

3811 Learn Well...How To Defend Yourself.
In Every Way.
Few...Will Fight For You.

3812 Leave No Divine Gift...Unexamined...
Unexplored...Nor Unopened.
NONE.

3813 Make Your World Small Enough...To Raise It To
Its Highest Level of Excellence.
(Too Much Weakens Focus.)

3814 My Love For You...
Will Address Your Wrongs.

3815 My Investment In You...Reveals
What I See.
Your Investment In Me...Reveals
What You See.

3816 Never Ignore An Offense.
It Contains Too Much Information.

3817 Never Make An Unnecessary Enemy.
Dumb...Never Hides.
Ever.
Kinda Reassuring.

3818 Never Permit An Enemy...
To Choose Your Weapons.

3819 Notice...Everything.
Focus...On One Thing.

3820 Remove Anything From Your
Environment...That Does Not
INSPIRE You.
Focus On What Inspires You. Only.

3821 RUN...RUN...From The Unthankful.
It Will Take 6 Months To Recover.
(Financially/Emotionally)

3822 Search Relentlessly For Opportunities
To Demonstrate Honor Toward Others.
Honor Creates Access.

3823 Set Small Goals.
Pleasures Are Immediate...
And Far More Frequent.
(Learned...The Hard Way.)

3824 Some Learn Best Through...
The Rose of Mentorship.
Some Learn Best From...
The Thorns of Experience.

3825 The Quality of Questions...Reveal
The Passion of The Protégé.

3826 The Most Powerful Habit On Earth...
Is Asking Questions.
Daily.
Of Yourself. Others.
Relentlessly.

3827 ~Those Without The Fear of God...
Will Never Admire You For Serving God.

3828 Trust No One...Who Does Not Trust Truth.
That Truth Rewards.
...Government.
...Friendships.
...Workers.

3829 Try To Avoid Shouting Instructions...
To Those Ahead of You In The Race.

3830 Two Classes On Earth:
Do Things...Happen To You?
Do YOU Happen...To Things?
FYI: I Am #2.

3831 When My Words Matter To You...It Shows.
When My Words Do Not Matter To You...
It Shows.

3832 When I Invest 10 Minutes In You, I Can
Then Determine Value of One Hour With You.
Time/Energy=Huge Investment.

3833 When You Stopped Asking...
You Stopped Learning.
When You Stopped Learning...
Your Present Became Your Future.

3834 Where Have You Chosen To Be...
Willingly Ignorant..?
That Is Where You Will...Flagrantly Fail.

3835 Who Is The..."Bully" In Your Life?
Do Not Embrace.
Do Not Honor.
Do Not Discuss.
Resist...Until He Flees.

3836 Whose Counsel Matters To You?
What Present Weakness Could Destroy You?
Who Has Invested The Most In You?

3837 You Cannot "Happen"...Where You Are Not
"Heard."
Think.

3838 Work Relentlessly...Relentlessly...
On Your FAITH.

3839 Your Actions...Revealed To Me What Your
Mouth Would Not.

3840 Your Competence...Established Your Salary.
Your Incompetence...Lowers Your Salary.

3841 Your Future Will Be Much Like...
The One You Admire Most.
(Elisha/Elijah)

3842 Your Harvest...Is Not A Picture of Your
Willingness To Give.
Your Harvest...Is A Picture of Your Ability
To Receive.

3843 Your Questions...Decide What You Learn
From Your Mentor.

3844 Your Reactions...Control The Future of Every
Relationship In Your Life.
Counsel Completed.

3845 Your Unwillingness To Listen...
Removes My Authorization To Teach You.

3846 Your Unwillingness To TRAIN...
Makes You...Unqualified To Reign.
The Fool...Cannot Rule.

3847 PURSUIT...
Is The Responsibility of The Protégé.

3848 PURSUIT...
Is The Proof You Are A Protégé.
(Ruth-Elisha)

3849 Pursuit And Trust...Identify The Protégé.
Not Need.
Not Love.
Not Pain.

3850 Pursuit Is The Price of An Experience.

3851 The Closer You Get...The More You Learn.

3852 The Passion of The Protégé...Determines The Impartation of The Mentor.

3853 The Passionate Protégé...Inspires The Mentor To Study More.

3854 The Protégé...Is Totally Unaware of What He Does Not Know.
...Only What He Wants.
(Elisha/Elijah)

3855 To Protégés~
NEWS...Avoid Problem-Zones Where You Have No Authority.
FOOLS...Compassion Does Not Change Them.

3856 When The Mentor Is Important To You...
~His Instruction Is Important To You.
If He Is Not...Neither Is His Instruction.

3857 Your Ignorance...Does Not Make You A Protégé.
Your Learning...Makes You A Protégé.

QUALITY

3858 Quality Conversation...Cures Depression.

3859 Quality-Questions~
...Need Solitude.
...Outcome-Oriented.
...Caring.
...Circular.
...Non-Positional.
...Relentless.

3860 The Quality of My Friends...
Makes Their Opinion And Approval
VERY Important To Me.

3861 The Quality of My Friends... Greatly Surpasses
The Hatred of My Enemies.
:)

3862 The Quality of My Friends Unleashes Incredible
Self-Confidence In My Value.

3863 The Quality of The Questions...
Reveals The Passion of The Protégé.

3864 The Quality of Your Questions...
Reveals The Depth of Your Interest.
(Solomon-Queen of Sheba)

3865 The Quality of Your Search...
Reveals The Depth of Your Passion.

3866 The Quality of Your Servanthood...
Has Created Your Reward System.

QUESTIONS

3867 A Master Listener...
With The Right Questions Can Ignite
That Spark of Desire Within You...
Into A Raging Fire.

3868 A Single "Question"...Can Instantly Increase
The Value of A Moment.

3869 An Unanswered Question...Often Reveals Even
More Than The Answer.
...Disrespect.
...Deception.

3870 An Unasked Question.
A Missing Conversation.
An Unthankful Attitude.
An Ignored Instruction.

3871 ASK QUESTIONS Until...
~You Know What You REALLY Want...NOW.
~You Can Identify What You Love/Hate/
Fear/Enjoy/Resent.

3872 Ask The Question Relentlessly... Until The
Answer Is Clear.

3873 ASK...Where The Good Way Is.
Walk...In It.
THEN...You Will Find Rest For Your Soul.
(Jeremiah 6:16)

3874 Asking Questions...Is The Most Important Thing
I Do Every Day.
Has Changed My Life.

3875 Every Reoccurring Problem Continues...
Because You Will Not Keep Asking Questions
Long Enough.

3876 Every Significant Question You Ask...Will
Create A Significant Change.

3877 If Your Question Reveals Little Thought...Little
Thought Should Be Invested In Answering It.

3878 Increasing Your Questions...
Increases Your Solutions.

3879 Midnight Questions~
I Wonder What Part of Me...
Is Bringing Sorrow To God..?
What Small Change...
Would Remove The Stress?

3880 MY QUESTIONS...
Impregnate My Environment~
With Explosions of Revelation And
Instant Understanding.
Penetrates/Dominates.

3881 Past Questions...Created Your Present.
NEW Questions...Will Create Your Future.

3882 Does He...Listen To God?
Does God...Listen To Him?
Your Answers Decide Your Heaven/Hell, Sis.

3883 How Are You Measuring Your
Improvements?
What Small Change-Would Make A BIG
Difference?
When Will You Make IT?

3884 Master The Art-of-Asking The Unexpected
Question.
RELENTLESSLY.
(1,001 Wisdom Keys/WisdomOnline.com)

3885 ~What Are You Unwilling To Live Without?
~What Is The Price You Will Pay For It?
~What Must You Change?

3886 ~What Are You Unwilling To Pursue With
Passion?
~What Are You Refusing To Make Your
Life-Quest?
~What Will Your Pride Cost You?

3887 What Are You Wrong About?
What Will Unforgiveness...Cost You?
What Little Change...Could Make
A Difference?

3888 What Change Are You Delaying?
How Important Is Your Credibility
To You?
What Is The Future...You CRAVE?

3889 ...What Hidden Prejudice Is...Robbing You?
...What Missing Conversation...
Could Really Change Everything?

3890 When The Question Is Clear...The Answer
Will Be Also.
(Ask Again...Again Until It Is Clear.)

3891 Whose Counsel Do You...PURSUE?
Who Pursues...YOUR Advice?

3892 What Serious 90 Changes Have You Made In
The Last 90 Days?

3893 Whose FAVOR Matters Most To You..?
WHY..?
What Is The Price To...Keep It?
What Is The Cost...of Losing It?

3894 Your Avoiding My Question...Revealed
Much More Than You Would Want.

3895 Whose Advice Do You...Follow?
Whose Loyalty...Have You Not Rewarded?
Does Accuracy...Really Matter To You?

3896 Questions @ 66~
What Will I Become...Next?
What Do I Have...To Invest In Others?
Where Should I Invest...Next?

3897 Questions Are...The Seeds...For Safety.

3898 Questions @ 66~
Where Do You Seek...
..."Increase?"
...Wisdom?
...Money?
...Love?
...Favor?
...Peace?
...Productivity?

3899 Questions..."Create" Your Answers.

3900 Questions...Can Turn Any Conversation
Into...Another Layer of Knowledge.

3901 QUESTIONS...Cure Confusion.
Questions Hosts Answers On Earth.
I Never Seek Answers.
They Only Work For/Respond To~Questions.

3902 QUESTIONS...Force Reactions, Which Then
Reveal All.
(Nothing On Earth Is...As Powerful As
Relentless Questioning.)

3903 Questions Increase The Value of Your Time With
Others.

3904 QUESTIONS...Make Decisions Easy.
Questions Are Magnets For Information.
Information Is Secret To Making Decisions.

3905 Questions...Make Decisions Very, Very Easy.

3906 Questions...Multiply The Value of Moments
Dramatically.

3907 Questions Often Reveal Hunger...
For Knowledge.
Questions May Reveal Hunger...
For Contention.
Questions Often Reveal Need...
For Attention.

3908 Questions...Summon Solutions.

3909 Questions...Summon Wisdom.

3910 Questions...Will Take You Where You Never
Dreamed of Going.

3911 The Better Your Questions...The Better Your
Decisions.

3912 The Master Secret of Life Is...QUESTIONS.
Ask Relentlessly...Recorder, Pen, Notebook.
One Skill? A-S-K-I-N-G.

3913 The Most Important Skill On Earth Is...
Learning To Ask Effective Questions.

3914 The Most Important Thing I Do Daily...
...Is Ask Questions.
Relentlessly.

3915 The Most Powerful Thing I Do Every Day Is...
Ask Questions.
Relentlessly.
Within Myself.
To Others.
To The Holy Spirit.

3916 The Most Powerful Thing On Earth...Is
A Conversation.
The Most Important Part of A Conversation Is...
Your Question.

3917 The Questions You Ask...
Will Decide The Future You Experience.

3918 The Unanswered Question...
Is An Important Conversation.
Listen Well.
I Do.

3919 What Is..."The Unasked Question"..?
In Your Relationship?
In Your Dilemma?
In Your Stress?
In Your Decision?

3920 What Questions Does He Not Answer?
What Is His Relationship With Pastor?
Do You Know His Financial History?

3921 You Become A Disappointment...
The Moment You Ignore My Question.

3922 YOUR QUESTIONS...
Decide The Speed of Your Learning.
Your Speed of Learning...
Determines How Fast You Succeed.

3923 Your Questions...
Have Created Your Lifestyle.

3924 Until You Ask A Question...Your Information Is Mostly Accidental.

3925 Every Question I Ask...Improves My Decision-Making.

3926 Questions...Expose Liars.

3927 One Question...Can Open 1,000 Doors.

3928 The Best Way To Win An Argument...Is By Asking A Question.

3929 3 Thoughtful Questions...Can Resolve Your Crisis.

REACHING

3930 Adaptation Is...The Burden of The Pursuer—Not The Pursued.

3931 Are You Pursuing...
...An Experience?
...A Lifestyle?
...A Conclusion?
...A Relationship?
...A Feeling?
...A Goal?

3932 Ask...Your Answer Is Present.
Seek...Leave Your "Comfort Zone."
Knock...What You Want Is Hidden From You.

3933 If You Have Not Found...You Have Not Truly Sought.

3934 If You Never Reach...You Will Become A Hostage To Predators.

3935 Only Pursuers...Qualify.

3936 Reaching...Accelerates Rejection.
Rejection...Accelerates Freedom.
Freedom Is...The Seed For Experiences.

3937 Reaching Is A Very Small Price...
For What You Receive.

3938 Reaching Is Not...
Evidence of Your Desperation.
Reaching Is...
Evidence of Your Discernment.

3939 Reaching Is...Proof of Passion.
Everything Unreceived...
Was Not Lawfully Pursued.

3940 Reaching...Is The Seed For An Experience.
...Hope.
...Love.
...Relationship.
...Knowledge.
A Question...Is "Reaching."

3941 Reaching...Qualifies You For Almost Everything.
Just "Reach."

3942 The A.S.K. System~
Ask...3 More Questions.
Seek...Counsel From 3.
Knock...On 3 Closed Doors.

3943 The Hungry...Hunt.

3944 THE UNPURSUED...
Will Never Be Experienced.
Never.
...A Relationship.
...A Conversation.
...An Opportunity.

3945 What You Are Refusing To Seek...
You Will Never Find.
(Jesus/A.S.K./Ask/Seek/Knock)

3946 What You Never Pursue...Will Never Be
Experienced.

3947 When You Know What To Pursue...
You Will "Find."

3948 When You Know What You Want...
You Will Know What To Seek.

3949 You Do Not Qualify...For Anything You Are
Unwilling To Reach For.

3950 What Are YOU PURSUING?
...An Experience?
...Mastery?
...A Friendship?
...Good Health?
...A Feeling?
...A Goal?
...A Change?

REACTIONS

3951 10 REACTIONS REVEAL CHARACTER
Your Reaction To...
~Authority
~Correction.
~Debt.
~A Gift.
~Greatness.
~Injustice.
~Instructions.
~Opportunity.
~Your Mistakes.
~The Bible.

3952 A Reaction...Teaches Far More Than Time.

3953 Class Is...A Reaction, Not A Decision.

3954 Class Is...The Ability To Discern A Fool Without Reacting To Them.

3955 Countenance...Can Be A Costly Reaction.

3956 Dumb...Has An Unmistakable Odor, Hidden In Reactions.

3957 I Entered...As A Door.
Your Reaction...Turned Me Into A Wall.
Bye.

3958 I React...When It Cures.
I Do Not...When It Will Not.

3959 I Study My Bible...To Know God.
I Study Reactions...To Know People.

3960 If You Jerk The Chain, Make Sure You Can Handle The Dog.
...Pearl Harbor/Hiroshima.
...Iraq/Hussein.

3961 Your Reactions...Explain Your Character.

3962 Make Every Reaction...
A God-Moment Today.
Triumph Is...An Hourly Event.

3963 My Reaction...
Decides The Power of Every Experience.
Good or Bad.

3964 My Reaction...
Decides The Strength of My Enemy.

3965 One Reaction...Is More Accurate
Than 1,000 Affirmations of Love.

3966 Reaction...Should Decide Where
You Invest Your Time.

3967 Reactions~
My Thoughts...
Reactions of A Woman...
Inspire A Man To Commitment.
Not Her Desperation...For Sponsorship.

3968 REACTIONS Are...Golden Wells of Wisdom.
They're Reactions To
...Authority.
...Greatness.
...Correction.
...Instructions.

3969 Reactions...Are Instant Answers.

3970 Reactions...Are Instructions.
...For Parents.
...When Dating.
...To Teachers.
...In Marriage.
...For Changes.

3971 Reactions...Are Irrefutable Divine Answers, Even If They Break Your Heart.

3972 Reactions...Are Prophecies of The Relationship.

3973 Reactions...Are Your Greatest Source of Wisdom About People.

3974 Reactions...Decide The Future of Every Relationship.

3975 Reactions...Determine Who Qualifies For Your Time.

3976 REACTIONS...Reveal Everything You Need To Know About Someone.
...To Correction.
...To Instructions.
...To Authority.

3977 Reactions Reveal More Secrets...
Than 100 Conversations.

3978 The Success of Every Relationship...Depends On
Reactions.

3979 Their Behavior Towards You Reveals Their
Perception of You.
Duh..!!

3980 To Know God...I Study The Bible.
To Know People...I Study Their Reactions.
...To Authority.
...To Correction.
...To A Gift.

3981 What KEEPS A Man Attracted To A Woman?
Her Reactions.
Few-Get-It.

3982 You Can Lose Lifetime of Favor...In One
Inappropriate Reaction.

3983 Your REACTION...Decided The End.
...of Favor.
...of Conversation.
...of Relationship.
...of Access.

3984 Your Reaction...Decides The Life And Death of Everything.
...An Offense.
...An Attack.
...Favor.
...Marriage.
...Honor.

3985 Your Reaction...Decides What Happens Next.
Think.

3986 YOUR REACTION...Has Greater Consequences...Than Any Offense.
(So, Invest More Thought Into It.)

3987 Your Reaction Is...A Serious Investment of Your Thoughts, Attention And Energy.
Invest...Wisely.
In Proven Soil.

3988 Your Reaction To A Gift...Is A Photograph of Your Character.
Your Reaction To Gift #1 Decides If You Get Gift #2.

3989 Your Reaction To An Instruction...Decides Your Income.

3990 Your Reaction To An Instruction Determines...
Future Access.

3991 My Words...Are My Investments.
Your Reaction...Is My Return.

3992 Your Reaction To Every Gift Is...
A Description of Your Character.

3993 Your Reaction To Me...
Reveals My Desirability.
Your Reaction To My Needs...
Reveals Your Love.

3994 Your Reaction To My Instruction Reveals The
Importance of My Favor.
Further Conversation Is Unnecessary.

3995 Your Reaction To My Instructions...Explains
Our Future Together.

3996 Your Reaction To My Simple Request...Made My
Decision Easy And Instant.

3997 Your Reactions...Decide The Success of Every Enemy.
Give Them Time To Make Mistakes.

3998 Your Reactions...Will Decide Our Future Together.
Advised. :)

3999 Your Reactions...Will Decide What Continues.
...Argument.
...Abuse.
...Friendship.
...Hunger.
...Mentorship.
...Instructions.

4000 Your Reactions...Are Deciding What Will Continue In Your Life.
...Favor.
...Open Doors.
...Opportunities.
...Credibility.

4001 Your Reactions...Can Greatly Limit The Joy of Your Enemies.

4002 Your Reactions...Decide If I Love or Leave.

4003 Your Reactions...Decide What Stays In Your Life.
...Friends.
...Credibility.
...Opportunities.
...Access.

4004 Your Reactions...Decide Your Success or Failure.

4005 Your Reactions...Decide The Future of Your
Marriage.

4006 YOUR REACTIONS...Explain All Your
Successes And All Your Failures.

4007 Your Reactions...Have Just Scheduled Another
Environment For Me.
Thanks For Clarity.

4008 Your Reactions...Tell Me A Hidden Story.

4009 Your Reactions To Me...
Determine...Your Future With Me.

4010 Your Reactions...Increase My Trust or Removes
It.

RECEIVERS

4011 Everything God Gives...
Is Not Necessarily Received.
You Only Possess...What You
Willingly Received.

4012 Few...Possess All The Gifts God Has Offered.
We Only Possess...The Gifts We Were "Willing To
Receive."
John 1:11

4013 FEW WILL UNDERSTAND THIS...
Learning HOW To Receive...
Is As Important As Giving.
(Gift of Access/Correction/Advice)

4014 I...Am A Door.
A Receiver.
I Have Decided...What Enters or Stays.
I Am A Receiver...of Every Divine Gift.

4015 I Receive...The Blood of Jesus.
I Receive...The Wisdom of God.
I Receive...My Assignment.
I Receive...Peace.
I AM...A RECEIVER.

4016 If You Decide To Trivialize The Protocol of Asking...Do Not Expect A Life of Receiving.

4017 MASTER RECEIVING..!
~Instructions.
~Opportunities.
~Invitations.
~Differences.
~Correction.
~Advice.
~Change.
~Mentorship.

4018 Master...The Art of Receiving.
Receiving...Is Seed For Your Future Sowing.
Jesus...Searched For Receivers.
John 1:12

4019 Never Confuse...Receiving And Taking.

4020 Receiving Is...The Birthplace For Sowing.
Receiving...of Difference/Opportunity/
Correction/Instruction...

4021 The Most Important Part of Receiving...Is Discerning The Value of What Was Given.
Access~
$$

4022 What God Can Give...Rarely Arrives.
What You Can Receive...Always Arrives.
John 1:8-12
Gold.

4023 What You Call A Miracle...God Calls A Gift.
He Searches For..."Receivers."
Are You Mastering The Art of Receiving?
John 1:12

4024 Whatever You Have...Is What You Have Been
Willing To Receive.
(Much More Has Been Given.)

4025 World-Class Forgivers...
Become World-Class Receivers.

4026 You Only Possess...
What You Have Been Qualified
To Receive.

REJECTION

4027 Wouldn't You Feel Stupid...
If A Fool Enjoyed You..?
Duh. :)

4028 Dating~
Rejection...Does Not Stop My Love.
Rejection...Stops The Rewards of My Love.

4029 Rejection Is...
Departure From A Yesterday Season.
(Comforts Abort Your Future.)

4030 Rejection Is...
Divine Purging of A Distraction.
A Miracle...God Scheduled, Instead of You.

4031 REJECTION Is...A Divine Decision You Were
Unwilling To Make For Yourself.

4032 Rejection Is...A Divine Dismissal.

4033 Rejection Is...A Divine Detour Around A
Scheduled Tragedy.

4034 Rejection...Is A Divine Delay In A Human Mistake.

4035 Rejection...Is A Divine Interruption To Your Misplaced Hope.
Think.

4036 Rejection Is...A Divine Ejection From A Small Place.
Think.

4037 Rejection Is...A Divine Interruption of A Human Tragedy.

4038 Rejection Is...A Divine Interruption To An Unexpected Tragedy You Were Entering.

4039 Rejection Is A Divine Opportunity...To Improve Your Future.

4040 Rejection Is...A Divine Opportunity...To Secure An Upgrade.

4041 Rejection...Is A Miracle Before You Asked For It.

4042 Rejection...Is A Recovery System.

4043 Rejection Is...A Second-Chance That God Is Giving You To Sow In Quality Soil.

4044 Rejection Is...A Wise Decision Made By Someone Else.

4045 Rejection Is An IMMEDIATE Solution...To A Future Problem.
Think.

4046 Rejection Is...Divine Closure of An Imagined Door.

4047 Rejection Is...Divine Ejection From Where You Are No Longer Assigned.

4048 Rejection...Is Divine Protection.
Dumb...Does Not Know It.

4049 Rejection...Is Divine Removal of A Future Odor You Have Not Yet Detected. :)
Rejection...Is Divine Removal of The Unnecessary.

4050 Rejection Is...Divine Removal From Where You Were Too Weak To Remove Yourself.

4051 Rejection Is...Divine Surgery: Removal of What Would Destroy Your Future.

4052 Rejection...Is God Making A Decision You Were Too Weak To Make.
:)

4053 Rejection...Is Not Someone Wanting You Out of Their Life.

4054 Rejection Is Someone...God Wanted Out of Your Future.

4055 Rejection Is...Simply Divine Deliverance Through A Surprise Door.
For Real.

4056 Rejection...Is Simply Divine Protection.
I Really Believe This.

4057 Rejection Is...Simply Someone Intimidated By Your Greatness.
Kinda Obvious, Isn't It..?

4058 Rejection Is...Simply The Divine Conclusion of A Wrong Season.

4059 Rejection Is...Simply Unexpected Freedom.

4060 Rejection Is...The Divine Ejection From Where
We Do Not Belong.
(A Miraculous Exit From Yesterday.)

4061 Rejection Is...The Divine Ejection From Where
You Were Overqualified.

4062 Rejection Is The Proof...Somebody Could Not
Master You.

4063 Rejection Is The Reaction of The Weak To...Your
Difference.

4064 Rejection...Is Usually A Divine
Interruption To A Developing Tragedy.
(God Likes You More Than You Like Yourself.)

4065 Rejection Is...When God Abruptly Stops My
Determination To Enter...A Lower World.

4066 Rejection Is...When God Disqualifies Someone
He Knew You Would Not.

4067 Rejection Is...When God Unhooks The Poisonous Fish You "Caught."

4068 Rejection...Is When God Removes Someone Unqualified For The Future He Has Planned For You.

4069 Rejection Is...When Someone Else Removes You From A Danger Zone.

4070 Rejection Occurs...When God Does Not Want Someone In Your Future.

4071 Rejection Occurs...When The Best Part of A Relationship Has Been Used Up.

4072 Rejection Occurs...When The Right One Just Became Available.

4073 Rejection...Schedules Divine Connections. Joseph...Butler...Pharaoh.

4074 Rejection...Simply Reveals Who Did Not Qualify For You.

4075 Rejection...Is A Divine Step Forward.
Joseph/Brothers.

4076 Rejection Is When God Stops...
Someone Who Is Stopping You.

4077 Rejection Is Often...A Divine Interference.

4078 When God Wants To Protect You...He Removes
Someone From Your Life.

RELATIONSHIPS

4079 A Costly Relationship Is...Always Too Costly.

4080 An Apology Does Not Replace...
"Understanding."

4081 An Apology...Does Not Remove
The Consequences.

4082 An Apology...Creates A 60-Second Miracle.

4083 An Undesirable Reaction...Creates A Lifetime
Memory.

4084 Are You An..."Enjoyable Experience?"
How Often..?
For Whom..?

4085 Attention Is...Not Admiration.
(A "Look" May Hide...A Very Different Thought.)

4086 Attention Is...Oxygen To The Soul.

4087 Attraction...Is Not Assignment.
It Is An Invitation...To Learn.

4088 Attention-Seeking...Is An Attempt
To Control Your Focus.
Via~
~Complaints.
~Anger.
~Silence.
~Flattery.
~Insults.
~Disrespect.

4089 Backstabbers...Are Usually In Front of You.

4090 Can I Trust...Your Words?
Are Your Reactions...Mature?
Are You Relentless...To Understand Me?
Does Your Tone...Convey Honor?

4091 Destroyed Relationships...
Occur Because of A Missing Conversation.

4092 Distractions Qualify For...Removal.
Jonah

4093 Do Not Plan A Relationship...Without Including Their Flaws.
Part of The Equation.

4094 Do Not Use Up All Your Energy On Adversaries...Save Some For A Picnic With Your Friends.

4095 Every Relationship Account Moves.
Deposits.
Withdrawals.
Toward Full...
or Empty.

4096 Every Relationship...Contains A Hidden Test.

4097 Every Relationship Has Hidden And Unexplainable Qualifications.

4098 Love...Increases Our Expectations.
Dramatically.

4099 EVERY RELATIONSHIP...Has A Cost.
Energy. Time. Focus.
Sometimes, The Cost Exceeds The Pleasure.
EVERY PLEASURE...Has A Price.

4100 Every Relationship...Has A Cost:
Seen/Unseen.
Some~$.
Some~Emotions.
Some~Time.
Nobody...Is Worth Bankruptcy
In ANY Area.

4101 Esther's Diary~
When You "Enter" Appropriately...
Your Stay Is Longer.

4102 The First 5 Minutes...
Is A Qualifier For An Hour.
The First Hour...
Is A Qualifier For A Return.
The-Esther-Diary.

4103 Every Relationship...Has Rules.
...Known or Unknown.
...Spoken or Unspoken.
...Ignored or Embraced.
...Honored or Dishonored.

4104 Everything You Do...Educates Others About You.

4105 Gentleness...Will Spoil You.

4106 Harassment Is...Not Determination.
One Creates...An Adversary.
One Creates...Admiration.

4107 I Believe:
...A Judas Is Discernible.
...An Absalom Is Predictable.
...An Enemy Is Defeatable.

4108 I Have Never Had An Enjoyable
Relationship With...A Non-Learner.

4109 I Know Not...How To "Read" A Woman.
But, I Know Well...How To "Read" A Man.

4110 I Will Give My Friends...The Stars.
I Will Not Give My Adversary...An Inch of
Ground.
"Neither Give Place To The Devil."
(Ephesians 4:27)

4111 If I Experienced You...
What Would I Experience?
Truth?
Honor?
Kindness?
Self-Absorption?

4112 In Many Relationships...
...One Is A Giver
...One Is A Taker.
Which One...Are You?

4113 Interest...Is Not Proof of Admiration.
Lion/Gazelle
Hunters/Deer

4114 Listeners...Last Longer Than Lovers. Think.

4115 Men Have...Position~
Women Have...Influence.

4116 My Incompatibility With Doubters...Has Lasted
65 Years.

4117 Never Confide...In "The Disinterested."

4118 No Relationship Is...Equal.

4119 Not Every Rose...Is Accompanied By Thorns.

4120 Overcoming The Uncaring...Is A Huge Success.

4121 Odor In A Refrigerator...
Is Explained By The Expiration Date.
Odor In A Relationship...
May Be Explained The Same Way.

4122 Pink Chains...Are Still Chains.

4123 Relationship Banking~
Stop Attempting Large Withdrawals...
Where You Have Made Tiny Deposits.
Inappropriate.

4124 Emotional Bankruptcy...Is The Proof Somebody
Is Draining Your Account.
(You Are The Responsible Banker.)

4125 Conversation...Is Not Relationship.
Understanding...Is Relationship.
(Twitter Can Give Illusion of Relationship.)

4126 LOVE Is...
The Unexplainable Desire To Be Owned.

4127 "Drip-Drip" Conversation Will Not Create...
An Ocean of Understanding.

4128 Relationship~
Hope...Is An Electrifying Seed.

4129 Do Not Invest...Proportionately.
Invest Your Very Best.
Each Relationship.
Accurate Feedback.
Fast.

4130 I Will Always Read Your History...
Before I Believe Your Prophecies.

4131 The Greatest Wealth On Earth...
Is The Friendship of God's Best.
I Am Speechless...At The Quality of My Friends.

4132 When The Music Stops...Leave.

4133 When You Understand Their Past
Experiences...
...You Will Understand Their Present
Behavior.
Really Important.

4134 You Want Me To Grade You...
Without A Test..??

4135 Your Expectations of Me...Are Your Own.
Not Mine.
Advised.

~

4136 Your Reactions...Have Become
Divine Instructions.

~

4137 Relationship Controlled By Discernment Is...
An Illusion.
Conversation...Unlocks Us.

~

4138 Relationship Is...An Investment.
...of Energy.
...of Time.
...of Thoughts.
...of $$.
Examine Profit And Loss Statements.

~

4139 Relationship...Is A Recovery System.

~

4140 Relationship Protocol~
~I Do Not Answer To "Hey!"
~I Am Not Moved By Tears/Perfume.
~I Do Not Always Answer The Phone.

~

4141 Do Not Build A Room...For Those Who
Simply Drop By Your Life.

4142 RELATIONSHIP-KILLER:
~When You Demand From Someone...
Something They Do Not Possess.
(Time-$$-Love-Romance-Servitude)

4143 Close Doors...Gently. Always.
Close Doors...With Promises Fulfilled.
Close Doors...In Tone of Honor.

4144 Demands...Diminish Access.
Inappropriate Demands...Destroy Access.
Counsel Delivered.

4145 I Do Not Fear...Your Anger.
I Fear...Mine.

4146 I Do Not Stay On A Highway...
That Destroys My Car.
I Take A Different Road.

4147 RELATIONSHIPS:
Imagine Depositing $$ Daily~
Only To Discover One Year Later~
The Bank Put It In
The WRONG ACCOUNT And You Lost
It All?
DISCERN.

4148 Relationships~
I Measure Growth By...
...What I Become In Their Presence.
...What They Become Through My Influence.
(Jesus/Zacchaeus)

4149 Freedom Is...Discovering Who You Can Live
Without.

4150 Rules...Create Freedom.
...For Others.

4151 Relationships~
It Will Get Harder And Harder To
Dislike...Someone Who Likes You.

4152 Marriage...Is A Covenant of Consequences.
(You Marry Their History And The Divine
Consequences To It.)

4153 Relationships~
Never Enter A Room...Uninvited.
Never Enter A Conversation...Unprepared.

4154 The Sound of Love Is Very Different Than
The Sound of Desire.

4155 Your Demands...Have Changed
Our Relationship.
More Than You Would Enjoy Knowing.

4156 Restore Relationship?
List 3 Steps That Would Restore Credibility.
If Ignored, Give Others The Opportunity.

4157 SELF-ABSORPTION Is...
The Enemy of Relationship.
Not Mere Attitude;
It Is A Philosophy Toward Life.
Self-Worship.

4158 SELF-CARE...Is Doing Something That
Improves Your Life. SELFISHNESS...Is
Keeping What Really Belongs To Another.

4159 Smart Women...Seek Control.
Smart Men...Permit Their Fantasy.
:-) Joking.
(About The Men.)

4160 Some Want You To Be...A Friend.
Some Want You To Be...A Confidante.
Some What You To Be...A "Ladder" To Their
Future.

4161 Somebody Longs To Pleasure You.
Teach Them How.

4162 The Higher Your IQ...The Fewer There Are Who
Can Enjoy You.
:)

4163 Dating~
The Quality of The Conversations...Will
Determine The Quality of The Relationship.

4164 TIME...Does Not Make You Knowledgeable of
Someone:
Attentiveness...Does.
(To Their Reactions, Honor, Etc.)

4165 DearSon~
Stay In Relationship...Until Her IQ Is
Confirmed.

4166 We All Want Companionship.
If It Is...
Meaningful.
Integrity.
Discerning.
Gentleness...With The Fire.

4167 When Admiration Steadily Diminishes...Prepare
For The Death of The Relationship.

4168 What Kind of "Experience"...
Have You Chosen To Become For Others..??
...Cold?
...Kind?
...Memorable?
...Inspiring?

4169 What Kind of Experience Are You..?
...For Your Mate.
...For Your Pastor.
...For Your Boss.
...For Your Child.
It-Matters.

4170 When The Boat Leaks...Float A Second Boat.
Wherever There Is Intimacy...
Something Is Born.

4171 Who Have You Decided To....
...Protect?
...Heal?
...Train?
...Listen To?
...Ask Questions?
...Ignore?
...Bless?
When?

4172 Who Trained You...
In Relationships..?
Think.

4173 Why Do You Think...You Are An Enjoyable
Experience?
Your Past History Confirms...
Your Expectations Are Easily Met.
It Also Confirms...You Won't Meet Mine.

4174 YOUR PRESENTATION Is...
An Explanation...of Your Perception of Me.

4175 If You Are Easy To Replace...
You Will Be.
The Odor of Incompetence...
Can Only Be Cured By Replacement.

4176 What Makes You...Difficult To Replace?
...As A Friend?
...As An Employee?
...As A Mate?
...As A Date?
...As A Confidante?

4177 Once You Have Been Treated Right...You Will Never Permit Being Treated Wrong.

4178 Happy People Are Wonderful For Relationships. Unhappy People Are Marvelous Resources For Ideas.

4179 Uncommon Friends...Create An Uncommon Life.

4180 Dating Is...Exploring For A Lifetime Investment.
Searching For A "Qualified" Owner.
:):)

REPENTANCE

4181 Leaders~

Confessing Laterally...Creates Chaos.

Confessing Upward...Creates Comfort.

4182 Repentance Is...The Seed For Recovery.
"If You Repent...I Will Restore You..."
(Jeremiah 15:16, 19.)

4183 The First Proof of Repentance...
Is To Repay Those You Have Wronged.
(Zacchaeus)

4184 The First Proof of Repentance Is...Restitution.
(Zacchaeus/Returned 4 Fold of Overtaxation)

4185 The Proof of Repentance...Is Change.

4186 Those Without Regrets...Are Also Without A
Conscience.

REQUEST

4187 A Single Request...Reveals
An Ocean of Knowledge.

4188 An Inappropriate Request Is...
Never Forgotten.
Your Costliest Mistake.

4189 An Inappropriate Request...
Reveals An Inappropriate Person.
The Signs Are There.

4190 An Inappropriate Request...Destroys Your
Credibility.
Credibility Is...The Highest Currency
On Earth.
Advised.

4191 My Request...Was Your Test.

4192 Say No...
...To Inappropriate Requests.
...When It Breaks The Rhythm of Your Day.
...To The Unproven.
...When The Spirit Warns.

REST

4193 Fatigue...Will Change Your Goals.
Rest...Is A Command.

4194 Rest...Changes Your Decisions.
Radically.

4195 Rest...Guarantees The Return of Hope.
Hopeless People Are Always...
TIRED People.

4196 Rest Is...A Receiving Position.

4197 Rest...Is A Significant Achievement.

RETALIATION

4198 Retaliation...Creates A Feeling,
But Not Your Future.

4199 Retaliation...Creates Energy For An Event That
Is Over.
Think.

4200 Retaliation...Is A Decision To Keep Evil Alive.

4201 Retaliation...Is Proof You Were Damaged.

4202 Retaliation...Is Using Tomorrow
Energy On A Yesterday Project.

4203 Revenge Focuses Your Life Energy
To Move...BACKWARDS.
Kinda Dumb.

4204 The Trap of Retaliation Is Ever Subtle...Yet,
Impossible To Hide.
Just FYI.
Loss In Favor Is...Profound.

REWARD

4205 DO YOU EXCEL...WHERE YOU ARE?
You Are In Your Test Zone.
You Are Qualifying For "The Reward Zone."

4206 Goliath: "I Am Your Biggest Problem."
David: "Nah, You Are My Happiest
Problem."
David: "First Rocky" :)

4207 Dog-Talk~
I Refuse To "Roll Over" For An Owner...
Who Does Not Reward Me.
Politics
Government

4208 Energy Is The Immediate Reward...For Being
Where You Belong.

4209 IF EVERYONE IS TREATED EQUAL...
How Do You Reward Loyalty?
Competence?
Passion?
Determination?
Faithfulness?

4210 OVERCOMING...
Has More Rewards Than Forgiveness.
(Revelation 3)

4211 Rewards of An Enemy:
~Expose The Judas In Your Life.
~Makes You Attentive To Accuracy.
~Confirms Loyalty of True Friends.

4212 REWARDS of KNOWLEDGE~
Stops Painful Losses/Experiences.
Explains Past Failures.
Creates Pleasures.
Makes Success Easier/Quicker.

4213 Small Changes...Can Create Huge Rewards.
Huge.

4214 The Kingdom of God...Is A Divine Reward
System.
My Persuasions~

4215 The Reward of Integrity Is...Fearlessness.

4216 The Reward of Truth...Is Instant Peace.
The Proof of Error...Is Instant Confusion.

4217 What Are The REWARDS of A Friendship With You?
...Listener?
...Encourager?
...Confidentiality?
...Energy?
Just Think About It.

4218 Your Rewards Are Determined By...Who You Pleasure.
Duh.
:)

4219 Your Rewards Reveal...
The Quality of Your Servanthood.

RIGHT

4220 I Make No Effort...To Be Bold.
I Make Every Effort...To Be Right.

4221 My Hatred of Wrong...Equals My Passion For
Right.

4222 "Right"...Creates More Joy Than "More."
"Right"...Is An Intoxicating Feeling.
Gloriously Irreplaceable.

4223 Mysteries~
The Reward of Doing Right...Is Immediate.
The Consequence of Doing Wrong...
Is Eventual.

4224 Never Strive...To Be "Great."
Simply Strive...To Be "Right."

4225 Right Decisions...Create Instant Peace.

4226 Right...Does Not Always Win.
The Prepared...Win.
(Cain/Abel...Ahab/Naboth...
Stephen/Stoning)
LEARN.

4227 Right Is...Not The Decision of A Crowd.

4228 Right People...Are Problem-Solvers, Not
Problems.

4229 RIGHT PEOPLE...Birth GLAD Seasons.
(Joseph/Boaz/Rebekah/Abigail)

4230 Right People....Can Be Trusted.
Anywhere.
Anytime.

4231 Right People...Place Great Value On Your Time.

4232 Right People...Place Huge Importance On
Dependability.

4233 Right People...Will Discern Your Value.
Nobody Else...Matters.

4234 Right Questions...Dismantle Every Crisis.

4235 Right Questions...Fix Anything.
Believe It. ASK.

4236 The Master Secret To EVERY Dilemma Is...To
Ask Enough Questions.

4237 Right Questions...Make Decisions Easy.

4238 Right Words...
Are Bridges To Favorable Change.

4239 Right Words...
Can Change Consequences.
(i.e. Repentance of Thief On Cross/
Nineveh)

4240 Right Words...
The Greatest Investment On Earth.

4241 Right Words...Are The Oxygen That Decides
How Long A Relationship
Will Stay Alive.

4242 Right Words...Decide The Longevity of
Every Relationship.

4243 What Was...The Legitimate Instruction?
Who Ignored...The Instruction?
What Should Be Done Next?
Who Owes...Who?

4244 Right Words...Without Right "Timing"...Are
Wrong Words.

4245 The First Responsibility of Being Right...Is
Correcting Those Who Are Wrong.

4246 The Right Cause...Never Guarantees Victory.
Never.
The Right Strategy...Guarantees Victory.

4247 The RIGHT Man Values Customized Training.
You Are The ONLY Qualified Trainer.
You Teach By What You Permit.

4248 The Right Man...Will Be Costly.
And...Worth It.

RIGHT ONE

4249 Most Men Are Not Attentive. At All.
The Right One...Will Notice Almost
Everything.
...Including Lies.

4250 One Right Voice...Can Conquer The Pain of
10,000 Wrong Voices.

4251 The Right One Will Not...
ENDURE Your Difference.
The Right One Will...
REQUIRE Your Difference.

4252 The Right One...
...Comforts Your Heart.
...Stimulates Your Mind.
...Excites Your Body.
...Empowers Your Spirit.

4253 The Right One...
Does Not Happen Until The "Game"
Becomes Your...QUEST.

4254 The Right One~
...Makes You Want To TALK/Every Secret.
...Unlocks Energy For Your Dreams.
...Makes You Long To Be "Owned."

4255 The Right One...
Will Immerse Herself In Your Goals...
If She Has Discerned You
As Her Divine Assignment. (Ruth)

4256 The Right One~
...Will Not Ask Inappropriate Questions.
...Attempt "Control By Contact."
...Evade Direct Questions.

4257 The Right One...Is Not Dangerous.
...Removes Fear.
...Is Easy To Trust.
...Inspires Conversation.
...Feels Your Pain.

4258 The Right One...Wants To Know Your Wisdom.
The Wrong One...
Wants To Know Your Weakness.
(Delilah/Queen of Sheba)

4259 The Right One...Will Discern You,
Too~Unless...You Have Been Asking God...For
His Most Ignorant.

RUTH

4260 Ruth's Diary~
If You Do Not Enjoy His Field...
You Will Not Enjoy His Future.

4261 Ruth's Diary~
Ruth Qualified In The Workplace...
Before Boaz Qualified Her For His Bedroom.
Few-Get-It.

4262 Ruth...Made Herself Available,
Not Unavoidable.
Boaz Made The Decision.
Ruth Created The Option.
Boaz Made The Decision.

SAILOR'S JOURNAL

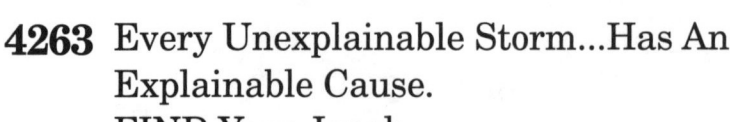

4263 Every Unexplainable Storm...Has An
Explainable Cause.
FIND Your Jonah.

4264 When The Storms Come...Find The Rebel Who
Boarded Your Ship.
Jonah On Board.

4265 When Wrong People Leave Your Life...
Wrong Things...Stop Happening.
Jonah Overboard.

SEASON

4266 Do Not Rush Away From Your Present
Season...Until You Have Discovered The Gold
Hidden Within It.
Wisdom.
Favor.
Mistakes.

4267 Look For The Hidden Stream...
In Your Desert Season.
"He Cutteth Out Rivers...Among The Rocks..."
(Job 28:10).

4268 One Wrong Person...Can Launch A Deadly
Season In Your Life.
Schedule Your Next Season...
With Someone Who Knows Your Value.

4269 The Difference In Seasons...Is
Who Likes You.
(Ruth/Boaz...Esther/King...Joseph/Pharaoh)

4270 You Do Not Have To Change Yourself...
To Change Your Seasons.
(Joseph...Esther...Daniel...)
Thrillingly True.

4271 SEASONS Are Scheduled By
~A Decision.
~Reaching.
~Recognition of Your Difference.
~An Instruction.
~Embracing A Quest.

4272 The Most Dangerous Season In Life Is When
You Do Not Have A Need.
God Seems...Unnecessary.
Your Faith Is...Unused.

4273 Was Your Present Season Scheduled...By Your
Faith or By...
Your Impatience..?

4274 What If Something You Are Reaching/ Racing
Toward...Was Hidden In Your Present?
Undiscovered?
Unexplored?
Unnoticed?

4275 What If This Present Small Test...
Was Actually The Big Test...
Just Before The Blessing..?
(Joy Comes In Morning..!)

4276 What If Your Present Season...Was Actually
Your Future...Awaiting Your
Recognition of Its Hidden Gold?
What If..?

4277 When The Music Dies...It Is The Season For A
New Song.
Motivation.
Disappointment.

4278 Your Next Season Begins...
One Person From Now.
Joseph/Pharaoh
Ruth/Boaz
Esther/King
Change

4279 Your Next Season Begins...
One Question From Now.

SECRETS

4280 Extraordinary Secrets...Lie Well Hidden In
Ordinary Moments.

4281 Golden Secrets...Are Hidden In Hard Places.

4282 Intimacy...Is The Nest For Secrets.

4283 Master Secret~
Many Do...All They Can Do.
The Wise...Focus On Doing What Others Cannot
Do.
Think.
Again.

4284 Scripture Nobody Believes.
"God Will Do Nothing, But He Revealeth His
Secret Unto His Servants The Prophets."
Amos 3:7

4285 Secrecy Is Hiding...
What Should Be Revealed.
Discretion Is Hiding...
What Should Be Concealed.

4286 Secret of Life?
Find The Consistent Ingredients of...
One Good Day.
Repeat That Equation...Daily.
24 Hour MasterPiece.

4287 Secret of Life...
Choose One Goal...At A Time.
Invest ALL.

4288 Secret of Success Is...To Live In Recovery Mode.
...From Offenses.
...Disappointment.
...Failure.

4289 Secret of The Queen of Sheba...
Was Not Mere Questions.
She Asked Solomon Questions...
He WANTED To Answer.
Rare.

4290 Create Short Easy Goals.
Fruit? Instant Completions And Pleasures.
Focus On 24 Hour MasterPiece Days.

4291 ~Identify WHAT Inspires You.
~WHO...Inspires You.
~How You Become Inspired.
Build.
Permit Others To Die.

4292 Pour Mentorship Into 12 Who Honor
You Most.
Invest Into Most Trusting Protégé.
Create Unique Reward System ACCESS.

4293 Wrap Every Conversation...
With The Sound of Gratitude.

4294 Secrets-of-Life...Ask Questions...
Relentlessly.

4295 Secrets-of-Life...Solve The Problem Closest To
You...Cheerfully.

4296 The Secret To All Success Is Simple: Effective
Listening.
I Really Believe This.
Almost Nobody Does.

4297 The Secret To Wisdom Is Simple...
A Question.
Increase Your Questions...
Increase Your Wisdom.
No Mystery, Really.

4298 Love...Is The Secret To Life.
Everything Else...Is An Experiment.

4299 When You Learn How To Keep Yourself
Inspired...You Have Learned The Golden Secret
of Life.

4300 Jesus Made No Attempt To Help Anyone...
Who Distrusted Him.

4301 Jesus Never Allowed His Own Compassion...
To Hold Him Hostage To Expectations.
Lazarus Dead 3 Days.

4302 Jesus...Never Chased A Non-Follower.

4303 Jesus Taught...The Multitudes.
Jesus Trained...The Twelve.
Jesus Taunted...The Scorners.

4304 Never Invest...In The Disinterested.
...Attention.
...Time.
...Energy.

4305 Questions...Are The Quickest Way To Expose A Deceiver.

4306 Questions...Silence Fools.

4307 Remain Poised At Mealtimes With...Your Judas.

4308 You Cannot Always Train...Those You Love.
You Can Always Train...Those Who Receive.

4309 The Smaller Your Circle...
The Greater Your Joy.
The-Secrets-of-Jesus.

SEED

4310 An Unassigned Seed...Is Still Awaiting Your Instruction.

4311 Any Good Thing That You Do For Another Person..."The Same"...You Will Receive From The Lord.
I Believe This.
Ephesians 6:8

4312 Doubt...Is The Seed For Research.

4313 Hurry Is...The Seed For Regret.
Delay Is...The Seed For Your Replacement.

4314 I Believe...In The Law of The Seed.
It Works In My Life.
Whatever You Choose To Believe...
Is Working For You, Too.

4315 I Have Never Regretted...My Seed.
I Have Often Regretted...The Soil.

4316 Law of The Seed~
So...You Disagree With The Law of Sowing
And Reaping.
What Other Plan Do You Have...To Improve
Your Life?

4317 My Seed...
Is The Only Voice My Future Obeys.

4318 Poverty Explained.
"Believe In God.
Be Established.
Believe His Prophets...So Shall Ye Prosper."
2 Chronicles 20:20

4319 Poverty's Worst Enemy Is...The Seed.

4320 Radical Seed...Creates Radical Harvest.
Rolls-Royce Faith...Creates Rolls Royce
Harvests.
Honda Seed=Honda Harvests.

4321 Regret...Is The Seed For Change.

4322 Romance Is...The Seed For Unending Energy.
Energy Is...The Reward For Loving.
Divine Design.

4323 Seed-Faith~
HER: "I Have Given MUCH To God~
He Has Never Given Me A Harvest!"
ME: "Why Are You Telling Me?
Tell GOD He Is A Liar."

4324 Seed-Faith~
HIM: "I Have Given And Given To God... But,
He Has Never Given Me A Harvest!"
ME: "Then, Quit."

4325 Words Are Seeds For Feelings.
Listening Is Seed For Learning.
Knowledge Is Seed For Change.
Conversation Is Seed For Understanding.

4326 Seeds of Honor...Can Create Any Future You
Desire.

4327 Seed-Sowers~
The Soil...Is As Important As The Seed.
Examine.

4328 Seed-Talk~
Hell Is Not Angered By Your Seed...But Your
Faith In God For Your Harvest.

4329 Something You Have Now...Is The "Exchange Price" For Something You Are Wanting In Your Future.

4330 Words Are Seeds...That Create An Immediate Harvest.

4331 The Seed of Favor...Grows Faster Than Any Seed For Favor.
Advised.

4332 The Seeds Within You...
Can Create Any Future You Desire.
...Inventory.
...Find Quality Soil.
...Obey Voice of Spirit.
...Expect.

4333 When Seed Does Not Grow...Try New Soil.

4334 Your Seed of Honor...Into The Unqualified Is Even Greater..!!

4335 Your Seed...Is The Only Master Your Future Will Obey.

SELF-CONFIDENCE

4336 The Social Posture of Males...Creates
Their Unjustifiable Self-Confidence.
Think.
:)

4337 There Is No Self-Confidence...Like A Woman
Who Has Found A Weak Man.

4338 What You Like About You...
Creates Self-Confidence.
What You Hate About You...
Creates Humility.

SELF-PORTRAIT

4339 Find The Broken Pieces...
Within You.
Nobody...Is Born "Whole."

4340 If You Are Not Excited About Yourself...You
Have Not Yet Discovered The God-Part of You.
Kinda Sad, Huh..?

4341 If You Can Be Only ONE of These...What Is
Most Important To YOU?
Interesting.
Inspirational.
Fun.
Dependable.

4342 Knowing Who You Are...Keeps You Very
Contented With What You Are Not.

4343 Self-Portrait~
Your Opinion of Me...Matters.
My Opinion of You...Matters More. :)

4344 The Divine Cure For Insecurity Is...Divine
Presence.

4345 Two Classes:
Looks In Mirror...
1) "I Came From An Ugly Gorilla."
Looks In Mirror...
2) "I Came From An Awesome God."
Both May Be Right. :)

4346 Treasure The "You"...That God Sculptured,
Designed, Assigned...To
The Earth.
His Designs...Are Flawless.

4347 YOU~
You Don't Decide What You Need...
You DISCOVER What You Need.

4348 YOU Are A Bank:
7 Accounts...
Energy.
Money.
Time.
Hope.
Health.
Spiritual.
Mind.
Who Makes Deposits? Withdrawals?

4349 YOU Are A LIFE-TRAIN...
Running On The Track of Instructions.
Every Derailment Is Caused By Ignored/
Forgotten Instructions.

4350 YOU Are A Special Treasure To God.
"Obey My Voice...Keep My Covenant,
THEN...You Shall Be A Special Treasure To Me."
Exodus 19:5

4351 You Are...AN EVENT.
Where Should You Happen...TODAY?
Where Should You Happen...FIRST?
WHO...Should You Happen To?

4352 YOU...Are A Bank.
Who Are Your Major Depositors?
Investors?
Borrowers?

4353 You Are Becoming...Whatever You Admire.
(Elisha/Elijah)

4354 You Are Not What You Have Been...Taught.
You Are What You Have...Believed.

4355 You...ARE The Environment.
(Decide To Be The Seed...That Sculptures
The Desired Atmosphere.)

4356 You Are The Only Person On Earth...Who Can
Decide What Is Important To "You."
Startling.

4357 You Are The Seed Into Your Job Environment;
You Either Improve The Equation...or Disturb
It.
You Are...Whatever You Are.
Think.

4358 You Can Have Everything You Need...And Then
Ruin It By Something You Do Not Need.
...40 Extra Pounds.
:) :)

4359 You Can Only Do Something...That You Have
SEEN.
In Room of Your Experiences.
In Universe of Your Imagination.

4360 YOU...Decide...Every...Change...
In...Your...Life.

4361 You Did Not Make It This Far...
Being Stupid.
You Are Not.
Your Brain Is...GOD-Designed.
Remember It...Every Second.

4362 You Never Live...What You Were Taught.
You Always Live...Who You Believed.

4363 YOU Will Always Act Like The Person You
Think You Are.
(Self-Portrait Decides Self-Conduct.)

4364 Your Self-Portrait...Is More Powerful Than Any
Opportunity.

SERVE

4365 A True Servant...Discerns Unspoken Desires.

4366 Hospitality Is...A Ministry of Comfort.
To Whom Are You Assigned?
Whose Comfort...Matters Most To You?

4367 Hospitality Is...A Ministry of Comfort.
Mastered By Abraham.

4368 Servants...Cannot Hide.
Snakes...Can.

4369 Servanthood~
Immerse Yourself...In The World of
The Person You Serve:
~Preferences.
~Agitations.
~Fears.
~Pleasures.

4370 Who Do You Long To Bless?
Master...Doing It.

4371 Servanthood~
The One You Pleasure...Will Choose
Your Rewards.
Nobody-Gets-It.
Joseph/Pharaoh.
Esther/King.

4372 Servanthood Is...First Step Toward Becoming A
Wealth Manager.
(Rebekah/Eleazar)

4373 Servanthood...Is A Serious Investment.

4374 Servanthood Is...The Investment of Your Life.
Study Well...The Soil.

4375 Servanthood Is...The Passion To Fulfill The
Vision of Another.
Easily Discerned.

4376 The Happiness of One Man Is... Sometimes
Worth The Anger of 1,000 Others.
Servanthood.

4377 "The Person You Serve"...Is The Divine
Designated Blesser of Your Life.
Took 65 Years To Grasp This.

SILENCE

4378 SILENCE...Is The Seed
For Misunderstanding.
Conflict...Is Caused By A
Missing Conversation.

4379 Silence During Slander...
Could Be Your Greatest Test.

4380 Silence...Is A Boundary.
A Wall.
A Fence.

4381 Silence Is...A Control Weapon, A Favorite Among
Deceivers.

4382 Silence...Is A Conversation.

4383 Silence...Is Not Mere Temperament.
Silence...Is A Strategy.

4384 SILENCE...Is Often The Seed For Peace.

4385 Silence Is Not Always…Agreement.
Silence Is Sometimes…Hopelessness.

4386 SILENCE…Is Permission.
Abuse.
Government.
Bullying.
Injustice.

4387 Silence…Is Permission.
(I Am Not A Silent Partner In Experiences
Thrust On Me.)

4388 Silence Is…The Least Used Weapon, Yet Often
The Most Potent.

4389 Silence…Is The Loudest Response.

4390 Silence…Is The Odor of The Disloyal.

4391 Silence Never Communicates Agreement.

4392 The Silence of A Man…Often Explains The
Emptiness of His Mind.

4393 Words...Are Life.
Silence...Is Death.

4394 The Silence of Ingratitude...Is Deafening.
The Wise...Listen.

4395 Your Silence...Is A Disturbing Weapon To An
Adversary.

SINGLE-TALK

4396 "Disagreement"...Explains Singleness.
:)

4397 FOR SINGLES ONLY.
Single For 33 Years.
Invest...To Really Know Someone.
Integrity...Is First.
Cannot Build On A Liar.
Explore. Reach.

4398 Reasons For Singleness...
Deception.
Dishonor.
Disagreement.
Disinterest.
Combative.

4399 SINGLE-MAN CHECKLIST:
1) Is She An Occasional Liar?
2) Does Her HISTORY Inspire Your Trust?
3) Is She Excited About YOUR Dreams?

4400 SINGLES..!
If You Ask Someone For A "Video Letter" To
Increase Understanding of Them And They
Refuse...You Received A Divine Answer.

4401 The "Right Woman"...Has No Competition.

4402 A King...Discerns Royalty.
And...It Is Absence.
(Likewise, A Queen.)

4403 A Kiss Is...Not A Relationship.
Neither Is...A Meal or Conversation.

4404 A Single Sentence Is...Often A Powerful
Explanation.
Accept It.

4405 Boaz...Was Not In Moab.
The-Ruth-Diaries

4406 Eve Was Not The Last Woman Who Lost
Her Paradise...By Listening To A Third Voice.

4407 If I Do Not Improve Your Life...I Am Not
Authorized To Stay In It.

4408 ~Manipulation.
~Conversation.
~Complication.
~Agitation.
~Exhilaration.
~Correction.
What Matters Most To You??

4409 Never Trust A Man...
Who Can Forget His Debt.
Nor Woman.
:)

4410 One Hour of Conversation...Reveals More
Than 1,000 Hours of Imagination.

4411 Pursuit Is...A Seed.
Inappropriate Pursuit Is...
An Inappropriate Seed.
Male/Female.

4412 Sexuality...Has Many Rivals.
Servanthood...Has Few.

4413 Since My Presence Did Not Improve You...
I Will Remove It.

4414 Singleness...Remains Because
Agreement Ended.

4415 Some View Kissing...As A Proposal.
Some View Kissing...As A Test.
Some View Kissing...As An Investment.

4416 The More You Talk...
The Clearer The Answer Becomes.

4417 The Right One Is...Worthy of Making
Your QUEST.
(A.S.K./Jesus)

4418 Unequal Investments...Create An Unbalanced
Relationship.

4419 Who You Think Is Your Harvest...Is Often
Just The Soil.
(Where You Sow, Not Reap.)
:)

4420 You Cannot Build A Relationship of
Influence...Without Presence.
...Parents.
...Dating.
...Management.

4421 There Is ONE True Reason You Have Chosen To
Stay Single...
...2 Different Definitions of Love.

4422 You Are...Still Single..?
There Is A Reason.
Probably...A DIVINE Reason.

4423 YOU KEPT TWO PEOPLE...
HAPPY TODAY.
You Remained Single.
(Smile!!! Too Cute)

4424 An Hour of Questions...Can Reveal More Than A
Year of Dating.

SOWING

4425 ECSTACY...To A Giver Is Discovering Someone Qualified To Receive.

4426 Every Giver Is A Magnet...For Parasites. Parasite Soil Is...The Deadliest Trap Satan Has Ever Set For A Giver.

4427 EVERY GIVER Is Searching For The Qualified...To BLESS.

4428 Everything Multiplies. Even NOTHING...Multiplies.

4429 God Always Judges My Giving...By What I Keep.

4430 Giver$~ You Do Not Owe Your Harve$t...To Anyone. Allow Others Responsibility of Sowing... For Their Own Harvest.

4431 If You Are Satisfied With Your Sowing...Be
Satisfied With Your Harvest.
Giving To The "Needy"...Is A Command.
Giving To The "Deserving"...Is Pleasure.
Giving To The "Thankful"...Is Ecstacy.

4432 Is Giving To God...
REALLY Repulsive To You?
Are You REALLY...Angry Over Scriptures On
Blessing?
WHY..?

4433 My Challenges~
Sowing Seed...Has Been Easy For Me.
Discerning Fertile Soil...Has Been My
Greatest Challenge.

4434 Strategic Sowing=Happy Harvest.

4435 The Only Way Satan Can Destroy A Giver
Is...Placing Wrong Soil In Front of Him.
Be Discerning.
Advised.

4436 Whoever Gives First...
Creates The Greatest Debt.
Nobody Gets It.
Master Secret.

4437 Why Keep Sowing...
Where You See No Harvest..?
Seed...In Wrong Soil Is Insanity.
Good Soil Is...Close.

4438 Your Most Productive Soil To Sow...Is Your Local
Pastor.
...Energy.
...Time.
...Money.
Will You Believe It?

STRESS

4439 2 Stress Removers...
"Unfollow."
"Block."
:)

4440 I Never Feel Stressed To Fulfill
The Expectations...of Stupid.
Never.

4441 STRESS...Is Merely A Puzzle To Be
Dismantled~One "No" At A Time.

4442 STRESS...Is Proportionate To Your Caring.

4443 Those Without Your Stress...Disdain It.

4444 STRENGTH...Is The Ability To Remain
Unstirred By World Currents Around You.

4445 Unreasonable Expectations...Create Stress.
No Wise Man Pursues...Stress That Has No
Reward.

STUDY

4446 Never Quit Studying The Divine Mystery...of You.

4447 Reject Nothing...You Have Not Thoroughly Examined.
...A Person.
...An Opportunity.
...An Idea.
...A Change.
...A Belief.
...Mentorship.
...Love.
...Friendship.

4448 Study...Offenses.
Forgive..."Quietly."
Ask...More Questions.
Believe...Conquerors.
Teach...A Learner.
Identify...Liars.

4449 Write Down 10 Questions...10 Minutes Daily.

30 Days.
Unleash Your Genius.

4450 Study Your Bible...To Know God.
Study Reactions...To Know People.
Study Opportunities...
To Know Your Assignment.

4451 Wisdom Excites Me...More Than Dreams.
:)

So...I Explain My Inability To Sleep. :)

4452 What You Study With Great Joy...
Is Where You Belong.

STUPID

4453 Amazing~
Stupid...Is Often My Greatest Inspiration
For Profound Thoughts.
:)

4454 If You Are Stupid...
or Think I Am Stupid...
We Are Not Compatible.

4455 Land of Stupid~
Do Not Enter MY Turf...
And Announce Yourself King.
...or Queen.
:-)

4456 Rebellion...Is The Proof of Stupid.

4457 Remembering Your "Stupid Days"...
Will Keep You Gentle With Others.
Maturity.

4458 Stupid...Does Not Offend Me.
Stupid...Disappoints Me.
:)

4459 STUPID...Does Not Make Someone Your Enemy; It Makes Them A Prayer Focus.

4460 Stupid...Has An Unmistakable Odor, Hidden In Inappropriate Reactions.

4461 STUPID...Is A Bloodline.

4462 Stupid...Is A Decision.
(Not...A Mistake, Experience or Sickness.)

4463 Stupid...Is Not Always "A Condition."
Stupid..Is Sometimes "A Moment."
:)
That Is How I Comfort Myself. :)

4464 The Words of Imbeciles...Rarely Edify.
:)

4465 STUPID...May Actually Be Genius In Disguise; Its Survival Ability Is Unmatched On Earth.

4466 Stupid...Never Remains Hidden.
Fortunately. :)

4467 The Closest Thing To A Devil...Is A Dumb Man.
:)

SUCCESS

4468 #1 Day Success...Key To Life.
Create A "Top 10 Day-Masterpiece."
Ingredients Needed?
Focus.
Completions=Success.

4469 3 Success Keys~
Write Down Instructions...On Checklist.
Follow Checklist.
Report Questions/Needs.
Enough.

4470 Direction...Matters.
Arriving...Matters More.
(The Landing of A Plane Matters More Than
The Flying.)

4471 Every Success Equation Contains...An
Adversary.
Every Success Story...Contains A Judas.
Just Discern Who.

4472 Every Unasked Question...
Delays Your Success.

4473 Where Have You Decided...To EXCEL..?
What Is The Proof..?
What Is Your Reward..?
Who Is Grading Your Progress..?

4474 First Rule of Success~
Put Great Value...On Time.
...Your Own Time.
...Others' Time.
My #1 Agitation: Abuse of Time.

4475 If Success Matters To You...Your "Time" Should
Matter To You.

4476 If You Succeed In Love...
You Have Succeeded.

4477 Measure Your Success...By Your JOY.

4478 Some...Endure Their Experiences.
Some...Decide Their Experiences.
Schedule...Small Successes.

4479 Regret...Is Proof of Progress.

4480 SUCCESS~
Create YOUR Personal Definition.
Identify Circles of Friends...
Comfort...Motivators...Heroes...Wisdom.

4481 SUCCESS~
Picture...Lifestyle You Desire.
Pursue...Mentorship From Who You Admire.
Plan...Changes In Daily Success Routine.

4482 SUCCESS
1~The Proof of Success Is...Joy.
2~Success...Is A Daily Experience.
3~Your Success Is Not...A Divine Decision.

4483 Success~
What Part of The Formula...
Have You Decided To Ignore..?

4484 Success Is...
When You Love What Mastered You.

4485 Success...Is A Daily Experience.
You Alone...Can Schedule It.
Success...Is A "Feeling."
Few-Get-It.

4486 Success Is...A One-Time Event...
With A 24 Hour Fragrance.
A 24 Hour MasterPiece Day~

4487 Success Is...An Hourly Event.
Scheduled.

4488 Success Is...An Opinion.
Continuously Changing.
When Defined...You Find.

4489 Success Is Decided...By Who You Ignore.

4490 Success...Is Hidden In Your Daily Equation.
Every Feeling You Are Pursuing In Your
Future...Was Hidden Inside Today.

4491 Success Is...Not A Divine Decision.
Success Is...Not A Divine Destiny.
Success Is...The Reward For Right Decisions.

4492 Success Is...Not A Miracle.
Success Is...A Decision.

4493 Questions...Create Movement In Your Life.
Profound...If You Believe It.

4494 Success-Secrets~
Whoever You Serve Well...Contains Your Future.
Elisha/Elijah
Ruth/Naomi
Rebekah/Eleazar

4495 The Basic Key To All Success...
Is The Willingness To Say "No."

4496 THE MASTER SECRET TO SUCCESS...
Is Simply Knowing Who To Please.
(Joseph/Daniel/Ruth/Esther/Jesus)

4497 When I Cannot Find A Highway...I Look For A
Road.
When I Cannot Find A Road...I Look For A
Path.

4498 When Success Is Your History...Your Prophecy
Has More Credibility.

4499 You Have Chosen...Your Own Definition of
Success.
That Explains Your Stress...or Your Joy.
:)

4500 Your Personal Definition of Success...Creates
Your Stress.

4501 Your Success Depends On...
...How Quickly You Discover Liars.

4502 Your Success Depends On...
...How Quickly You Discover What You Want
Most.

4503 Your Success Depends On...
...The Pain You Are Willing To Overcome.

4504 Your Success Depends On...
...The Weakness You Are Willing To Admit.

4505 Your Success Depends On...
...Whose Advice You Are Willing To Pursue With
Passion.

4506 Your Success Depends On...Your Focus.

4507 Your Success Depends...On Who Enjoys You.

4508 Your Success Depends On...Who Trusts You.

4509 Your Success...Depends On Who You Ignore.

4510 Your Success Is A Divine Desire...But,
A "Human" Decision.
Think.

4511 Your Success Is Determined...By The Offense
You Are Willing To "Ignore."

4512 Your Success Is Determined By...Who Likes You.

4513 Your Stress Is Determined By...Who Does Not.
:)

4514 Your Success...Is Not A Divine Decision.
Your Success...Is A Divine Reward...
For Honoring Divine Laws.
Think.
Again.

4515 Your Success Is The Decision...of Someone You
Have Decided To Please.
Nobody-Gets-It.

4516 Your Success Is...Waiting For You In Someone
You Decide To Please.

SURVIVAL

4517 Remember~
FLOW...Like Water.
...Especially Around Dissenting Rocks.

4518 Survival...
Is Not The Proof That You Are Improving.

4519 Survival Creates The Illusion...
That You Know Enough.

4520 Survival Is A Yesterday Miracle...
Not A Prophecy of Your Future.

4521 Your Survival Is The Proof of Divine Mercy...Not
The Proof of Your Wisdom.

TALK

4522 Self-Talk~
What Life Topic...Should I "Master?"
What Daily Task...Should I Assign?
Who...Do I "Enjoy?"

4523 Self-Talk...Can Become Your Most Effective
Source of Inspiration.

4524 Self-Talk~ Who Am I...Neglecting?
Whose Friendship...Should I Be Growing?
What Questions...Should I Be Asking?

4525 Talk To Me...I Will Listen.
Talk To Me Kindly...I Will Respond.
Talk To Me With Honor...I May Become
Your Friend.

4526 TALK YOUR FUTURE...
Until You Are Doing It.
"Forget The Former Things.
I Am Doing A New Thing."
Isaiah 43:18-19

TEACH

4527 If You Have A Passion To Teach...Focus On
Someone Who Does Not Know.
:)

4528 If You Have Anything To Teach Me,
...Teach Me Love!
If You Want The Way To Reach Me...
...It Is Through Love..!

4529 Never Teach Anyone...
That You Do Not Love.

4530 Repetition 3 Times Comes From Teaching
Slow/Argumentative People...

4531 Strong Teaching...Does Not Change Your Judas.

4532 Teacher-Talk...
Do Not Teach Anyone...You Don't Love.

4533 The Most Important Person In Your Life...Is The
One Willing To Teach You.

4534 The Non-Listener...Is
The Untaught.
"...The Comforter, Which Is The Holy
Ghost, He Shall Teach You All Things."

4535 THE SEASONS of The Unteachable...Never
Change.
THE FUTURE of The Unteachable...Is
Happening Now.
THINK.

4536 The Skill of The Teacher...Often Decides The
Passion of The Learner.

4537 Those Unwilling To Come Hear You Teach...
Disqualify Themselves For Private Counseling.

TEAM-TALK

4538 I Don't Hire...A "B" Team.

4539 If You Do Not Like My Speed...Do Not Get Into My Car.

4540 If You Want To Do It Differently...
Write Your Own Paycheck To Yourself.
Ain't Gonna Happen.
:)

4541 My-Team-Only~
My Requests...Are Opportunities.

4542 Staff-Talk~
Rebellion Is Not An Event...Rebellion Is
A Person.

4543 Accuracy~
"Righteous Lips...Are The Delight of Kings.
They Love Him...Who Speaks What Is Right."
Proverbs 16:13

4544 Anger...Is A Very Costly Luxury.
Disinterest...May Even Be Costlier.

4545 Avoiding My Question...
Revealed Much More Than The Answer.

4546 Being Hard To Reach...Makes You Easy To Fire.

4547 Difference In Our Goals...Explains
The Disagreement In Our Decisions.

4548 Do Not Ever Forget...
Who You Are Talking To.

4549 Every Problem You Create...
Diminishes Favor.

4550 If You Follow My Instruction...
You Are Never Wrong.
If You Do Not Follow My Instruction...
You Are Never Right.

4551 Every Question You Ask...Multiplies Your
Wisdom.

4552 Nobody...Expects Perfection.
I DO Expect...Completion of My Instructions.

4553 One Completion...Has More Value Than
A 100 Beginnings.
Completers Create Favor.

4554 Some Love...To Talk.
Some Love...To Plan.
Some Love...To Do.
Some Love...To Think.

4555 The Season You Learn...Schedules
The Season You Lead.

4556 The Silence of Defiance...
Does Not Remove Its Odor.
Workplace.

4557 The Squeaky Wheel...Gets The Attention.
It Is Also...The First To Be Replaced.
(John Murdock, Jr.)

4558 The Unwilling...Are "The Unaware."
Unaware...of Consequences.
Unaware...of Reward Potential.

4559 Your Doubts...Create Your Limitations.
Your Mountains...Create Your Opportunities.

4560 When The Favor of Your Leader Becomes
Unimportant To You...Resign.

4561 Your Accuracy...Increases Your Credibility.
Your Credibility...Determines Your Favor.

4562 Your Reaction...To An Instruction Will
Build Your Credibility or...Destroy It.

4563 The Dangerous...Are The Unnecessary.

4564 The Unsupervised...Remain Uncorrected.
The Uncorrected...Remain Untrained.
The Untrained...Remain Useless.

4565 My Pain...Is Your Opportunity.

THANKFUL

4566 If You Ever Smell The Fragrance of
Thankfulness...You Will Want To Live
Around Them The Rest of Your Life.

4567 The Aroma of The Thankful Is...
Intoxicating.
Addictive Really.

4568 The Closest Thing To God On The Earth Is...A
Thankful Person.
Invested Entire Day Into...5.
A Very Happy Day.

4569 The Most Thankful Receivers...Become The
Most Generous Givers.

4570 The Thankful...Are The Qualified.
The Unthankful...Are The Unqualified.

4571 The Thankful...Cannot Fail.
The Unthankful...Cannot Succeed.

4572 The Thankful...Produce Your Joy.

THOUGHTS

4573 A Meaningful Thought...Is Great Progress.

4574 A Single Divine Thought...
Is A University.
Hanging-Around-God.

4575 Boss...Your Mind.
Instruct It. Aloud.
Command It.
Focus It. Ruthlessly.

4576 Your Mind...Is A Clever Servant.
Rule It.

4577 Every Thought...Is An Investment.

4578 Great Thoughts...Are Great Moments.

4579 Great Thoughts Die...In Wrong Places.
Environment Determines What Grows.
Or, Dies.

4580 Choose The Thought...That Masters Me.
I Command It...Audibly.
My Mouth...Rules It.

4581 I "Love"...The Thoughts God Gives To Me.
That Is Why He Gives Me...More.
:)

4582 I MAGNIFY...
3 Different Pleasure-Thoughts Every Day~
Until...Painful "Problem-People" Disappear
From My Agenda.

4583 Injustice Happens Once...
But Your Mind Can Make It Happen 5000 More
Times.
Focus...Creates Feelings.

4584 Mind-Talk~
Make Tomorrow So Huge...
Yesterday Is Ashamed To Discuss Itself.

4585 My Thoughts At 65~
The Greatest Secret To Life Is...
Ask Questions...Relentlessly.

4586 My Thoughts...
Honor...Is The Seed That Flourishes In
Every Environment.
So Want Spirit To Help Me Master
The "Law of Honor."
Solves 90% Problems.

4587 NEEDS OF YOUR MIND:
...A Goal.
...Conversations.
...A Hero.
Invest.

4588 Never Confuse Your Mind...With YOU.
You Are Not...Your Mind.
Your Mind...Is Your "Servant."

4589 Sculpture A Mind...That Rejects Small
Thoughts.

4590 Some Thoughts Are Too Glorious...
To Be Spoken.
Only The Discerning...Qualify For Them.

4591 Some Thoughts Should Remain
Unspoken...Until Those Worthy of Them Show
Up.

4592 The Greatest Thoughts...Are Unspeakable.

4593 The Mind Always Finds...Whatever It Is
Looking For.
Always.
A Reason To Quit or...
A Reason To Finish.

4594 The Mind Without A Future...
Becomes Homesick For The Past.
Command It.

4595 THINK.
Nothing Is...Priceless.
Nothing.

4596 THINK~
Success Is...
Simply Trusting The Right Voices.
Failure Is...Simply Trusting
The Wrong Voices.
Duh. :)

4597 THINK OF ONLY 3 THINGS TODAY.
THAT GREATLY INSPIRE YOU.
3 THINGS...ONLY.
Nothing Else.
Life Will Excite You Again.

4598 Thinkers: The Non-Thinkers Greatest Stress.

4599 Thinking...Creates Changes.
"I Thought On My Ways, And Turned..."
(Psalm 119:59)
~Questions.
~New Goals.
~Decisions.

4600 THINKING...Is Simply Emotional Jogging.

4601 Thinking...Is The Seed For Progress.
What Can Be Improved?
Who Should I Train?
Who Should I Host On Earth?

4602 Thoughts...Inspire Tweets.
Persuasions...Inspire Books.

4603 You Are Only One Thought Away...
From Radical Change.
Every Day of Your Life.

4604 You Cannot Walk Away From A Thought;
You Can Only Walk Toward
A DIFFERENT Thought.
Discoveries.

4605 Your Mental Conversation...
Makes It Bigger And Bigger.

4606 Your Mind...Is An Ocean.
Your Mouth Is An Aquarium
Do Not Confuse Them.
:)

4607 Your Mind...Is Your Servant;
Archiving Memories, Pleasures And
Possibilities Feed:
~A Focus.
~A Hero.
~A Conversation.
~Sounds.

4608 Your Mind...Needs An Instruction.
Your Mind...Is Your Servant, Not Master.

4609 Plane-Thoughts~
Thinking...Reveals Hidden Longings.

4610 Plane-Thoughts~
Thinking...Produces Movement.
A Shift.
A Departure.

TIME-MANAGEMENT

4611 5 Timesavers~
"I'm Sorry."
"I Misunderstood."
"I Forgot."
"I'm Confused."
"Forgive Me."
Two-Word Genius.

4612 10 Minutes Invested In You...Enables Me To
Determine The Value of An Hour With You.

4613 An Apology
...Is A Time-Management Technique.
:)

4614 He Who Steals Your Time...
Has Stolen More Than Your Money.
...With Your Cooperation.

4615 I Know How Important An Hour Is To Me.
What I Don't Know...Is How Important My Hour
Is To You.

4616 Never Wake Me Up.....To Sit, And Sit And Sit.
Never.
Never.
Never.

4617 Procrastination...Is
The Re-Assignment of Time.

4618 Routine...Is Your Road To A Desired Future.
Powerful Secret.

4619 SCHEDULE The Experiences...
That Move You Toward Your Next Goal.
~Conversations.
~Mentorship.
~Reading.

4620 Stuffing Your Mouth...Does Not Make The Food
Tastier.
Stuffing Your Schedule...Does Not Make Life
Happier.

4621 TIME Is...More Important
Than Money.
Money Is...Replaceable.

4622 Time-Management...
A Small Completion Is...More Important
Than A Great Beginning.

4623 Time-Management~
My Clock...Does Not Assess My Progress.
My Completions...Assess My Progress.

4624 Time-Management~
Never Invest Rolls-Royce Time...
On A Honda Problem.
:)

4625 Time-Management~
Never Invest Rolls-Royce Time...
On A Bicycle Problem.
Never.

4626 Time-Management:
~Standardized Reward Systems.
~Simplify Mail Responses.
~Pay Trust (Bills).
~Distribute Authority/Tasks.

4627 Time-Management Tips!
Always Say, It Is...MY Fault.
Saves Two One-Hour Conversations...Daily.
730 Hours A Year.

TITHING

4628 NOTE TO NON-TITHERS...
Distrusting God...Will Be The Costliest
Decision of Your Lifetime.
Money.

4629 If You Do Not Want To Tithe And Give To
God...DON'T.
I Am Sure You Will Offer Him...
The Same Freedom.
:)

4630 TITHING Is...
Not Your Payment of A Debt...
But The Acknowledgment of Your Debt.
...The ONLY Proof...You Conquered Greed.

4631 TITHING Is...The Only Tangible
Documentation of Your Trust In God.
(Surpasses "Feelings"...of Trust.)

4632 Tithe Is Proof of Honor.
God Is Not Poor.
Bring Tithes...Malachi 3.
God Wants Your Honor.

TODAY

4633 Another Day.
Another...Masterpiece In The Museum of
My Life.
Every 24 Hours.
Another Masterpiece.
I Paint.

4634 Beautiful, Peaceful Day...
In The Presence of God.
"His Mind Is Kept In Perfect Peace."
Focus...Chooses Our Feelings.

4635 Choose 3...Small Goals Today.
Magnify...In Your Mind.
Plan A Reward Time...Tonight.
Tell The Person...Who Rejoices With You.

4636 Daily Focus~
Identify 3 Happy Things In Your Life...And
Build Your DAY Around Them.
EVERY Day.
Inspiration.

4637 Day Test~
What Happened Today...That You Should
Make A Habit..?
What Happened Today...That Should Never
Happen Again?

4638 Day-Analysis~
What Have You Decided...
...To Remember?
...To Forget?
...To Do Again?
...To Do Differently?
...To Ignore?

4639 Day-Power~
Prophesy Your Day. (Assign A Theme.)
Create A Knowledge-Map.
~What To Learn.
~Questions To Ask.

4640 Do Not Leave Your Present...Without Mining
The Gold Divinely Hidden In It.
Linger A Little Longer...

4641 Earth Is...Simply A Menu of Possible
Experiences.
Today...Was "Your Choice" of Experiences.

4642 Every Day Is A Painting...In The Museum of
Your Life.
Your Choice of Sounds...People...Words...
Can Make It...A MasterPiece.

4643 Every Day Is...My Harvest~
From A Yesterday Decision.

4644 Every Day...Contains Divine Opportunities.
Identified or...Ignored.
Treasured or...Trivialized.

4645 Everywhere YOU Happen Today...
GOD Should Happen.
Allow Him.

4646 Feelings.
Quality of Friends.
Inner Peace.
Energy.
Hope For Change.
How Do You Grade A "Day In Your Life?"

4647 HAVE A 3-DAY..!!!
3 People...You Really Enjoy!
3...Completed Priorities..!
3 Miracles...You Are Enjoying Today!

4648 I Did So Many Things Right Today...Yesterday
Was Embarrassed.

4649 I Have Decided To...HAPPEN.
Every Day.
Everywhere I Go.

4650 Your Same Ability That Created TODAY...Is
Building Your Future.
Satisfied? Or, Troubled..?

4651 I PROPHESY TO YOUR DAY!
For New Things!
New Ideas!
New Streams of Honor!
New Hope!
New Strategies!
New Connections!

4652 I Prophesy Today~
"You Will Receive 3 Distinct Revelations
From The Spirit...Exposing
One Wrong Person And Two Changes.
One Person Will Become Disqualified Today...For
Your Future Confidences.
Two Changes...Implemented."

4653 I Prophesy!
You Will Have...A "Daniel Week!"
Perfect Decisions And Spirit of Excellence.
Embrace It.
Journal It.

4654 I Prophesy~
Two People Will Leave Your Life
Within 21 Days...
...And Your Joy Will Double.
Journal It.

4655 NAME 3 THINGS...You Did Right Today.
Relax.
Smile.
Savor.
Ignore...Satanic Taunts And Turbulence.
God Is Satisfied.

4656 Prophesy To Your Day.
"Thou Shalt Decree A Thing...It Shall Be
Established Unto Thee..."
Job 22:28

4657 Prophesy...Whatever You Intend To Experience.

4658 Some Days Are...Rewards.
Some Days Are...Seeds.

4659 Simplify Your Days.
Limit Desires.
Identify Small Pleasures.
Sleep Longer.
Become Conversational With God.
Focus.

4660 Some Days...Are Seeds.
Some Days...Are Harvests.
Every Day...Is A Divine Investment In You.

4661 Stop Peering Into The Fog of Life...
And Identify The "Profoundness" of Today.
A Single Day.
Now.
Colors.
Laughter.

4662 Subtraction...Is The Hidden Secret To
Multiplication.
Think.
Until Today Ends...Tomorrow Cannot Begin.

4663 TAKE THIS INTO YOUR HEART...
God Will Speak 3 Times To You...TODAY.
Listen.
Look...For Divine Messages.
Journal.

4664 TODAY.
Lavish Honor...
Into Your Environment For 72 Hours.
Journal...Your Joy.
Assess Changes...In The Aura.

4665 Today...
I Will Downsize...My Problems.
I Will Resize...My Future.

4666 TODAY..!
I Will Paint A "24 Hour MasterPiece."
My LIFE..!
Faces...Energize Me..!
Colors...Inspire Me..!
Sounds...Excite Me..!

4667 TODAY...
...Is Your Resumé...For Tomorrow.
...Is An Opportunity To Qualify For
Your Future.
...Is Your Seed For NEXT.

4668 Today...Could Cure Yesterday.
Today...I Decided To Enter My Future Early.
My Future...Has Been Nervous Without Me To
Instruct It.

4669 Today...I Planted Seed For Tomorrow.
Good Seed.
Great Soil.
Uncommon Harvest.
So, Tomorrow Is...Not Unpredictable.

4670 Today...I Trained For Tomorrow.

4671 Today I Will Reap My Harvest...
From My Yesterday Seed..!

4672 TODAY...Is My Favorite Servant.
She Erased...Yesterday.
She Deposited...1,440 Minutes Into
My Life-Bank.

4673 Today...Is The Best Gift God Has Ever Given
You.
Repair...A Mistake.
Forgive...An Offense.
Invest...In Your Family.

4674 Today Is...The Future That Has Been Waiting
For You.
An Excited Servant.

4675 TODAY...Is The Future You Have Been Planning
An Entire Lifetime.
Were You Effective?

4676 Today Is The Proof...God Enjoyed You Yesterday.

4677 Today...Is Your Servant.
Instruct It...Relentlessly.
TODAY Revealed Your Skill...At
Planning A Future.

4678 Today...Seed of Honor.
Tomorrow...Harvest of Favor.

4679 Today...Was A Divine Table.
You...Chose The Meal.

4680 Today...Was Exactly Like Your Future.
...Unless You Change A Habit.

4681 TODAY...Was The Future You Have Discussed
For A Lifetime.
Was It What You Planned?
What Would You Change?

4682 Today...Was The Future You Have Pursued Your Whole Lifetime.
NOTHING Changes...Unless It Is In Your Daily Routine.

4683 Today....Was Your Opportunity To Build Credibility With Your Boss.
Did You..?

4684 TODAY...Was Your Seed For The Future You Have Been Passionately Describing.
So...What Was Different About It?

4685 What Is Your Greatest Agitation Today..?
What Are 3...Possible Solutions?
Do This...Hourly.

4686 What Were Your 3 HAPPIEST Thoughts Today?
How Often Have You Decided...
To REPEAT Them?
Thoughts...Are Directional.

4687 Whatever You Learned TODAY Is...The Only Thing That Will Make Tomorrow Different.
Think.

TOMORROW

4688 Another 24 Hour MasterPiece.
I Paint...With Freedom...Laughter...
Comfort...Rest.
Better Than Ever.
Gold.

4689 When You Get To Where You Are Going...
Where Will You Be?

4690 Tomorrow...Another Wave of Harvests From My
Lifetime of Sowing.
Wow.

4691 Tomorrow Begins...One Decision From Now.

4692 Tomorrow...I Will Succeed.
Again.
I Do It...Every 24 Hours.
Another...MasterPiece.

4693 Tomorrow Is...
The Divine Cure For Yesterday
Goals.

4694 Tomorrow Is...Your Servant.
Instruct It.
Clearly.
Decisively.
It Knows It Is A Divine Gift...From God
To You.

4695 TOMORROW...Is Your Future.
Duh.
:)
Think.

4696 Tomorrow...Will End Today.
And...That Is A Good Thing.

4697 What Are 3 Things That INSPIRE YOU..?
Keep Those PICTURES...
In Your Mind All Day Tomorrow.
That Is "The Secret of Life."

4698 What Will Make Tomorrow...
Totally Different Than Every
Previous Day In Your Life?

TRIVIALIZE

4699 I Never Trivialize...
The Achievements of Others.

4700 I Never Trivialize...
The Opinions of Those I Love.

4701 I Never Trivialize...A Divine Instruction.

4702 I Never Trivialize...A Lie.

4703 I Never Trivialize...A Threat.

4704 I Never Trivialize...Disrespect.

4705 Trivializing The Desires of Your Leader...
Launches A Search For Your Replacement.

TRUST

4706 3 ZONES of TRUST
Caring...(Mother).
Competence...(Surgeon).
Character...(Mate).

4707 A Single Act of Betrayal Can Sabotage Years of
Bonding.
Trust Is A Gift.
Guard It.

4708 A Trustworthy Person...
Is God's Fifth Greatest Gift To You.
Jesus. Bible. Life. Access.

4709 Elijah Papers...
Your Legacy Is...
In The One Who Trusts You.
(Elijah/Elisha)
Truth.

4710 I Trust No Man...Who Is Cruel To Another.

4711 I Trust No One...
Who Is Incapable of Anger.

4712 I Love...Everyone I Trust.
I Do Not Trust...Everyone I Love.
Think.

4713 I Will Trade The Counsel of 100 Experienced
People...For One Voice I Trust.

4714 My Greatest Treasure...Is The Discovery of A
Trustworthy Person.

4715 Never Trust Anyone...
Who Can Forget A Debt.
Never Trust Someone Who Does Not
Love You.
Never.

4716 Never Trust...Your Instincts.
VERIFY...Your Instincts.

4717 No Feeling On Earth...
Compares With Trust.

4718 Distrusting The Right Voice...Is The Deadliest
Mistake You Will Ever Make.
Eve/God

4719 No Greater Pleasure...Than The Company of A
Trustworthy Person.

4720 The Difference Between Seasons...
Is Who TRUSTS You.
Few-Get-It.

4721 The Voice You Trust...
Has Created Your Future.

4722 Those I Cannot Trust...
May Find Me An Unhappy Experience.

4723 Those Who Do Not Cherish Trust...
Rarely Become Trustworthy.
In You.
In Themselves.

4724 Those Who Do Not Trust Me...
Have No Place In My Future.

4725 Trust Is Rarely Valued. Ever.
Proof? Little Effort To Build/Maintain It.
No Regret When Lost.
Forgiveness Is Goal/Not Trust.

4726 TRUST 7 TEST:
Can You Trust His~
Competence?
Caring?
Character?
Discretion?
Accuracy?
Decisions?
Discerning?

4727 Trust Any Man...Persuaded of His Own
Ignorance.

4728 Your Deadliest Mistake In Life...Is Trusting The
Wrong Person.
Caution...Is The Seed For Safety.

4729 Trust...Can Be The Costliest Experience of Your
Lifetime.

4730 Trust...Produces Peace.
Distrust...Produces Stress.

4731 Trust...Creates Credibility.
Credibility...Creates Access.
Access...Creates Opportunity.
Opportunity God's Greatest Gift.

4732 Trust Nobody...
Who Can Hide Their Enjoyment of You.
;)

4733 Trustworthiness...
Makes Lifetime Friendships.

4734 Trustworthiness...
Decides The Lifetime of A Friendship.

4735 Your Trustworthiness...Makes Your Love
Believable.

4736 Someone You Trust...Is Trusting Someone You
Don't.

TRUTH

4737 A Drop of "Real" Satisfies Me...
More Than An Ocean of Ceremony.

4738 Fall In Love With Truth...It Has Immediate
Fruit.
Truth Has A Fragrance...Error Has An Odor.

4739 Knowing Truth...Creates An Indescribable
Responsibility.

4740 Slither Is...Any Snake Navigation Used To
Deceive Another of The Truth.

4741 Truth...Agitates Liars.
Truth...Infuriates Deceivers.
Truth...Excites The Trustworthy.
Study Reactions.
Relentlessly.

4742 Truth...Has Never Failed To Excite Me.
Ever.

UNDERSTANDING

4743 I Cannot Understand...What You Cannot
Explain.

4744 The Willingness To Listen...Is Different Than
The Ability To Hear.
Listening...Is Not Proof of Understanding.

4745 Understanding...
When I See Who Misinterprets Me...
I Wonder How Many I...Am Not Understanding
Either.
I Am So Sorry.

4746 Understanding...Is Not Permission.
"I Understand Why You Would..."

4747 Who God Authorizes You...To Love~
He Empowers You...To Understand.

UNTHANKFUL

4748 Do Not Make "The Unthankful"...
Your Focus.
Simply..."Re-Gift."
:)

4749 I Do Not Want Any Relationship With...
The Unthankful.
At Any Level.

4750 Neither Beauty Nor Sensuality...Ever Removes
The Stench of Unthankfulness.

4751 Santa Just Laughed...
...When I Handed Him "My List of My
Unthankful Friends."
Said I Saved Lot of $$.
The Unthankful...Are.
Duh. :)
FYI.

4752 The Unthankful...Are Never Well-Hidden.

4753 The Unthankful...Are The Malaria Flies Who
Thrive At The Campfire of The Benevolent.

VALUE

4754 The Greater The Treasure...The Higher The Cost.

4755 Currency Is...Anything of Value.
Patience...Forgiveness.
The Blood/Cross...

4756 Never Stay Around...
Anyone Who Does Not Know Your Value.

4757 Something WITHIN You Is...
Incredibly Valuable.
Find It.

4758 Those Who Ignore Your Value...Are Disqualified For Your Attention.

4759 Those Who Truly Value You...Value Your Time.
Those Who Truly Value You...Value Your Advice.
Think.

4760 Twitter-Talk~
Amount of Followers Is...Not Proof of Value.
Jesus vs. Ungodly.
Church vs. Evil.

4761 Value~
Everything...Has A Price.
Everything.
Whether You Paid It...or Another.

4762 What YOU Pay...
Determines Its Value To You.

4763 What You Value...
Determines "Who" You Value.
Truth.
Wisdom.

4764 You Do Not Attract...
What You Need.
You Do Not Attract...What You Love.
You Attract...What You VALUE.

4765 Move Mountains...But "Kill" Giants.

4766 Victory Is Not...A Divine Gift.
Victory Is...A Divine Reward.

4767 Your Mountain You Are Facing...
Will Never Reappear.
Ever.
"He Overturneth The Mountains By The
Roots."
Job 28:9

4768 Your Victories Are Hidden In...
The Mistakes of Your Enemy.

4769 WAITING..?
Unasked Questions...
Will NEVER Be Answered.
(Waiting Does Not Produce Information
Questions Can.)

4770 Waiting~
Law of Process...Births The Ecstacy of
Anticipation And Hope.

4771 Waiting...Is Not Absence of Movement.
Waiting...Is Not Absence of Progress.
Waiting...Is Not Delay.
Waiting...Is Seed.

4772 Waiting...Is Not Always Proof of Patience.
Waiting...Is Often Proof of Pride.

4773 Waiting...Is Often A Satanic Tool
To Paralyze Your Reaching.
(Blind Man Cried Out/Woman With Issue of
Blood)

4774 Waiting...Was Created For Slow People. :)

WARRIOR-TALK

4775 Every Warrior Needs A Nest.
Comfort Is...A Magnet No Man Forgets.
Man's Fantasy? Nest Without Thorns.

4776 Every Warrior Needs An Audience...of One.

4777 Every Warrior Needs~
Nest...Without Thorns.
Voice...Without Sarcasm.
Love...Without Fear.
Pleasure...Without Caution.

4778 The Low Quality of Your Enemies...Will
Embarrass You, Not Anger You.
:)

4779 If You Do Not Fear War...Do Not Fear Life.

4780 Satan Decides...His Entry.
You Decide...His Exit.
Luke 4

4781 The Hidden Weapon...
Is The Most Dangerous.

4782 War And Peace~
Integrity And Deception...Cannot Peaceably
Co-Exist.
But, Only Deception Knows It.

4783 War Is...The Fruit of Ineffective Conversation.
Sad. Sadistic. Sick.

4784 War...Is The Seed For Peace.
Ephesians 6

4785 WARFARE Is...Always...To Steal Your
Territorial Authority And Rights.
(Eden/Israel/Mosque/Politics...Your Life.)
THINK.

4786 Warriors Need...
Voice...Without Scorn.
Conversation...Without Disinterest.
Pleasure...Without Caution.

4787 Fearless Is...Not An Attitude;
It Is The Reward For Research.

4788 Fearlessness...Is Not Miraculous.
It Is The Reward For Discovering...
The God Within You.

4789 If God Fights All Your Battles...Why Did He
Command You To Put On Armor..?

4790 It Is Easy To Stay Strong...
When The Others Are Wrong.

4791 Some Fight...Noisily.
Some Fight...Silently.
Some Fight...Lawfully.
Some Fight...Unlawfully.
Know Your Enemy.

4792 Their Weapon Is Not A Command To Fight...It Is
Information To Shield For Protection.
THINK.

4793 My Own Decisions...Have Caused My Greatest
Pain.
...To Trust.
...To Wait.
...To Hire.
...To Ignore Whispers of Spirit.

4794 Never Enter A Battle...
That Has No Obvious Reward.

4795 Never Fight An Unnecessary Battle.
When Forced Into Battle...
Use The Deadliest Weapons.

WEAKNESS

4796 Do Not Feel Ashamed Because You Are Weak.
Be Ashamed Because You Won't Reach
For Help.
Pride Is...Deadlier Than Any Weakness.

4797 Weakness...Excites A Bully.

4798 Weakness...Is In Every Equation.
Acknowledging It...Is Wisdom.

4799 Your Weakness...
Creates A Future For Someone.

4800 YOUR WEAKNESS...
Creates Success For Someone.
i.e. Mechanic Fixes Car You Can't/
Interpreter—Translates Language You
Cannot Speak.

4801 Your Weakness...Does Not Dilute My Love.

WINNING

4802 And The Winner Is...The One Who Refuses To Quit.

4803 And...The...Winner...Is...Whoever Can Keep Themselves Inspired.

4804 And The Winner Is...Whoever Can Stay Focused.

4805 DELUSIONS:
Your Winning Is Not Decided By...
The Love of God.
Your Winning Is Decided By...
The WISDOM of God.

4806 Winners...Believe That Their Own Decisions Made Them So.
Losers...Believe The Decisions of Others Made Them So.

4807 Winning A Battle...Is Wise.
Avoiding A Battle...Is Wiser.

WISDOM

4808 #1 Reward of Wisdom...Is Mastery of Your
Reactions.
...To Criticism.
...To Correction.
...To Greatness.
...To Instructions.

4809 2 Ways To Get Wisdom:
People.
Pain.

4810 A Wise Quote...Does Not Make You Wise.
(Satan/Mount of Temptation)

4811 Difficult Days...Produce Profound Wisdom.
Every Experience Is...
Saturated With Wisdom;
Extract It And No Experience
Can Embitter You.

4812 Hair Is Important~
But Not As Important As My Blood.
Everything Has "Different Value."
Wisdom...Recognizes Difference.

4813 Mystery To Me~
I Wish Those Obsessed With The Love of
God...Would Treasure The WISDOM of
God.
Hosea 4:6/Proverbs 4:7

4814 New Places...Require New Wisdom.
Yesterday Instructions...Are Obsolete.
(Very Hard To Learn...
The "Purpose" of New.)

4815 Profound Sadness...
Is The Seed For Profound Wisdom.

4816 The Dominant Reward of Wisdom Is...
Recognizing Who You Should Honor.
Difference Between...The Wise...
And The Fool.

4817 THE WISDOM...You Need Depends On Where
You Are On Your Journey.
(Needs Differ.
Monday Manna...Does Not Arrive Sunday.)

4818 The Wise...Fight Endlessly To Establish Their
Credibility.
The Fool...Seeks Acceptance Without
Research.

4819 The Wise...Never Walk Through "Closed" Doors.
The Fool...Never Sees The "Open" Door.

4820 The Wise...Write Their Own Horoscope.

4821 Trouble Is...My Research-Servant,
That I Summon For New Wisdom.

4822 The Chief Role of Wisdom Is...
Identifying Who You Should HONOR.
(Wisdom Is...The Awareness of Difference.)

4823 Wisdom...
Decide Where You Want To Excel.
Identify Who Can Mentor You.
Ask...10 Questions Daily.
Focus.

4824 WISDOM...
~Is The Ability To Discern DIFFERENCE
(In People/Moments/Environments).
Is The Ability To Anticipate A Consequence/
Reward.

4825 WISDOM Begins...One Question From Now.

4826 WISDOM Creates...Progress.
Isaiah 1:17

4827 Wisdom...Is Brief.
Opinions...Are "Long." :)

4828 WISDOM FROM JOSEPH:
The One Who Trusts You Is...Worth More Than
10,000 Who Do Not.
(Joseph/Pharaoh)

4829 WISDOM FROM JOSEPH:
Your Future Is...Only One Conversation Away.
(Joseph/Pharaoh)

4830 Wisdom From Rebekah:
What Camel Did You Refuse To Water..?
Costly Rebellion.
(Genesis 24-Eleazar/Isaac)

4831 WISDOM Is...Knowing Who Should Be Ignored.

4832 Wisdom Is A Gift...
That Requires Receiving.
"For The Lord Giveth Wisdom: Out of His
Mouth Cometh Knowledge,"
(Proverbs 2:6).

4833 Wisdom Is...Always A Question Away.

4834 WISDOM Is...Awareness of Difference.
Honor Is...Rewarding of Difference.

4835 WISDOM Is...Knowing The Divine Reaction To
A Human Problem.

4836 WISDOM Is...Not Genetic.
Wisdom Is...Not The Fruit of Age.
Wisdom Is...A Choice.

4837 WISDOM Is...Recognition of Difference.
WHO...
~Comforts You?
~Motivates You?
~Energizes You?
~Mentors You?
~Protects You?
~Trusts You?

4838 WISDOM Is...Recognition of Value.
Everything-Everyone...Has Different Value To
You.
Consistently Assign Value. (It Changes.)

4839 WISDOM Is...Recognizing Difference.
Honor Is...Rewarding of Difference.
Prosperity Is...Reaping From Difference.

4840 WISDOM Is...The Ability To Anticipate The
Consequences of A Decision.

4841 Wisdom Is The Ability To Discern...
...Sugarcoated Bitterness.

4842 Wisdom Is The Ability To Discern...
...The "Difference" In Another.

4843 Wisdom Is The Ability To Discern...
...The Divine Deposit Hidden In The Moment.

4844 Wisdom Is The Ability To Discern...
...What Another Needs.

4845 Wisdom Is The Ability To Discern...
What Matters Most.
...In A Relationship.
...To God.
...In The Moment.

4846 Wisdom Is The Ability To Discern...
When To Be Silent.

4847 Wisdom Is The Ability To Discern...
...When You Are Wrong.

4848 Wisdom Is The Ability To Discern...
Who Is Ahead of You.

4849 Wisdom Is The Ability To Discern...A Lie.

4850 Wisdom Is...The Ability To Discern The Behavior
Appropriate For The Moment.

4851 WISDOM...Is The Reward For Loving.
(Love Children? Animals? Technology?
That's Where Your Wisdom Will Be.)

4852 Wisdom...Is The Seed For Good Decisions.
Good Decisions...Create A Successful Life.
Who Are You Blaming..?

4853 Wisdom...Is Your Protection.
A Righteous Life Is Not A Protected Life.
(Vulnerable-Cain Killed Abel)
Think...TWICE.

4854 Wisdom Keys...Do Not Merely Unlock: They Also "Lock."
Think.

4855 Wisdom Without Love...
Is Not Wisdom At All.

4856 Wise Words...Are Like Deep Waters;
Wisdom Flows From Wise...
Like A Bubbling Brook.
Proverbs 18:4.
Deep Cries Out To Deep.

4857 Your HISTORY...Explains Your Wisdom.

4858 Your Wisdom Enters...
At The Speed of Your Questions.

4859 Your Wisdom Is Easily Discerned...
When I See Who You Honor.
Unhidden-Secrets.

4860 Your Wisdom Is Increasing...At The Speed of Your Questions.

4861 Your Wisdom Is Revealed...By Who You Honor.

WOMAN-TALK

4862 A Man Knows...
...When There Is No Recognition Nor
Interest In His Stress And Responsibilities.
Impactful.

4863 A REQUEST Is...Often The Training
Curriculum.
Few Women Discern It.
Very Few.
Rebekah.
Kingly Elimination.

4864 A Smart Woman...Creates An Angry Man.
Hehe.

4865 A Woman Decides...How A Man Feels.
That Feeling...Decides Their Future Together.

4866 A Woman Is To A Man...What God Cannot Be.
But No Man Accepts That. :)

4867 Adam Himself...
Did Not Know What He Was Missing.

4868 You Think Your Husband Does..?
ALL Men Are Demanding.
WHAT...They Demand Is The Difference.
Listen...A Little Bit Longer.

4869 All Men Do Not Want The Same Thing In A
Woman.
Some Men Merely Want An Experience...
Not A Relationship.

4870 Any Man...Could Teach A Woman How To Please
Him.
Almost No Man...Will.
Reaction Aborts Training.

4871 Common Mistake...Among Women.
Every Male Is...Not Necessarily A Man.
A Man Protects...Not Hurts.
A Man Is Gentle...Not Crude.

4872 Create...The Environment He Does Not Want To
Leave.
The Addiction of A Man Is...
An Environment.
(Golf-Bar-Fish)

4873 Beauty Enters Every Competition...
But Trust Wins It.

4874 Esther Knew How To Correct Stupid Decisions...Without Making Her King Look Stupid.

4875 Every Man....Really Wants To Know.
No Man...Wants "You" To Teach Him.
:)

4876 If You Kill The "Giving Heart" of A Man...
Your Relationship Is Over.

4877 Know The Dog...Before You Jerk The Leash.
:)

4878 No Man Marries A Woman...For Her Beauty.
He Marries Her Because of...How He Feels In Her Presence.

4879 Treasuring His Words...
...Will Qualify You For His Private Thoughts.
Advised.

4880 You Can Teach A Man Anything...If You Can Remove The "Tone" of A Teacher.
Bad Childhood Memories.

4881 Your Presentation...Decides His Desire.
Or Not.
:)

4882 Your Words...Reveal Your Heart.
Your Tone...Reveals Your Attitude.
Your Schedule...Reveals Your Passion.

4883 If You Do Not Tell Us...We Will Not Know.
Like..."10 Times."
:)

4884 Men Are Trained Through...Your Reactions.

4885 Do Not Search For...Young.
Do Not Search For...Old.
Do Not Search For...Wealth.
Search For...The Man Who Honors.

4886 Eve's Diary~
"Listening...Can Be Costly."
Wrong Voices.

4887 Eve's Diary~
I Got...What I Wanted.
But, I Lost What I Had.

4888 Eve's Diary~
I Was Hoping Adam Would Say, "No..!"
Is There Any Man...Strong Enough To Tell
Me "No"..?

4889 Eve's Diary~
"The Garden Is So Huge...So It Took Me
A While.
But, I Finally Found It...The Forbidden Fruit."
:)

4890 What Top 3 Qualities...Do You Really Want In A
Husband?
Heart-Talk.

4891 How Do You Change...A Man?
Through Your... "Reactions."
It Is Also...How You Lose Him.
:)

4892
HOW TO CHANGE A MAN
Timing...Esther.
Questions...Queen of Sheba.
Directness...Ruth.
Credibility...Naaman's Maid.
Honor...Abigail.

4893 If You Must Explain Your Difference...
He Cannot Discern It.
What He "Has Not"...He Cannot.

4894 If You Need A Different Kind of Man...He May
Need A Different Kind of Woman.
Earn Him.

4895 The Energy of A Man...Is Determined By
The Reactions of His Woman.

4896 Ladies, Make Yourself...
UNFORGETTABLE.
Correct Him.
Correct Him.
Correct Him.
Truly, A FOREVER Memory.

4897 Man Profile 7:
His History.
His Weakness.
His Obsession.
His Heroes.
His Mentors.
His Integrity.
Who He Honors.

4898 Many Women Want A King...
With "Peasant" Expectations.
Ain't Gonna Happen.

4899 No Man Forgets...An Unkind Woman.

4900 Many Women...Have Enjoyed My Presents.
Few Women...Have Enjoyed My Presence.
:)

4901 Men?
Immerse Yourself In His World (Esther).
Prove Trustworthiness To Those He Trusts.
(Ruth).
Do Not Resent How He Uses His Time.
(Proverbs 31).

4902 Men Never Forget...A Female Critic.
Never.
:)

4903 My Mother...Never Spoke A Boring Word To Me
In Her Lifetime.
My Mother Was~
...Believable.
...Outspoken.
...Attentive.
...Corrective.
...A Reader.
...A Servant.
...Interesting.

4904 No Man Finds A Corrective Woman...Exciting.
Memorable, Yes.
Exciting, No.

4905 No Man...Has Ever Adapted To A Corrective
Woman.
:)

4906 No Man Lives...Without An Agenda.
Hidden or Known.
Holy or Unholy.

4907 No Woman Is Ugly...In A Fur Coat.
:)

4908 No Woman Is Ugly...When She Smiles.
:)

4909 Only One Woman...
Can Train A Man Effectively.
The One He Admires...Most.
(P.S. Great Men Crave Gentle Training.)

4910 Potiphar's Wife Was Not The Last Woman
Infuriated By "No."

4911 SHE~
Your Look...Decides If He Lingers.
His Lingering Decides...What He Learns.
His Learning Decides...If He Loves.

4912 PROVERBS 31 WOMAN:
She Seeks-13.
She Works-13.
She Brings-14.
She Rises-15.
She Stretches-20.
She Sells-24.
HER HUSBAND SITTETH~23.

4913 Q: "What Makes A Woman Memorable?"
A: Attentiveness.

4914 Some Women Want A Man...They Can Conquer.
Some Women Want A Man...They Cannot
Conquer.
Some Women Want A Man...God Has
Conquered.

4915 The Choice Is Always Yours:
Winning Our Argument...or Winning My Heart.

4916 The Deterioration of Women...Decides The
Deterioration of Every Culture.

4917 The Greatest Inspiration In The Life of A Man
Is...
...A Woman.

4918 The Interested Woman...
Outlasts The Interesting Woman.
I Know.

4919 The Most Beautiful Women...
Do Not Discuss It.

4920 The Non-Listening Woman...
Does Not Have A Chance In Keeping
A Good Man.

4921 The One Investment Women Will Not Make:
Questions...That Find The Oil
or Reveal The Sand.
Worthy Investment.

4922 The Only Rescuer A Man Has
From The Tyranny of Boredom.
The Unpredictability of A Woman...

4923 The Woman Who Corrects Her Man...Makes
Herself Quite Memorable.
...Like Fingernails On A Chalkboard.
:)

4924 Wives Decide...
What Their Husbands Remember.

4925 Uncommon Woman...Strives To Understand
Daily Responsibilities of Her Man.
Thoroughly.
Prevents Stressful Expectations.

4926 Uncommon-Wife~
She Asked.
Jesus Ignored.
She Worshipped.
Jesus Responded.

4927 What A Man Will Not Tell You~
He Wants His Opinion To Be Pursued...
On Almost Everything.

4928 What A Man Will Not Tell You~
He Wants...Immediate Admiration To
A Problem He Solved.

4929 What Angers A Woman...Often Excites A Man.
:)

4930 What-A-Man-Will-Not-Tell-You~
He Wants...Your Difference From Others
To Be Apparent, Instantly Discernable
To His Friends.

4931 What-A-Man-Will-Not-Tell-You~
He Worries...About The Trusts
You May Break With Your Girlfriends.

4932 When You Think You Know Him...
You Do Not.
Every Woman's Mistake.
:)

4933 Wish Women Knew...
...That Your Unspoken Disapproval Is A
Discernible Odor To The Male Spirit.

4934 The Secrets of Your Man...Will Be Shared
Proportionate To Your Reactions To His
Words.
I Know.

4935 Women~
Some Inspire...Conversation.
Some Inspire...Silence.

4936 Women~
Some Inspire...Trust.
Some Inspire...Distrust.

4937 Women of Wisdom~
Secrets-of-Esther~
"Immerse Yourself In His World."

4938 Secret-of-Ruth~
"Work In His Field."

4939 Women of Wisdom~
Servanthood...of Rebekah.
Adaptation...of Ruth.
Attentive To Timing...Like Esther.
Productivity...of Proverbs 31.
Women Rule The Domain
That Matters.
The Mind.
This Is Often Too Cumbersome For
The Male Mind.

4940 Those Who Abuse Women...Are Abusers.
The "Weakest" of Abusers.

4941 Your Biggest Mistake Will Be...
Misinterpreting His Stress Level.

4942 Nothing Intimidates A Man...Like A Godly
Woman.

WORD OF GOD

4943 Family...Mark My Words.
Scorn For The Word of God...
Is A Deadly Mistake.
Mark My Words.

4944 FAVORITE-SCRIPTURE~
"Acquaint Now Thyself With Him,
And Be At Peace:
Thereby Good Shall Come Unto Thee."
Job 22:21

4945 Top 10~
Identify Top 10 Scriptures That "Inspire"
You Personally...And Keep Them In Front
of You Daily.

4946 CLEVER WORDS...Are Rarely Wise Words.
~Rarely.
~Politics.
~Deception.
~Words.
~Conversation.

4947 HEALING WORDS!
If You Want To Talk...I Will Listen.
If You Want To Go...I Will Follow You.
If You Want To Cry...You Have My Arms
Open.

4948 If A Word Is A Picture...Tone Is The Frame.

4949 If Your Words Confuse Me,
I Refuse To Visit Your Thoughts.

4950 If YOUR Words Were The ONLY
Encouragement Your Family Would Ever
Hear...During Their Lifetime...Would It Be
Enough..?

4951 If Your Words Will Not Make A Difference...Why Speak Them?

4952 Make A List of 10 Words...That Make You Smile. :)
Now...Speak Them Quickly.
Words...Birth Feelings.

4953 My Words...Are Very Important To Me.
Engraved In My Heart Really.
Disturbed Greatly When There Is Disdain For Wisdom.

4954 My Words...Control Divine Behavior.
Nineveh.
Thief On The Cross.

4955 Pleasurable Words:
The ONLY Cure For The Pain of Life.
(Words That Explain...Motivate...Heal... Honor.)

4956 Quoting God...
Simply Means You Are Always Right.
ALWAYS.
Kinda Gets Addictive. :)

4957 Right Words...Heal.
"Pleasant Words Are Like Honeycomb...
Sweetness To The Soul...Health To
The Bones."
Proverbs 16:24

4958 The Only Cure For Wrong Words...
Is Right Words.
Your Tweets Are Healing Oil.

4959 The Words of Your Critics...
Do Not Explain Who You Are.
Their Words Explain...Who They Are.

4960 The Words You Speak...Are Opening Doors.
The Words You Do Not Speak...Are Closing
Doors.

4961 Those Dismissive of My Words... Have Lost The
Opportunity To Live In My Heart.

4962 Twitter Family...
Words Can Be Bullets.
Please Do Not Destroy Reputations of Good
People.
Please.
I Beg of You.

4963 What You Repeatedly Hear...
You Eventually Believe.

4964 When My Words Cease To Be Important To
You...I Realize I Have Ceased To Be Important
To You.

4965 When You Open Your Mouth...You Reveal Your
IQ.

4966 When You Talk...I Know How You Think.
(From The Abundance of The Heart,
The Mouth Speaketh.)

4967 When Your Words Do Not Matter...Leave.

4968 Word To Encouragers~
You Have No Idea How Much Your Words
REFILL...The Emptied Vessel.
Many "Empty" Us.

4969 "I Am Right"...Takes You A Mile.
"I Am Wrong"...Takes You 100 Miles.
"I Am Sorry"...Takes You 1,000 Miles.

4970 I Will Fight Your Pain...With My Words.

4971 If ALL of Your Words Are Not From Your
Heart...I Am Not Interested In ANY of Them.

4972 Some Speak Words That...Crush.
Some Speak Words That...Chisel.
"Father,
I Will Speak Words That...CARESS."

4973 Words of Caring...Are Not Always The Proof of
Caring.

4974 WRONG WORDS:
...Close Doors.
...Create Painful Memories.
...Stop Conversations.
...Assassinate Hope.
...Can Keep You Single.

4975 WRONG WORDS...
Often Close The Very Doors God Opened.

4976 Your Mouth...Has Revealed Your Heart.

4977 Your Words Are Birthing... Currents In Your
Environment.

4978 Your Mouth...Has Scheduled Every Failure In
Your Life.
Simple.
Yet, Remarkable.
Our Deliverer...Became Our Captor.

4979 Your Mouth...Will Cause Every Major Problem
In Your Life.
(Your Words or Silence...Cannot Think of
An Exception In My Personal Life.)

4980 Your Words Are Birthing...
Divine Reactions.
Thief On Cross.
Luke 23:42-43

4981 Your Words...Are Creating Your Experiences.
Your Words...Are Pictures of Your Mind.
Your Tone...Is A Picture of Your Attitude.
Your Focus...Is A Picture of Your Interest.

4982 Your Words Can Close Doors...
Quicker Than God Will Open.

4983 Your WORDS...Decide What I Feel.
What I Feel...Decides My Memory of You.
My Memory of You...Decides My Desire
For You.

4984 Stop Working...For The Man You Resent.

4985 The Obedient Worker...
Will Far Outlast The Genius Worker.
...In Honor.
...In Longevity.
...In Relationship.

4986 I Have Stopped Training Those...Who Need
Their Job.

I Train Those...Who "Love" Their Job.

4987 "Things Do Not Have To 'Change The World'...To
Be Important." -Steve Jobs Quote

4988 If Your Life Is Uninteresting...You Have Not Yet
Discovered Your Divine Difference From Others.

WORSHIP

4989 EVERY WORSHIPPER IS:
A Secret Warrior.

4990 I JOLT My Mind Into Reality...
~By Singing..."Yes, Jesus Loves Me!"
Loudly.
:)
Nothing Else Really Matters.

4991 Now Bring Me A Minstrel.
...When The Minstrel Played
...The Hand of The Lord Came Upon Him.
2 Kings 3:15

4992 Singing...Is Protocol For Entering Divine
Presence.

4993 Singing...Silences Demonic Whispers.
If You Can Sing, You Cannot Lose.

4994 Worship...Corrects Your Focus.
Focus...Decides Your Feelings.
Feelings...Affect Your Decisions.
Worship...Cures Fear.

4995 WORSHIP LEADERS~
When You Stir People To SING...
~Their CHAINS Are Broken.
~Their FOCUS Is Corrected.
~Their HOPE Returns.

4996 Astrology Is Simply Worship of The Creation
Instead of The Creator.

4997 An Uncommon God...Does Not Create
Common Things.

WORTH

4998 Calvary...Revealed Your Worth.
Never-Forget-It.

—

4999 I Know You Have An Assessment...
of Your Worth.
It May Be Very Different...Than Mine.
:)

—

5000 The Size of The Key Does Not Reveal...
The Worth of The Treasure.

—

5001 ~Identify...What Pleasures You.

~Limit Those...Who Access You.

~Choose...One Subject To Master.

~Exit...The Disrespectful.

—

- 840 -